Social effectiveness MPO's 79
measures
Utilization of service 75
Typology et

Managing Public Transit
Strategically

❖

goals & Objective — 8
strategic Management — 4?
Measuring & monitoring — 59
Chapters 8, 9 & 11

Gordon J. Fielding

Managing Public Transit Strategically

A Comprehensive Approach
to Strengthening Service
and Monitoring Performance

Jossey-Bass Publishers
San Francisco   •   London   •   1987

MANAGING PUBLIC TRANSIT STRATEGICALLY
A Comprehensive Approach to Strengthening Service and Monitoring Performance
   by Gordon J. Fielding

Copyright © 1987 by: Jossey-Bass Inc., Publishers
                       433 California Street
                       San Francisco, California 94104

                              &

                       Jossey-Bass Limited
                       28 Banner Street
                       London EC1Y 8QE

Library of Congress Cataloging-in-Publication Data

Fielding, Gordon J.
  Managing public transit strategically.

  (The Jossey-Bass management series)
  Bibliography: p.
  Includes index.
  1. Local transit—Management.   2. Urban transpor-
tation—Management.   I. Title.   II. Series.
HE4301.F54   1987   388.4′068   87-45497
ISBN 1-55542-068-0 (alk. paper)

Manufactured in the United States of America

The paper in this book meets the guidelines for
permanence and durability of the Committee on
Production Guidelines for Book Longevity of the
Council on Library Resources.

JACKET DESIGN BY WILLI BAUM

FIRST EDITION

Code 8744

A joint publication in
*The Jossey-Bass
Public Administration Series*
and
The Jossey-Bass Management Series

Contents

Contents

Transit Service • Politics of Public Transit • Managing Strategically

Preface

Transit is back in the mainstream of U.S. urban transportation. The downward trend of ridership was reversed during the 1970s; antiquated equipment was replaced; new rapid transit systems were built for San Francisco, Washington, D.C., Atlanta, Baltimore, and Miami; and modern buses were supplied to virtually every city and many rural areas. But the renaissance of transit has been achieved at high cost: Real costs per vehicle mile increased by 56 percent between 1970 and 1979, and by 1982, $7.6 billion in assistance from all levels of government was required to sustain this transportation network. Since 1982, the level of governmental assistance has declined in real terms. Now, the challenge is to ensure that the achievements of the 1970s are not lost. Contemporary transit agencies must be managed so that they produce service efficiently and ensure that it is used effectively.

This book will help transportation professionals and aspiring managers to think strategically; to collect information; to plan, deploy, and market service; and to monitor performance. Expansion of the transit industry has created employment opportunities for transportation professionals, many of whom have had little formal training in management. This book was written primarily to satisfy these managers' need for continuing education and, secondarily, to provide a resource for students seeking employment in transportation agencies or engineering and management consulting firms.

Public managers, urban planners, union officials, transit employees, students, and the informed public will find that *Managing Public Transit Strategically* provides constructive proposals for the operation and management of public transit agencies. This book outlines methods that will help professionals integrate planning and marketing studies or design better strategies for labor negotiations. It will assist public officials in developing new methods for allocating transit assistance and in monitoring the results; and it will enable journalists to present balanced accounts of transit performance.

Students in upper-division and graduate classes in public policy and management should find the book valuable reading. It can also serve as a training aid for transit organizations interested in managerial development. Examples and case studies from operating agencies are provided throughout the book.

Public managers need books that summarize research and place management within an intellectual framework suited to specialized endeavors. *Managing Public Transit Strategically* addresses both needs. It is the first book to address strategic management in the transit industry. In this regard, it fills a critical gap in the literature of transportation and public administration.

Strategic management has long been recognized as an important tool in private enterprise. With appropriate modifications, it can be an extremely effective tool for the transit industry as well. The strategic approach involves identifying the organization's basic mission; pinpointing internal and external factors that influence this mission; adopting a set of master strategies, policies, goals, and objectives; developing functional strategies; implementing these strategies; and reviewing and evaluating performance.

Managing Public Transit Strategically differs from other books on public transit. It is most similar to Gray and Hoel's *Public Transportation* (1979), which is now out of print. Two other books, Altschuler, Womack, and Pucher's *The Urban Transportation System* (1979) and Meyer and Gomez-Ibanez's *Autos, Transit and Cities* (1981), adopt a policy perspective that considers public transit as well as other transportation modes. Historical perspectives are offered by Smerk in *Urban Mass Transportation* (1974) and by Jones in *Urban Transit Policy* (1985).

Throughout this book, I have emphasized monitoring and control mechanisms. Most of my research during the last decade has involved the development of measures of transit performance. In this work, I explain why this approach to management is needed and provide illustrations from my experience with service provision, monitoring, and control during my work as a transit manager, consultant, and scholar. These conclusions are supplemented with references to the research achievements of other scholars and insights provided by practicing transit managers.

Overview of the Contents

Chapters One and Two explain the benefits of a strategic approach to managing transit. Chapter One describes the broad social context and the diverse goals for transit in the United States. The challenge for managers is to select appropriate goals and objectives and to organize transit to achieve them. Chapter Two explains why goals for transit became muddled, tracing changes in goverment policy toward transit from 1960 to 1985. Concluding the chapter is a section explaining the Reagan administration's "new federalism": an attempt to reduce governmental responsibility for operating assistance and encourage privatization.

Whereas Chapters One and Two focus on the external environment for transit, Chapter Three assesses the internal environment. Different modes of transit are explained as is the distribution of the transit enterprise from city to city. To facilitate this discussion, a typology of bus transit is presented to avoid confusing the management dilemmas of very large systems—like those in New York City, Chicago, and Los Angeles—with those of smaller systems, which have different kinds of problems. The steps in strategic management are explained and case studies are provided to integrate information presented about the external environment with the requirements for operating service.

Chapter Four closely parallels my own research. A methodology is developed for selecting measures of transit performance. Then their use as indicators for the major dimensions of transit performance is explained. Using this method, the performance of an agency can be analyzed over time and the results compared with the achievements of similar agencies. Without such a method for monitoring performance, managers cannot manage strategically; they can merely supervise.

Subsequent chapters summarize research on different functions of transit and demonstrate how the strategic approach can unite an organization. Chapter Five explains the budgets of transit organizations and their use for short-range planning, performance monitoring, and fiscal control. Fiscal planning is essential to strategic management, and budgets are essential tools for short-range transportation improvement programs. Methods for forecasting revenue and projecting operating costs are included as useful techniques in fiscal planning.

Chapters Six and Seven are devoted to labor relations. In the transit industry, labor is the largest cost under management's control. Trends in labor productivity are discussed and the diseconomies of scale in transit are analyzed. Approaches to labor negotiations are suggested, but major attention is devoted to methods for monitoring and analyzing labor efficiency, since productivity is management's responsibility. Improvements in labor efficiency have been achieved by agencies that plan work force needs carefully, set objectives for labor efficiency, and then monitor attendance, sick leave, and compensated leave to see whether objectives are being met.

Chapter Eight presents transit planning from a strategic perspective. Different methods for analyzing service are presented, followed by sections devoted to methods for scheduling service and estimating cost. Procedures are described whereby service needs can be matched to services that are feasible for an agency to supply. Too often, effort is wasted studying service desires that are not feasible for the transit agency to satisfy. Special attention is also given to transportation system management strategies for integrating transit with regional programs for reducing highway congestion.

Chapter Nine associates transit marketing with planning by matching travel preferences with feasible services. The problems of marketing transit are introduced within the context of marketing in nonprofit agencies. Service development, market segmentation, pricing, advertising, and customer service are each considered as elements of the marketing plan. The need to monitor the results of marketing is emphasized as a way to improve the strategic management of each agency.

Chapter Ten clarifies the political context of transit management. It returns to the external environment theme of the first two chapters by explaining the importance of different constituencies to transit development and the need for transit organizations to build and maintain these constituencies. Special attention is devoted to governing boards because they both reflect and filter the expectations of different constituencies and translate public demands into policy. The concluding chapter summarizes how the different responsibilities of management can be integrated. Managing strategically assists transit personnel to identify and pursue potential markets. It also helps them realize that service that is dependent on governmental assistance will be subject to political influence. In any case, management must identify feasible services that they can afford to supply and then ensure that those services are used effectively.

Reviewers have suggested that too much emphasis is given to producing transit efficiently and too little to ensuring that it is used effectively. The bias is intentional because management has more control over the production of service than over its consumption. However, management must be sensitive to both efficiency and effectiveness goals. Successful transit managers artfully combine both while recognizing that ridership response to transit strategies is dependent on factors largely beyond management's control.

A prescriptive approach is adopted in Chapters Three through Ten, where I focus on what *ought* to be emphasized, rather than what *is* emphasized. Current practice seldom matches this ideal, and I realize that local circumstances require modification to functional activities. However, deciding a mission, choosing strategies, and implementing and monitoring the results over several years will be useful to all transit managers. Focusing on what is wrong with public transit would not have accomplished my objective. There have been too many articles and books in this mold, written by authors who have identified what is wrong with transit without prescribing realistic solutions. These authors have had neither experience with trying to do the right thing nor appreciation for the complexity of managing a public agency amid conflicting objectives and under the full glare of media scrutiny. Criticism has made the need for change apparent without providing realistic guidelines for improving transit.

Acknowledgments

This book has developed through my experience in the classroom and revisions have benefited from comments by students and colleagues. The original version was developed for a course on transit management I taught at the Massachusetts Institute of Technology in 1984. Subsequent versions have been used in graduate courses in social science and management at the University of California, Irvine. Comments from students who approach transit management from different academic points of view have assisted me in revising the text for a broad audience. Detailed reviews by Stephanie Frederick, Marcy Jaffe, Nancy Kays, and Gregory Thompson were especially helpful. Gerald Haugh and Douglass Lee reviewed the initial draft, and many of their suggestions have been incorporated.

My association with the Institute of Transportation Studies has been extremely beneficial to my research. Charles Lave, James Perry, Lyman Porter, and Roger Teal have been colleagues on different research projects and have contributed to conclusions used in the chapters on measuring transit performance and labor relations. Lyn Long compiled the reference section and always knew where to find source material. Portions of the text have been used in the midmanagerial training course arranged by Lyn Long for the Institute.

My research on transit performance was funded by the University Research and Training Program of the Urban Mass Transportation Administration. James Bautz, Frank Enty, Philip Hughes, Nathaniel Jasper, Judy Meade, and Robert Trotter have managed a federal program that has facilitated numerous studies in management, planning, and public policy in an era when university research has been buffeted by changing federal policy. Both transportation research and scholarship have benefited from their willingness to sustain independent analyses of federal programs and policy.

The text was prepared by the word processing center of the School of Social Sciences at the University of California, Irvine. The professional efforts of Katharine Alberti, Dorothy Gormick, Margaret Grice, Cheryl Larsson, Susan Pursche, and Helen Wildman are gratefully appreciated.

Irvine, California   G. J. (Pete) Fielding
September 1987

The Author

Gordon J. Fielding is a professor of social science and management at the University of California, Irvine. He joined the University in 1965 and in 1976 was appointed director for the Irvine branch of the Institute of Transportation Studies. In 1983 he became the systemwide director for the Institute, which has branches at Berkeley and Irvine.

After receiving his B.A. and M.A. degrees from the University of Auckland, Fielding completed his Ph.D. degree in geography at the University of California, Los Angeles, in 1962. He then returned to New Zealand and taught at the University of Auckland until he moved to the Irvine campus in 1965.

Fielding was general manager of the Orange County Transit District (OCTD), Santa Ana, California, from 1971 to 1975. At OCTD he managed the development of an integrated bus and dial-a-ride system and helped plan a rapid transit system. Since his return to the University of California, he has been involved in transportation research and the teaching of public policy and public administration. He is the author or coauthor of twenty monographs and thirty-five professional articles on transportation policy. He has been appointed to both state and federal advisory boards and served for ten years as a director of DAVE Systems, a private operator of public transit systems.

In 1981, Fielding received the Outstanding Public Service Award from the administrator of the Urban Mass Transportation Agency (UMTA) for his research on transit performance. He has organized and taught a ten-day course on transit managerial effectiveness offered by the Center for Transit Research and Training at Irvine, which was funded, in part, by UMTA. More than 180 midlevel managers from transit agencies have attended that course.

Managing Public Transit
Strategically

1

The State of Public Transit in the United States

The challenge to the transit industry today is managerial. In the first years of publicly owned transit, the primary problems were insufficient resources, dwindling patronage, and obsolete equipment. Now in the mid 1980s the industry has modern equipment and facilities, and its employees are generously paid. Although nationwide the proportion of all trips made by public transit has declined, the industry has maintained its share of peak-period trips and is vital to the provision of transportation in the largest cities.

With the physical plant securely in place, today's managers must now make it work better and more competitively. In particular, they need to control the costs of transit production and position the industry so that it will profit from economic shocks and changes unfavorable to competing modes of travel. To these ends, management must upgrade its own abilities and furnish thoughtfully priced services in markets where transit enjoys a comparative advantage over the automobile.

Achieving these goals will not be easy. If managing a transit system was once relatively straightforward, it is now frustratingly complex. Gone are the days when market mechanisms helped managers decide how much service to provide, which vehicles to use and how to maintain them, how to assign employees, and how to finance service. With public ownership, agencies have grown larger and more complicated, in many cases serving entire regions instead of single cities. Transit unions have become more powerful as well,

1

with the result that long and exhausting negotiations are often needed before agreement can be reached on wages and work rules for drivers and mechanics. A continually shifting political scene further complicates matters for an industry dependent on public subsidies. Managers must be keenly sensitive to the vagaries of change acting on and through diverse political interests, for it is these, not demand in the form of farebox receipts, that determine how much service is placed on the streets, where, and at what price.

Systems Theory

In the circumstances of the 1980s and for the foreseeable future, managers must learn to think and plan strategically. What this means in detail and how to accomplish it are the subjects of this book. The topic will be presented in terms of general systems theory, which characterizes an organization as a unified system of interrelated parts. With this theory, one may also take the larger view, seeing the organization as just one of many interrelated parts that form its environment.

Systems analysis permits one to describe transit organizations in their historical and environmental contexts so that their dependence on governmental influence becomes apparent. It also serves to distinguish between service production and service consumption (Figure 1). This distinction makes it possible for managers to use operations-research techniques to evaluate methods of producing service and policy-analysis techniques to examine the distribution of service benefits. Once they have been clearly delineated and assessed, both production and consumption of service can then be more easily improved.

The systems diagrams that will be encountered throughout this book are analogue models of how an organization should function. Of course, real management systems are neither as static nor as interdependent as these models. Rather, the systems approach filters reality so that interactions and interdependencies can be understood in a constantly changing situation (Bozeman, 1979). They have been prepared to help students and managers understand the complexity of the transit environment and to evaluate the worth of various managerial strategies.

Figure 1. Societal Context for Transit and Its Managerial System.

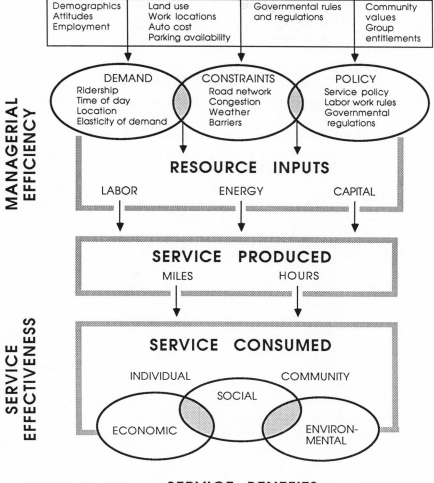

Transit organizations are resource-dependent, open systems. External influences affect the way in which management obtains and uses resources and how service benefits individuals and groups. Understanding of the managerial system is helped by distinguishing managerial efficiency—the use of resources to produce service—from service effectiveness—the consumption of service.

Several other considerations control the shape and content of this volume. First, although illustrations from other countries appear now and again, the book primarily addresses transit management in the United States. Second, transit is considered only as a public enterprise. Third, the focus is on motor bus rather than rail management.

American Orientation. It was necessary to limit the scope to one country because all transit environments are highly politicized and therefore unique. It was difficult enough to account for the federal, state, and local agencies of the United States without attempting to include the political cultures of other countries. However, this constraint should not limit the book's relevance and the technical and financial chapters should be particularly helpful to transit managers both inside and outside the United States. The need to generate clearly defined objectives and to evaluate performance against these objectives is shared by all transit organizations regardless of their political context. But given that public-sector management may call for skills that are only about 10 percent technical, 30 percent financial, and 60 percent political, readers should continually keep in mind that the book has been shaped by the American experience—a political culture where transit plays a minor role in urban passenger transport, and where its continued existence depends on government assistance.

Public Enterprise. Public agency management differs from private on two important counts. In the privately owned transit agency, the profit motive furnishes goals, and net returns provide measures of performance. Objectives are clear to employees, and the consequences of not achieving them quickly become apparent. In a public enterprise, however, goals are often contradictory, and employees may be confused about what constitutes satisfactory service. For this reason, a good deal of attention is devoted in this book to the determination of appropriate goals for public transit.

The "customers" for each type of agency also differ. A private transit operator need satisfy only a narrow segment of the market, namely, those who use transit frequently. A public agency, in contrast, must satisfy not just its immediate clientele but a broader political constituency as well. Even though most urban residents do not use transit services, public transit needs their support for its continued existence. In fact, transit agencies devote much effort to balancing the user demand for more and cheaper transit against nonuser demands for adequate but economical service.

This book focuses on public transit rather than private, because most transit services cannot be operated at a profit and are therefore not furnished by private enterprise. Private firms of course do have a role in providing public transit under contract to public agencies. Such firms are especially helpful in reducing peak-period demand when they furnish additional commuter service and specialized transit. Private agencies under contract are also cost competitive as providers of service in the outer suburbs and in smaller cities. However, their overall contribution is small.

The suggestion that transit ownership and management be returned to private hands has received much fanfare of late. In searching for ways in which to reduce federal expenditures on transit, the Reagan administration has repeatedly called for the "privatization" of services. While it is true that the contributions of private enterprise to the public transit system have reduced organized labor's demand for increased wages and benefits, the proportion of service operated by private companies remains small. Only 5 to 10 percent of transit service can be provided by private contractors at competitive rates. In the New York urbanized area, for example, where 74 percent of all private transit is provided, privately operated transit offers only a slight cost advantage compared with public operators of similar size and operating characteristics. The large cost differentials claimed by advocates of private transit have been based on spurious comparisons of small private operators with large regional public operators. In fact, if the private operators were asked to operate regional service and were subjected to the inevitable union constraints, their costs would quickly climb to the present public levels.

Bus Orientation. Bus agencies dominate transit in the United States. Of the 336 agencies that reported statistical information to the Urban Mass Transportation Administration (UMTA) in 1982, 174 were fixed-route bus operators. Another 137 were fixed-route bus operators with some demand-responsive service. Of the remaining 45 agencies, 32 were multimodal agencies in which bus operations predominated, 3 were exclusively rail, and the remaining 10 were small special-purpose operators providing service by ferryboat or by cable-powered, incline planes.

Because of the dominance of bus transit, this book will primarily address management problems connected with bus operations. In some ways, managing bus operations is a more complex task than managing rail operations. For example, service is dispersed, and schedules are difficult to coordinate. Supervision is also a problem, since operators must act independently and supervisors may not know where vehicles are or the conditions under which they are operating. Installation of mobile radios has aided supervision, but there is seldom the equivalent of a train-control system to aid management. Some chapters will not apply expressly to rail service, whereas others will be quite relevant to it. The techniques of effective financial management, labor relations, and employee development, for example, apply equally to both modes, and rail managers should find the chapters on these subjects useful.

External Influences, Goals, and Prospects

A discussion of strategic management brings up many other topics, such as performance evaluation, budgeting and financing, improvement of labor efficiency, transit planning, transit marketing, and preparations for operating in a political environment. Before plunging into these, however, it will be helpful to locate modern public transit more firmly in its time and place. In particular, we must recognize the external influences that affect public transit, understand its proper goals and objectives, and envision its potential.

External Influences. Although the management of transit could be narrowly defined in terms of service production and consumption, strategic thinking requires that it be connected with its larger social environment. External influences affect transit management in numerous ways and cannot be ignored. Demographic patterns, employment centers, parking availability, the road network, and street congestion all affect bus operations and must therefore have a place in management's development of strategic plans.

In particular, transit's relationship with its funding sources must be appreciated. Because service can no longer be supported by fare revenue, transit agencies have become reliant on federal, state, and local governments for assistance. As a result, governmental agencies are influential as both providers of resources and promulgators of rules and regulations. Their influence is manifold. For example, a host of application and reporting requirements must be complied with, service must be supplied equally to all social groups, and transit agencies must agree not to eliminate jobs when using federal funds to improve service.

Transit managers have only limited powers to shape these external forces. They may lobby for additional funding, try to alter customer preferences through promotion programs, and attempt to shape land use and highway plans so as to encourage development beneficial to transit operations. Compared with such interest groups as labor unions and highway advocates, however, transit's ability to shape its environment has been weak.

Since it cannot control its environment or even change it in any meaningful way, transit management's best strategy is to come to understand the transit environment as fully as possible and make use of this knowledge wherever possible. To be *effective*, managers must respond to the demands of individuals and groups. Because their agencies depend on the support of the communities they serve, transit managers must ensure that transit service supports the economic, social, and environmental goals of these communities. However, transit managers can make their greatest contribution by being *efficient*—that is, by supplying the desired services for the least amount of resources. To be both effective and efficient, managers must be ardent students of the social and political network in which they work. They need to realize that efficiency is under management's control, whereas service effectiveness is influenced by many factors in the environment that lie beyond management's ability to shape or restrain.

Efficiency and effectiveness are being used here in the context of public management rather than of economics. Efficiency is the relationship between the resources used (labor, capital, and fuel) and the service (miles and hours) produced; effectiveness is the deployment of service to accomplish goals (increasing passenger trips to produce more revenue or to reduce traffic congestion). Use of efficiency and effectiveness in this connotation is frequently debated in public management, because it could result in an agency being efficient while ignoring service goals. When economists examine the productivity of private firms, they define efficiency as maximizing net benefits (the value of output minus its cost). Reducing net cost per passenger or minimizing deficit per passenger would represent efficiency in this connotation. However, when organizations are more dependent upon governmental assistance than sales, definitions that separate the efficient production of service from its consumption are advantageous. The public management connotation is used in this book to clarify the strategic importance of producing transit efficiently. Additional discussion of these definitions is presented in Holzer and Halachmi (1986).

Goals and Objectives. Inappropriate goals are a major impediment to improved management. But before the consequences of placing effectiveness before efficiency objectives are explained, let me define the terms. Goals are general statements about what an agency should accomplish. Objectives are more concrete: they translate goals into specific aims that are to be accomplished within a designated time period. Normally, objectives are stated in such a way that their accomplishment can be measured. To control costs of production, for example, is a goal that can be translated into the objective to restrain cost increases during the next year to less than the change in the consumer price index. Some goals are easily translated into objectives that transit can accomplish. Others are not, and transit has suffered from too many of the latter.

Governmental agencies agreed to support public transit because enough people believed that a number of goals would be accomplished through increasing transit ridership. Increasing the effectiveness of transit by maximizing ridership therefore became the primary goal during the 1970s; transit agencies reduced fares, regardless of the revenue lost, and expanded service, regardless of the cost of serving low-density areas, as an inducement for people to switch from autos to transit.

Few of the predicted benefits of increased ridership have been realized, however, and the cost of public transit has become a highly visible political issue. Elected officials still express support for increased ridership, but they do so mainly to retain their cities' shares of government assistance for transit. In general, political support for this particular goal is waning. Nevertheless, as long as the stated political goal is ridership maximization, transit managers will be reluctant to abandon it in favor of efficiency. To some extent they are thus coerced by public policy into increasing ridership even as the reality of dwindling resources suggests that efficiency should be given the higher priority.

The pursuit of effectiveness rather than efficiency goals has increased transit deficits and made the industry ever more dependent on government assistance. Lave (1980, p. 72) has suggested:

> To the extent that it is useful to look for a villain behind the deficits, one should be careful to remember that the major fault does not lie with management or labor, but rather with the new goals that society has assigned to transit: transit has been asked to solve the congestion and pollution problems by running more service during peak hours to attract commuters out of cars; it has been asked to solve the mobility problems of the transit dependent by running frequent service through low-density suburban neighborhoods; and it is even asked to help solve the poverty problem by giving highly subsidized fares to the poor, and to senior citizens.
>
> The end result of these new social policies is that transit revenues cannot keep pace with costs: (1) fares must be kept low for everyone in order that they not harm the few poor people we are concerned with (no one has had the courage to try targeting the low fares to the relevant groups rather than shotgunning them through the entire population); and (2) buses

must run in low-density neighborhoods where they cannot possibly attract enough patronage to pay their costs.

It is common to find contradictory objectives holding sway in public administration. To see that transit is not alone in this regard, we need only observe the behavior of major public university administrators. It is well known that a university's prestige derives from the quality of its faculty's research, which requires generous funding. State legislators, however, are interested in educational opportunities for their constituents. When seeking annual approval of what are basically research budgets, university administrators shower state legislators with statistics on the numbers of students that the university has graduated and on the many achievements of these students. University administrators are caught in a double bind. They must gain funding for research by demonstrating that the university is devoted to an activity more or less incompatible with research.

In transit, prestige comes not only from the number of passengers carried but also from the size of operations. Running more vehicles, carrying more passengers, and constructing new rail lines are the things that excite management, since they enhance professional stature. Simply managing the transit system efficiently is not exciting. Of course efficient operation does concern managers, but it is seldom given high priority. Unfortunately, attempts to improve transit performance will be hampered as long as effectiveness goals supersede efficiency ones. It would undoubtedly help matters greatly if the transit profession itself were willing to redefine professionalism.

Appropriate Goals and Objectives. Transit management should strive for operational efficiency. Ensuring that service is used should remain a goal, but it ought to have a lesser priority than it now enjoys. In order to provide more and better service for each dollar invested, transit managers need quantifiable objectives around which all operational activities can be coordinated. The Greater Manchester (U.K.) Passenger Transport Executive proposed that the objectives listed below would permit the executive to control costs while maintaining its ridership (Cochrane and Tyson, 1980, pp. 1043–1044):

1. Provide a public passenger transport system that results in a leveling-off of patronage within three to five years. Patronage will be measured in terms of journeys per person.
2. Improve the load factor, measured in terms of passenger miles per vehicle mile.
3. Improve vehicle utilization, measured in terms of vehicle miles per hour.
4. Reduce in real terms the costs of operation, measured in terms of cost per hour, as adjusted for inflation.

The operative directive is the fourth, which requires costs to be controlled in real terms. Since this can be achieved simultaneously with improved vehicle utilization and increased patronage per vehicle mile, it does not conflict with the second and third objectives. Underlying the first objective is recognition that ridership should be allowed to level off, with no additional effort made to increase it during peak hours. The aggregate thrust of the four directives, then, is for efficient operation of the Manchester system.

Ideally, policy is always expressed in terms of measurable objectives. The Manchester objectives provide an excellent example. These are objectives whose intent all employees can understand. They are so straightforward that employees can judge for themselves whether the objectives are being met, and they permit employees to share with management a vision of the agency's purpose and functions.

Rarely in the United States does one encounter objectives stated as precisely as those proposed by the Manchester Executive. Most are vague, provide little managerial direction, and seldom suggest ways of determining whether objectives have in fact been achieved. One might expect that specific goals and objectives could be inferred from the apparent intent of federal, state, and local legislation. But a coherent program has not emerged from the many transit-assistance programs that have been voted into existence. Cervero and Brunk (1983) have shown that an assortment of federally legislated goals have been developed for UMTA. To UMTA's basket of policies must be added state and local directives that themselves have little in common. The result is a hodgepodge of policies that are largely ignored.

Guidance for appropriate objectives can be found in the wording of some federal and state legislation, but the intent has been obscured by legislative attempts to prescribe social and environmental goals. When Congress in 1974 amended the Urban Mass Transportation Act of 1964 to provide operating subsidies, it stated a clear goal for transit: "It is declared to be in the national interest to encourage and promote the development of transportation systems, embracing various modes of transport in a manner that will serve the states and local communities efficiently and effectively" (Section 5[g]Ii). Although this policy statement appears in only one section of the Urban Mass Transportation Act, its location in Section 5 is significant. Section 5 established the program under which financial assistance is allocated to states and urbanized areas for either capital or operating purposes. Before 1974, local governments were encouraged to seek federal funds for capital projects, because it was thought that reinvestment in deteriorating facilities would make transit more effective. However, when the federal government chose to subsidize operating costs, the stipulation that transit be provided in an efficient way was included.

The program audit guidelines of the U.S. General Accounting Office (1972) also spell out efficiency and effectiveness requirements. These guidelines specify three distinct aspects of transit performance that auditors are to evaluate: (1) financial performance and compliance with legislative intent, (2) economy and efficiency, and (3) program results or effectiveness. Under the first, auditors must look for simple procedural correctness in the conduct of financial and legal matters. The second "determines whether the entity is managing or utilizing its resources in an economical manner" (p. 2). Inquiry into the third aspect, program results, "determines whether the desired results or benefits are being achieved" (p. 2). The last two elements of the audit procedure can be considered efficiency and effectiveness policy statements.

Achievable objectives can be extracted from policy goals that require efficient and effective conduct of transit affairs. Such objectives can serve as organizers of the diverse activities of transit management. They also permit development of performance measures that do not have to be drastically revised as policy shifts over time.

Goals and objectives will naturally change over time. As will be seen in Chapter Two's documentation of transit history, the objectives of the past differed from and presaged those of the present. Future changes should be accepted as a matter of course, since the needs and desires of transit's constituencies will not be stable. With strategic planning, managers should be able to anticipate changes in goals and objectives.

Prospects for Transit. As noted at the beginning of this chapter, the transit industry of the 1980s is in good health. With the necessary capital investment made and base funding assured, the industry must now control the costs of transit production, compete with other modes where it has a comparative advantage, and profit from changes in its environment whenever possible. For example, managers should be aware of increasing congestion in urban areas and anticipate new opportunities afforded by commuter lanes on freeways and arterial highways.

Transit is not impossible to manage: current problems can be solved with sound approaches and reasonable effort. Transit agencies have sufficient authority to act, relevant knowledge is available, and the consequences of not acting are foreseeable. Transit also enjoys considerable public support. Although public support is not as enthusiastic as it was in the early 1970s, there is no organized opposition. In other words, the foundation exists on which to build efficient operations. What the industry needs now are managers sensitive to the transit environment and capable of formulating responsible plans for their agencies' futures.

Managing Strategically

When developing a strategic plan, transit managers must first define their agency's mission, its broad goals, and its specific objectives. They must then analyze the environment in which the agency operates, identifying institutions, persons, constituencies, and political trends that could affect the transit agency's goals. This first stage is called *situation assessment*. The environmental analysis, together with an assessment of the agency's strengths and weaknesses, is used to develop a set of possible plans. A cost-benefit analysis is performed for each possibility, and one plan is selected in light of estimated financial resources. This process is called *fiscal planning*. To carry out this plan, managers create a detailed program of implementation and allocate resources sufficient to support it. This is the *management* phase. Implementation is undertaken, and monitoring of performance against objectives is immediately begun to provide feedback to management. This phase is called *performance evaluation*.

Strategic management is a systematic approach to public administration that relates annual and short-run planning and budgetary cycles to a complex environment (Figure 1.) It is not a concept new to transportation. The Short-Range Transportation Plan (SRTP) and the Transportation Improvement Program (TIP) requirements published by the U.S. Department of Transportation on July 17, 1975, embody a similar cycle of analysis and action (Table 1). Monitoring performance has only recently been taken seriously by local agencies, however; it is still the most frequently slighted task in public management. Planning and budgeting have dominated operations, with little attention given to whether objectives are met. It cannot be overemphasized, however, that unless results are monitored against objectives, an agency is not being managed strategically.

Strategic planning is common in transit; strategic management is not. Alternative courses of action are evaluated, but they are not linked with fiscal planning or the monitoring of performance. Managers claim that strategic management is too demanding for public agencies, where choices must be made between needed programs. Alternative approaches are used where transit services are regarded as portfolios. Management chooses between those portfolios in which it enjoys a comparative advantage while easing out from those in which its services are inferior. When these marketing portfolios are integrated with fiscal planning and the monitoring

Table 1. Strategic Planning Compared to Requirements for Short-Range Transportation Planning (SRTP) and the Transportation Improvement Program (TIP).

Strategic Planning	*SRTP/TIP*
• Formulation of goals and objectives	• Plan shall be consistent with the area's goals and objectives
• Analysis of organizational environment—internal and external evaluations of status, strengths, and prospects, including financial resources	• A multiyear unified work program shall include discussion of the important transportation issues facing the area and a staged multiyear program of projects
• Identification and evaluation of alternative courses of action	• Analysis of alternative transportation investments to meet area-wide needs
• Selection of strategic actions	• Identify priorities for transportation improvements and include estimates of costs and revenues
• Implementation through work programs, operational plans, and budgets	• Update the program annually and group improvements of similar urgency into staging periods for implementation
• Control through monitoring progress and results of actions	• Monitor urban developments and transportation indicators

Source: Adapted from Meyer, 1983, and U.S. Department of Transportation, 1975.

of results, they represent a prudent approach toward managing strategically.

As stated earlier, transit is not impossible to manage. Successful managers will be those who can define goals and objectives appropriate for their agencies; select the means for accomplishing these and marshal the resources; motivate their employees; structure the organization; plan, deploy, and market the services; monitor, measure, and control service against the objectives adopted; and reward the performance of employees. This is a stiff order, but not impossible to achieve. Each of these tasks will be discussed in depth in the chapters to come. First, however, it will be illuminating to examine the consequences of not managing strategically. Such consequences can best be seen in a review of recent transit history.

2

How Expectations and Goals for Transit Have Changed

Public transit has been revived through the investment of federal, state, and local funds: no other domestic program has grown so rapidly. But in the course of this growth, transit has been assigned an array of poorly defined, often conflicting, and usually impossible-to-achieve goals. Solving social and environmental problems, rather than using resources efficiently, has had priority. This chapter summarizes the political events and changing policies that have benefited and buffeted transit systems since 1960. The purpose is to help transit managers understand how the environment in which transit now operates has come into existence, how poorly chosen goals have created many of transit's problems, and why current policy seeks a reduced federal commitment to public transit, greater operating efficiency, and the privatization of services.

A history of public transit is not intended. Smerk (1974, 1979) and Saltzman (1979) have explained the trends in transit ridership and the economic and institutional forces that contributed to the decline after 1946 when automobiles, gasoline, and tires became readily available and governments assisted highway building and suburbanization of housing. The financial reserves of most private bus companies were soon exhausted, which led to their appeal for either public assistance or public takeover. This chapter focuses on the period between 1960 and 1985 when public funds were provided for the takeover, modernization, and subsidization of public transit and describes the changing expectations with reference to federal legislation. During the first decade, a rational approach to urban problems was sought. Transit investment was expected to balance highway development and stimulate central city economies through urban renewal, employment opportunities, and improved accessibility. Between 1970 and 1978 environmental and social concerns were emphasized. An idealistic approach to urban problems prevailed, and transit was expected to reduce highway congestion, energy consumption, and air pollution. The need to provide transportation for the elderly and handicapped was given as an additional reason for assisting transit. Those were the golden years for transit. But the image soon tarnished when it became apparent that transit alone could not solve all these problems. After 1978, expectations were reduced, and concern was expressed over the size of transit deficits.

More economical approaches to urban transportation were sought, and transit was no longer expected to work urban renewal miracles. Transit policy evolved to suit societal issues, and each new agenda, along with its policies and regulations, was superimposed on those that had prevailed earlier. Obligations were cumulative, and management became muddled by poorly defined and often conflicting regulations and frustrated by planning and reporting requirements. It is somewhat prophetic that the two most successful rail developments in terms of economical construction and rider response were developed during this period without federal assistance. The Lindenwold line constructed from New Jersey into Philadelphia opened in 1969, and the San Diego Trolley opened on schedule in 1981. Developed with state and local funds, both began operations under budget and with a higher ridership than projected.

Federal assistance to transit was initially meager. But like so many other governmental projects begun as limited loan schemes, transit assistance did not remain small. The first loan program, enacted in 1961, was the proverbial camel's nose under the tent edge. By 1976 the camel had gotten its whole head in, and the federal program had increased to almost $2 billion. It continued to grow to $3.5 billion in 1981. With the advent of the Reagan presidency in 1981, however, came notice that subsidies for operating expenses were to be reduced and that transit must become more self-reliant. By 1984, federal assistance for all programs had declined to $3.4 billion.

Balanced Approach, 1961–1970

Federal funding of transit began as an attempt to help cities preserve commuter rail service threatened by the Federal Transportation Act of 1958. This act contained a provision that allowed railroads to stop providing interstate passenger service after thirty days if the Interstate Commerce Commission did not investigate the request. Previously, railroads had been obligated to obtain state approval before filing for abandonment. With passage of the act, several railroads immediately gave notice of their intention to abandon service. This alarmed the residents of cities along the eastern seaboard who depended on commuter railroads for suburban travel (Danielson, 1965). Having recently passed the Federal Defense Highway Act, Congress at first showed little sympathy for these commuters. Rail transit was considered to be important to only a few cities, whereas automobile and truck traffic was growing, and the proposed highway network was regarded as superior to rail transit systems. But when it became apparent that many states would have difficulty financing their share of the federal highway network, Congress grew more sympathetic to the needs of cities with large transit-dependent populations.

The election of President Kennedy in 1960 brought a symbolic commitment to urban problems that helped big-city mayors who were seeking federal assistance for transit as well as highways. Mayor Dilworth of Philadelphia had been the major proponent of legislation to aid the nation's cities. Eventually he succeeded in having a mass transit loan program approved as part of the Housing Act of 1961. A small amount was also included for demonstration projects. Only $42.5 million was approved, and the Housing and Home Finance Agency, which was authorized to administer the program, restrictively interpreted Congress's directive to loan money only "when repayment was reasonably certain." Since loans were seldom granted, it was the demonstration programs that influenced future transit legislation. They furnished highly visible examples of how transit might be improved with capital assistance.

Changing attitudes toward transit were apparent in legislative attempts to find a more comprehensive and balanced approach to urban planning. The Housing Act of 1961 required that mass transportation planning be included as an element of comprehensive planning under the Section 701 planning grants. A similar requirement was included in the Highway Act of 1962. Under Section 9, the secretary of transportation was to ensure that, after 1965, proposed highway projects would be based on a comprehensive, continuing, and cooperative planning process; alternative modes were to be considered when highway projects were being planned. These bills formalized the legislative goals that urban areas should have balanced transportation plans, that comprehensive transportation should be available to carless households, and that rail rapid transit could be used to facilitate commuting between the new suburbs and the central city. Such ideas seldom went beyond the planning stage, however, because federal grants, other than for demonstration projects, were not available for transit projects.

Following President Kennedy's 1962 transportation message, Senator Williams of New York introduced a bill authorizing capital grant assistance for the transit industry. The labor and automobile lobbies gave only cautious support to the proposed legislation. Labor welcomed the prospect of additional jobs but worried about the possible loss of the "right to strike" if municipalities used federal grants to purchase private transit companies. The legislation was opposed by the Farm Bureau and the U.S. Chamber of Commerce as an unwarranted extension of federal activity into domestic affairs, and the bill was finally defeated in the House Rules Committee.

Development of Consensus. The defeat of the 1962 legislation demonstrated that balanced transportation systems had not yet attracted cohesive support among legislators. In response to the bill's defeat, the Urban Passenger Transportation Association (UPTA) was formed to lobby for transit legislation. The association represented the mayors of large cities, the transit industry, the commuter railroad industry, and organized labor. Labor had joined after a clause (Section 13 [c]) was added to the proposed legislation that provided job protection for employees of private bus companies purchased by public agencies. Also protected was the right to bargain collectively.

The anxieties of labor were well founded. Modernization of public transit was being promoted in San Francisco and Miami, with claims that new capital investments would reduce dependence on labor. Since no employees would be required to operate them, the arguments went, automated transit systems would require only capital funding. Not only was automated rapid transit to be underwritten, but cities were to be assisted in the purchase of failing private bus companies. Because several states precluded third-party bargaining by public employees, labor's concern over job retention and collective bargaining rights was warranted.

The political strength of organized labor was apparent in the early attempts to obtain federal assistance for transit. Labor had initially withheld support for transit funding, and the 1962 bill had failed. Only after labor endorsed the legislation did President Johnson place the Urban Mass Transportation Act on his "must pass" agenda (Schneider, 1968). The bill was approved on June 30, 1964, and signed into law by President Johnson on July 9. To the goal of balanced transportation was now attached the principle that existing workers should not be adversely affected by future grants. This provision, administered by the Department of Labor, has given organized labor a means of delaying any transit project not beneficial to transit union members.

The act also contained provisions assigning transit a role in downtown urban renewal projects, requiring transit management to offer construction jobs to inner-city workers, and giving citizens affected by proposed transit plans the right to comment on them at public hearings.

Smerk regards the 1964 Urban Mass Transportation Act as the cornerstone for subsequent legislation: "Not only [did it] provide aid for the improvement and development of mass transportation systems, but [it also encouraged] the planning and establishment of areawide coordinated transport" (1974, p. 56). However, the planning and engineering studies that qualified projects for federal assistance were not funded, and grant applicants had to cover one-third of total project costs themselves (as well as justify projects on urban renewal grounds). Both requirements severely constrained requests for capital assistance; few cities had either planned for, or accumulated sufficient funds for, capital projects. Transit assistance remained a small program beneficial to cities with rail programs that were willing to protect employee status as facilities were modernized.

Establishment of UMTA. The 1966 amendments to the Urban Mass Transportation Act expanded the guidelines. The authorizations from 1964 had expired, and increased capital funding was needed for the purchase of equipment, including the assets of bankrupt private companies. In addition to renewing the capital funding authorizations, Congress in 1966 also provided support for planning, design studies, and management training and made research grants to colleges and nonprofit institutions. As part of the massive Housing and Urban Development Department, however, the transit program was somewhat stifled, since the department gave preference to grants that directly assisted urban renewal. A new Department of Transportation was established by Public Law 87-670 in 1966. This law required the secretaries of the two departments to determine whether the Urban Mass Transportation Program was an urban program or a transportation program. Allan Boyd, the first secretary of the Department of Transportation, had a broad view of transit and its potential role in a balanced transportation program for urban areas. He promised to give transit equal status with the federal highway program within his department, and the decision was announced by President Johnson to move the transit program to the Department of Transportation in 1968 and create the Urban Mass Transportation Administration (UMTA).

Despite all the legislative activity of the 1960s, not much was accomplished in public transportation. Between 1965 and 1970, only $768 million was provided for transit capital assistance—a very small amount compared with the $24.8 billion allocated to highways from the Highway Trust Fund. Even at the state and local levels, financial support for public transit was minimal. The principal activity was the public takeover of private bus companies that could not survive without public assistance.

Nevertheless, political support was growing. Transit was a timely issue for the 1960s: it was urban, inner city, and socially oriented. It was supported by influential leaders (mayors) and by constituencies with access to votes and campaign support (labor). These resources were used skillfully by transit advocates. This coalition was even more successful in the 1970s when it embraced environmental and energy issues. These issues attracted support from suburban voters and introduced new obligations for transit to add to its existing goals of developing balanced transportation, assisting urban renewal, protecting employees, hiring minorities, and soliciting community participation in transit projects.

Idealistic Approach, 1971–1981

Both the scope and amount of federal support increased substantially during the 1970s. When adjusted to 1980 dollars, the amount of federal assistance increased more than fourfold, from $772 million in 1971 to $3,367 million in 1980. State and local support for public transit also increased and, by 1980, thirty-nine states were providing financial assistance to transit. Whereas federal intervention in the 1960s grew out of society's desire to preserve transit systems and use them to stimulate economic development, the escalation in federal assistance during the 1970s was a product of the national preoccupation with environmental and energy issues.

Federal requirements promulgated as the result of the National Environmental Policy Act of 1969 and the Clean Air Amendment of 1970 focused attention on the harmful environmental effects of the automobile. New anxieties superseded pollution worries with the energy crisis of the winter of 1973–74. Republicans, then in control of the administration, promoted a program that would demonstrate the federal commitment to environmental quality and energy conservation yet would avoid the heavy cost of President Johnson's Great Society initiatives. The transit program was ideal and became what Altschuler, Womack, and Pucher (1979, p. 36) have described as "a policy for all perspectives":

The explanation, we judge, lies in the fact that transit proved to be a policy for all perspectives on the urban problem. Though its direct constituency was relatively small, its ideological appeal proved to be extremely broad. Whether one's concern was the economic vitality of cities, protecting the environment, stopping highways, energy conservation, assisting the elderly and handicapped and poor, or simply getting other people off the road so as to be able to drive faster, transit was a policy that could be embraced. This is not to say that transit was an effective way of serving all these objectives, simply that it was widely believed to be so. Additionally, because the absolute magnitude of transit spending was so meager at the beginning of this period, it was possible to obtain credit for rapid program growth with quite modest increases in the absolute level of expenditures.

Republican support for transit had its background in the 1960s, when the transit lobby needed the votes of Republican suburban legislators to offset the opposition of Southern Democrats to the urban spending of the Johnson administration. Transit advocates acquired support from suburban interests by allocating capital assistance on a discretionary basis. This meant that suburban cities were eligible for funding along with large central cities. Although more than 90 percent of the federal funding went to the ten largest cities with rail transit operations, federal transit administrators did a good job of "sprinkling" buses around in suburban communities. They also effectively extolled the ability of rail rapid transit to reduce congestion along arterial corridors between suburban communities and the central cities. Although the transit program was spearheaded by the big-city mayors and guided through Congress by lobbyists for organized labor, Republican representatives from suburban communities realized visible benefits for their constituents through federal transit assistance. And these grants carried the same obligations that were intended for central city transit systems.

Table 2. Service Produced, 1960–1985.

	1960	1965	1970	1975	1980	1985
Passenger Vehicles						
Rail[a]	11,866	10,664	10,600	10,660	10,697	11,153
Bus[b]	53,426	51,053	50,750	51,514	60,234	79,923
Total	65,292	61,717	61,350	62,174	70,931	91,076
% Change		(5.5)	(0.6)	1.4	14.1	28.4
Total Vehicle Miles						
Rail (millions)	465.7	436.9	440.8	448.4	402.8	407.8
Bus (millions)	1,677.1	1,571.3	1,442.3	1,541.3	1,690.2	1,787.0
Total (millions)	2,142.8	2,008.2	1,883.1	1,989.7	2,093.0	2,194.8
% Change		(6.3)	(6.2)	5.7	5.2	4.9
Miles of Route[c]						
Rail	3,935	2,173	2,081	---	1,186	---
Bus	56,696	61,266	57,063	---	125,630	---
Total	60,631	63,439	59,144	---	126,816	---
% Change		4.6	(6.8)	---	114.4	---
Employees						
Number	156,400	145,000	138,040	159,800	187,000	211,933
% Change		(7.3)	(4.8)	15.8	17.2	40.1
Operating Cost per Vehicle Mile						
All Modes ($)	0.64	0.72	1.06	1.89	2.98	4.92
1980 $[d]	1.65	1.72	2.06	2.67	2.98	3.97
% Change		4.2	19.8	29.6	11.6	33.2
Federal Funds All Programs						
($ millions)		11.2	154.3	1,410.1	3,367.3	3,529.4
1980 $ (millions)		26.8	299.3	1,607.5	3,367.3	2,844.7

Table 3. Service Consumed, 1960–1985.

	1960	1965	1970	1975	1980	1985
Passenger Trips						
All Modes (millions)	9,395	8,253	7,332	6,972	8,235	7,889
% Change		(12.2)	(11.2)	(4.9)	18.1	(4.2)
Passenger Revenue						
All Modes ($ mill)	1,334.9	1,340.1	1,639.1	1,860.5	2,556.8	4,661.8
% Change	(1.8)	(0.4)	22.3	13.5	37.4	82.3
Total (1980 $)[d]	3,449.4	3,196.8	3,183.3	2,629.3	2,556.8	3,757.4
% Change		(7.3)	(0.4)	(17.4)	(2.6)	47.0
Av Fare per Passenger						
All modes ($)	14.2	16.2	22.4	26.7	31.1	40.2
1980 $[d]	46.0	47.0	53.6	46.6	40.4	32.4
% Change		2.2	14.0	(13.1)	(13.3)	19.8
Passengers per Vehicle Mile						
All modes	4.4	4.1	3.9	3.5	3.9	3.7
% Change		(6.8)	(4.8)	(10.3)	11.4	(5.1)

Table 3. Service Consumed, 1960–1985, Cont'd.

	1960	1965	1970	1975	1980	1985
Operating Revenue per Vehicle Mile						
All modes ($)	0.66	0.72	0.91	0.94	1.23	2.19(e)
1980 $d	1.71	1.72	1.77	1.33	1.23	1.77
% Change		0.6	2.9	(24.9)	(7.5)	43.9
Ratio Operating Revenue to Operating Cost per Mile						
All modes	1.02	0.99	0.86	0.54	0.42	0.40

aIncludes subway, surface (light) rail, and cable (after 1975) in all rows. Automatic guideway and commuter rail excluded all rows until 1980. Nineteen eighty-five includes all rail modes.

bIncludes trolley buses in all rows.

cAdapted from U.S. Department of Commerce, 1974, and U.S. Department of Transportation, 1982.

dGross Domestic Product "Implicit Price Deflator" base year 1980=100. U.S. President, 1986.

eNineteen eighty-five figure includes auxillary and other nonoperating revenue.

Sources for Tables 2 and 3: Adapted from American Public Transit Association (APTA), 1985, Tables 5A, 7A, 9, 11, 13, 18. Nineteen eighty-five estimates were provided by APTA. Includes all modes for 1985 and many small rural systems formerly not reported by APTA.

Transit advocates used the support of their enlarged constituency to urge federal funding for operating assistance, so that public systems could be expanded without passing the full cost on to patrons. Operating revenue per vehicle mile had remained fairly stable between 1960 and 1970, but operating costs had begun to increase quite sharply (Tables 2 and 3). Operating revenue no longer covered costs for many systems, and they clearly required new sources of operating revenue. These needs coincided with changing federal priorities. In the 1960s the problems of crime, poverty, urban decay, and education were paramount, and transit was advocated as an urban renewal strategy. By 1970, Americans were beginning to realize that these problems could not be solved by money alone. What was sought was a new commitment to urban areas that stressed preservation of existing communities, improvement of environmental quality, and encouragement of economic revitalization through reduction of traffic congestion. Opposition to the federal highway program aided this policy shift. Interstate highways in urban areas only eased congestion for a short period.

By making it possible for people to drive farther and more
frequently and encouraging the use of private automobiles for
urban commuting, new freeways soon became as congested as
surface streets during peak hours. Freeways and their interchanges
were also prodigious consumers of urban land. Although they
increased the attractiveness of adjoining land, thereby benefiting
individual property owners, freeways removed substantial private
property from the tax rolls so that bisected communities seldom
came out ahead in terms of revenue. Public transportation was seen
as a substitute for the freeways. Once again, advocates for transit
called for balanced transportation, not so much for the sake of
urban renewal but as a way to respond to the new issues of highway
congestion and air pollution without destroying the urban tax base.

   The Urban Mass Transportation Act of 1970. This act
passed both the House and the Senate by overwhelming majorities,
committing the federal government to spending at least $10 billion
over a twelve-year period for urban mass transportation. Contract
authority was provided for grants totaling $3.5 billion during the
first five years. Local governments could now use federal funds not
only to plan and design major transit projects but also to construct
them.

   Transit had become a popular issue after almost a decade of
effort on the part of organized labor, city leaders, and the industry
itself. Even cities without previous aspirations to build rapid transit
systems now requested transit assistance. Small, privately operated
systems were going bankrupt, and local governments sought federal
funds to buy them up and expand service. Senior citizens did a great
deal to make transit popular. Through the regional conferences
preceding the 1971 White House Conference on the Aging, senior
citizens clearly communicated to elected officials that improved
public transit was their second most important issue after increased
Social Security benefits.

   Even the highway interests were forced to acknowledge the
momentum for transit. During the 1960s they had for the most part
ignored transit and had opposed suggestions that the highway trust
fund be used to finance transit services or facilities. However, in the
early 1970s, opposition to the highway program was so strong that

only by yielding some funds for public transit construction could its lobby achieve support for completing the interstate highway system. The Highway Act passed by Congress in 1973 allowed local authorities to exchange transit projects for interstate highway projects and increased the proportion of total cost for transit projects that were eligible for federal funding. Expenditure for transit capital projects was increased from two-thirds to 80 percent of a project's net cost. Significant policy changes were also introduced. For the first time, local and state authorities could utilize highway funds for constructing exclusive bus lanes and fringe parking lots and for purchasing buses or rail cars. This same legislation also required transit agencies to provide full access for individuals with disabilities, a provision that ultimately led to a very costly and controversial program.

Although federal capital funding for transit was discretionary, ample funding was easy to secure. To obtain capital grants, urban areas had only to comply with federal regulations and produce a 20 percent local match for federal dollars. New vehicles and renovated maintenance facilities began to appear in suburban communities and small cities as well as in major metropolitan areas. As it renovated, consolidated, and grew, the industry enlarged its constituency by portraying transit as the solution for urban congestion and polluted air. And the industry made the most of the energy crisis that occurred in the winter of 1973–74, advertising itself as a desirable transportation alternative.

Operating Subsidies. While operating revenue per vehicle mile had remained fairly stable between 1960 and 1970, operating costs had risen quite sharply (Tables 2 and 3). Revenues no longer covered costs for many systems. However, transit managers were unwilling to increase fares because the resulting decrease in ridership would have reduced their ability to fulfill social and environmental goals. States such as Pennsylvania, California, Massachusetts, and Connecticut began to provide transit operating subsidies early in the 1970s, but the federal government rejected such a policy in 1971. Federal transit policy was patterned after its highway policy—the federal role was to provide capital assistance only. Maintenance and operating support were delegated to state and local governments. Opinion changed, however, as a result of the 1973–74 oil embargo, when transit was heralded not only as a substitute travel mode but also as a means of conserving petroleum.

Congress authorized federal operating subsidies in the National Mass Transportation Act of 1974. Section 5 of the Urban Mass Transportation Act of 1964 was amended to authorize the use of federal funds for "payment of operating expenses to improve or to continue such services by operation, lease, contract, or otherwise" (Public Law 93-93-503, Section 103 [a]). The funding authorized under Section 5 could also be used for capital expenses, although in practice very little money was used for this purpose. Because Section 5 funding was allocated to urbanized areas based upon population criteria, some medium-sized cities, such as Memphis, Tennessee, were eligible for more operating assistance than they could match with local funds and used Section 5 funds to purchase vehicles. Matching the federal funds was not a constraint for most transit systems who used federal funds to expand services and decrease fares.

Employee protection, formalized in earlier legislation, was reaffirmed by the 1974 legislation. Transit managers had hoped to eliminate the labor protection clause (13 [c]) from the Urban Mass Transportation Act or at least to prevent its application to operating assistance, fearing that the protection clauses would impair management's attempts to improve labor efficiency. Subsequent events have proved them correct: service increased by 11 percent between 1970 and 1980 at the same time that assistance from all levels of government increased by almost 800 percent to $6.8 billion. Management bears responsibility for the decline in transit productivity, but its options were limited by the protection afforded to employees under Section 13 (c).

To employee protection was added the principle of reduced fares for the elderly. Given impetus by the White House Conference on the Aging in 1971, groups representing older Americans had since become skillful lobbyists. They agreed to support operating assistance for transit only when guaranteed that language in the 1974 act would reduce fares for elderly, low-income, and handi-capped persons.

By 1975 transit had become the beneficiary of an enormous amount of capital and operating funding. Capital was available not only to complete the Bay Area Rapid Transit (BART) system in San Francisco and the METRO system in Washington, D.C., but also to begin new systems for Baltimore, Atlanta, and Miami. In addition, light rail systems were modernized in Philadelphia, Boston, and San Francisco; and planning and design started in Buffalo, Portland, Santa Clara County in California, Sacramento, Los Angeles, and Detroit. New buses began to appear in almost every urban area from Tampa, Florida, to Orange County, California, and in many rural areas as well.

Availability of federal, state and local assistance motivated transit managers to repeat earlier mistakes. Service was expanded to the suburbs and beyond in search of passengers as it had been in the streetcar era. Expansion was pursued regardless of cost in the belief that success was determined by ridership growth. Careful appraisals of the cost of providing services and financing future deficits were neglected while expansion was promoted. Route miles were increased at the expense of service frequency. Route miles of bus service rose from 91,000 to 125,600 between 1970 and 1980, but vehicle miles of service per route mile actually decreased. Transit was marketed to new groups unlikely to use transit services. As a result, transit systems became overextended during the 1970s, with the cost of service bearing little relationship to revenue. As a result, transit confronted the same specter as it had during prior decades, when many systems went bankrupt or were forced to curtail services and increase fares.

National Surface Transportation Act of 1978. Between 1974 and 1978, considerable debate took place in Congress over the wisdom of providing operating subsidies to transit. Not only were such subsidies costly, but they posed numerous problems. The larger cities complained that the government's population-based formula allocated insufficient funds to large systems and compensated small cities too generously. It was estimated, for example, that in 1978 the transit rider in New York City was subsidized by four cents per trip, whereas transit riders in Santa Barbara, California, received a subsidy of fifty cents per trip. Such problems were likely to arise when uniform national goals for transit were pursued under very different urban conditions. However, congressmen could not agree on more equitable methods for allocating funds, and the population-based formula was retained with minor changes in the National Surface Transportation Act of 1978. Apart from an extension until 1982 of slightly increased Section 5 funding, no substantial changes were made in the laws applying to public transit. Transit had reached its zenith in public support. Thereafter, it would have to become more self-supporting.

Changing Attitudes. Division within the transit lobby was apparent. Whereas in the early 1970s a united coalition had convinced federal legislators to support funding for transit, by 1978 the lobby had fragmented. Large urban areas with rail systems argued for an allocation formula based on route and vehicle miles of service, a methodology opposed by transit managers and mayors from urban areas served by buses only. They preferred a formula based on population and population density. Both groups criticized the unions, claiming that labor demanded more than its fair share of subsidies. The support of handicapped groups for transit began to wane; these groups were disappointed by the failure of transit authorities to provide the handicapped with full access to transit services. The escalating costs of transit in urban areas—especially the high per-passenger deficit for new rail systems and for express bus systems from suburban park-and-ride lots—began to alarm business groups that had formerly supported public transit in the belief that it would solve urban congestion problems.

Legislation was proposed in 1980 to extend the federal subsidy program, but this initiative collapsed when the competing transit interests refused to compromise on the funding formula. Soon thereafter, the transition report of the incoming Reagan administration stated its categorical opposition to providing federal subsidies for transit operating expenses. Opposition to continued operating support developed at other levels of government. Alarmed that transit deficits had been increasing at twice the rate of inflation, city governments and state legislators knew that changes were required. When Boston closed its system down for twenty-six hours in December 1980 because of insufficient funds, the debate in the

Massachusetts legislature over "bail out" funding indicated the extent to which transit had lost political support at the state level. Funds were provided, but in the following year Massachusetts passed strong "managements' rights" legislation that restored the flexibility and rights that management had lost to labor at the bargaining table. The new legislation transformed the Massachusetts Bay Transportation Authority. Management was encouraged to contract out for the rebuilding of rail cars and station cleaning, hire part-time workers, assign workers and overtime on the basis of availability rather than seniority, plan and determine levels of service, and establish productivity standards.

Also in the early 1980s, the city of Chicago fell $80 million short of balancing its 1982 fiscal year budget, and for several months the Transit Authority paid none of its bills except those for wages and fuel. The budget reduction required for the system's survival was accomplished through drastic changes in the labor agreement as well as service cutbacks.

Cost-Effective Approach

As indicated above, the inauguration of President Reagan in 1981 signaled a shift in federal transit policy. Responding to public concern over the rising cost of federal programs, the incoming administration unveiled its policy of New Federalism. This philosophy promoted local control of public programs (including responsibility for expenditures), fiscal prudence and accountability, elimination of costly regulations, and greater private-sector provision of public services.

These principles, which represented sharp changes from the social and environmental goals that had previously guided transit policy, met opposition in Congress. Nearly every urban area in the nation and many rural areas as well had benefited from federal transit assistance, and labor and management were able to construct an intense and successful lobbying effort to prevent funding reductions. In the end, the administration achieved only regulatory reform; other issues were stalemated. Federal operating assistance continued, but both the increases sought by transit agencies and the phase-out desired by the adminstration were stalled in Congress until an infusion of new money provided an opportunity to restructure the transit program.

       Surface Transportation Assistance Act of 1982. Once again transit found an ally. In the early 1960s transit had been supported by big-city mayors and labor unions. In the early 1970s environmentalists, energy conservationists, and the elderly allied themselves behind transit. In 1982, it was the highway lobby and national concern over deteriorating infrastructure that gave transit the support it needed.

       Highways and bridges, many of them built with federal assistance, were deteriorating because revenues from gasoline taxes were declining in real terms. Many governors and most state highway officials joined the trucking industry, contractors, and representatives of the automobile and oil industry in urging the Reagan administration to increase the excise tax on fuel by five cents per gallon. This revenue would be used for maintaining highways and completing the interstate highway. However, in order to obtain sufficient votes in Congress, the highway lobby had to agree to share one cent of the tax with transit. The Reagan administration quickly made use of the tax proposal, insisting that New Federalism precepts appear in the enabling legislation in return for administration support. The Surface Transportation Assistance Act was approved in December 1982. As of April 1983 a five-cent-per-gallon federal tax was imposed on gasoline, with one-fifth of the revenues dedicated to a transit trust fund.

       Additional funding was now available for transit, but the provisions of the Surface Transportation Assistance Act posed a large structural problem. In fact, a marvelous opportunity to develop a unified transportation fund was missed. Some American urban areas such as New York, Boston, Philadelphia, and San Francisco are heavily committed to transit. Others, such as Los Angeles, Detroit, Miami, Houston, and Dallas-Fort Worth much prefer the automobile. But both groups shape their transportation policies so as to maximize federal funding rather than accommodate local preferences for travel modes. A unified transportation block grant could have helped cities choose *between* transit and highway programs in terms of net community benefits. However, current policy does not permit such choices. When a city rejects a project that was to have received federal funding, the city cannot reallocate funds to "parallel" transportation projects. A case in point is Los Angeles. Had the city rejected its Metro Rail subway, federal transit funds could not have been spent for improvements to the paralleling Santa Monica Freeway. These funds would have been sent elsewhere, perhaps to expand rail systems in San Francisco or San Diego. Given the choice of undertaking a dubious project or losing federal money altogether, no city will sit by and let funds go to competing cities.

In addition to establishing the transit trust fund, the 1982 Surface Transportation Assistance Act modified the old allocation formula and its application. Henceforth, a larger percentage of the subsidy total was to be allocated by formula (two-thirds versus one-third under the 1978 act), and the basis for allocation itself was altered. Whereas the bulk of formula funds had been allocated according to population and population density under the old Section 5 formula, the new Section 9 formulas allocated funds primarily according to the amount of transit service supplied in each urban area (vehicle miles and route miles). Use of the funds was also regulated so that a decreasing proportion of each region's allocation could be spent for operating assistance.

Managerial Challenges. The 1982 legislation and subsequent shifts in the government's transit policy represent another set of changes in federally assigned goals—and another set of challenges for transit managers. Transportation policy in American cities has shifted from one simple panacea to another without taking into account the complexity of human behavior that underlies travel preferences. Transportation managers understand these preferences, but the segmented nature of funding policies and federal regulations precludes undertaking transit improvements that would better match travel needs in different cities or even in different areas of the same city. The Reagan administration has emphasized the need to return local service and operation decisions to state and local levels, but applicants for federal funding still have to comply with a host of financial requirements, planning regulations, and reporting obligations.

American transit is still at the mercy of political decisions and the interest groups that shape those decisions. Testifying before the House Subcommittee on Investigation and Oversight, Altshuler (1981) criticized the federal government for its lack of consistent goals and objectives for transit. Similar concern was voiced by the U.S. General Accounting Office: "It became clear during [our] review . . . that mass transit has been assigned an array of goals to accomplish by federal, state, and local governments and that these goals were poorly defined, not prioritized, and, in some cases, conflicting. The end result has been confusion as to what mass transit is supposed to do and an inability to determine what mass transit is accomplishing" (Bonnell, 1981, p. 555).

The heavy hand of politics has frequently been apparent on transit policy since 1960, with the result that attempts to improve the management of transit operations have been sporadic. Transit has been expected to revitalize central cities and create jobs; reduce congestion and air pollution and save energy; improve transportation for carless households, the elderly, and persons with disabilities; and protect the working conditions of transit employees—and to accomplish these goals while providing safe and reliable service. Each set of expectations brought new rules and regulations with which transit managers had to comply. And each set has been cumulative. Most of the regulations contained in the UMT Act of 1964 still apply. Once-small administrative staffs now constitute 9 percent of the work force. Most of these additional employees are needed to comply with federal, state, and local regulations rather than to supply safe and reliable service.

Changes will be necessary now that it is clear that funding from all levels of government is declining. Transit managers will be called on to provide a reasonable level of service within this new framework that is attractive to regular users. Their primary objective will be to preserve the ridership gains made during the 1970s within a fiscally austere environment. They will have to strike an equilibrium between revenues, service, and ridership. Use of private providers will help to make transit more self-reliant, but an uneasy truce exists between private companies and public agencies. Private companies believe that public agencies are obstructing their expansion, while public managers believe that the only advantage held by private firms is that they can employ less costly, nonunion labor. Public managers doubt that this cost advantage will last if private companies assume more than 10 percent of service in any region.

The new equilibrium will require managerial skills of a high order. Application of demonstrated techniques of performance measurement, cost analysis, market segmentation, service diversification, and resource allocation will be required. Whether the industry can shift its operational strategies in time to avert a downward spiral of ridership is still unclear. However, there is growing evidence that among the more innovative and sophisticated agencies, beneficial changes are already being made. The viability of American transit may hinge, simply, on the ability of its current generation of managers to manage.

3

A Strategic Approach
to Transit Management

Transit would not have survived in most cities without governmental assistance. Critics may denounce the high cost of this achievement and the way in which transit is organized and provided, but few will deny its benefits for urban Americans. The challenge now is to develop leaner, more efficient transit systems in areas where transit ridership is high and to encourage a greater diversity of services and service providers in other markets.

This chapter outlines a strategic approach to transit management that emphasizes the assessment of organizational strengths and weaknesses, the selection of development strategies or scenarios, and the monitoring of performance. It begins with an assessment of American transit, including a brief description of service modes and variations in service provision. It concludes by outlining a more systematic approach to transit management—an approach that will be further developed in subsequent chapters.

In contrast to the historical perspective of Chapter Two, this chapter describes the geography of American transit: where it is provided, by what modes, how it differs from place to place, and what its opportunities are. The two orientations—historical and geographical—place transit management in its situational context. Just as a grasp of transit's changing objectives enables managers to understand why various constituencies have different expectations for transit, so too can a knowledge of how transit functions in different environments suggest possibilities for transit development. Both perspectives provide the necessary background for the strategic approach to transit management outlined in Figure 2.

Figure 2. Steps in Strategic Management.

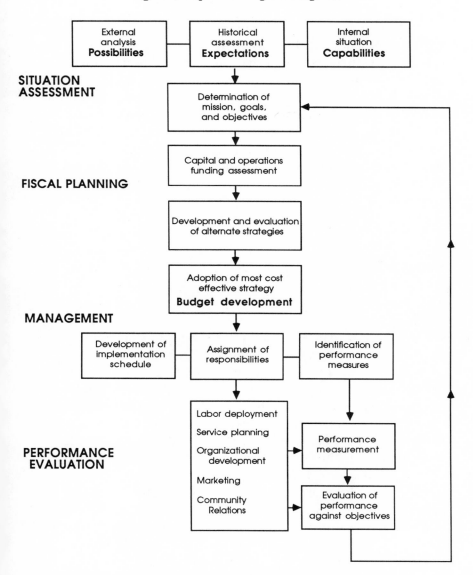

Strategic management can be subdivided as follows: situation assessment, fiscal planning, management, and performance evaluation. It is a continuous process that is structured by budget development, adoption, implementation, and evaluation of results against budget proposals.

Transit Modes

More than 1,000 public and private agencies provide transit service in America. Of these, 336 have reported data to UMTA in accordance with Section 15 of the Urban Mass Transportation Act of 1964, as amended. The remainder are small, usually owner-operated companies that provide charter service and express commuter service for major metropolitan areas or in rural areas. In this book, two types of agencies are not included as public transit because they provide exclusive-ride services. These are taxis and private and nonprofit agencies that serve special clients such as hospitals, social centers, churches, and schools. However, when taxis provide share-ride service under contract to public transit agencies, they are included as public transit.

Unless otherwise cited, statistics used in this chapter come from two sources: the *National Urban Mass Transportation Statistics: 1982 Section 15 Annual Report* (U.S. Department of Transportation, 1983) and *The Status of the Nation's Local Public Transportation: Conditions and Performance* (U.S. Department of Transportation, 1984). Information for both documents is based on the 336 agencies that reported under the Section 15 requirements. No reliable data are available on the other operators.

Transit is provided in a variety of modes. This chapter is primarily concerned with conventional bus service, rapid, light, and commuter rail service, trolleybus service, and demand-responsive service. The operating characteristics of these modes are summarized in Table 4, but readers desiring more detail should refer to Gray and Hoel (1979), Vuchic (1981), or Reno and Bixby (1985).

1. *Conventional fixed-route, bus transit* is the most widespread and predominant form of service. Nationally, it provides 83 percent of the revenue service hours and accommodates 72 percent of the passenger trips. It operates under a variety of conditions: as local service (averaging thirteen to fifteen miles per hour), as express service on arterial streets (fifteen miles per hour), on freeways (twenty-eight miles per hour), and on grade-separated busways (forty-five miles per hour). Operating speed depends on passenger boardings, urban density, and congestion. Service is used predominantly for short trips averaging 3.6 miles. Patrons generally do not

Table 4. Transit Operating Characteristics by Mode, 1982.

	Motor Bus	Rapid Rail	Light Rail	Trolley Bus	Demand Response	Ferry Boat	Other	All Modes	Comm. Rail[c]
Operating Expense by Function (%)									
Vehicle Operation	59.5	30.7	36.2	60.7	37.5	14.4	49.6	50.7	49
Vehicle Maintenance	21.0	19.2	26.7	17.2	9.6	4.9	11.4	20.3	23
Nonvehicle Maintenance	2.8	22.0	23.9	7.6	1.1	0.8	17.5	8.4	19
General Administration[a]	16.8	28.1	13.2	14.5	51.9	79.9	21.5	20.6	9
Total %	100	100	100	100	100	100	100	100	100
Total Operating Expense (millions)	4,851.4	1,954.4	111.2	66.2	83.1	41.7	14.0	7,122.0	1,161
Number of Systems	311	9	8	5	147	3	6	336[d]	7
Active Vehicles	56,109	9,615	1,089	768	1,966	16	250	69,813	
Route Miles	11,430	1,142	392	426	NR	NR	NR	14,390	
Employees	122,401	47,945	3,526	1,779	2,264	850	309	179,074	
Annual Vehicle Revenue Hours (thousands)[b]	110,238	19,640	1,410	1,514	3,306	46	NR	132,254	
Annual Passenger Trips (millions)	5,287	1,809	132	153	12	25	12	7,667	285
Annual Passenger Miles (millions)	19,139	8,588	377	251	70	113	63	30,423	7,055
Trip Length (miles)	3.6	5.3	2.9	1.7	5.8	4.5	5.3		25

[a]Services purchased from private operators reported as General Administration Expense.
[b]Passenger car revenue hours reported for rapid rail and light rail.
[c]U.S. Department of Transportation, 1984. Not included in All Modes column.
[d]Multimode agencies only reported once.
NR No data reported.
Source: U.S. Department of Transportation, 1983.

ride much further unless they are using express service. Fixed-route service utilizes full-sized heavy-duty buses operating by schedule. Articulated buses based on European designs are now constructed in the United States, and they are increasingly being used for heavily traveled routes and on busways. Minibuses (less than thirty feet long) are used in small cities and for central city circulation. Frequency of service varies with the time of day. Frequent service is provided in the morning and afternoon peak-demand periods. During the midday and on weekends and holidays, the elapsed time between buses (the headway) is longer, or service may even be discontinued. Service in the evenings is reduced, with very few agencies operating all-night, "owl" service.

2. *Demand-responsive service* comprises a broad range of public transportation such as dial-a-ride, shared-ride taxis, jitneys, commuter buses, and van pools. Collectively these services are labeled *paratransit* (Kirby and others, 1974). Many of these services are provided by private carriers under contract to public agencies. Rural transit systems are frequently operated on a demand-responsive basis because where the density of population is low, service can respond to demand rather than operating by schedule. Many small systems report under this category, but they carry only 0.16 percent of passenger trips.

3. *Rapid rail transit* is frequently called heavy rail service. This mode is defined as urban rail service operating on exclusive rights-of-way and using electrically powered, multiple-unit vehicles. Vehicles are entered from floor-level platforms, and fares are generally collected at turnstiles. Nine systems operated rapid rail in 1982. Four of these are exclusively rail agencies. The remainder operate rail systems along with buses and other modes of transit. For example, the transit authority in Boston operates both heavy and light rail and buses and contracts for paratransit, commuter rail, and ferryboat service. These nine rail systems produce 12 percent of the national vehicle revenue hours of service and carry 23 percent of all passengers. Passengers travel an average of 5.3 miles per trip (the speed of rapid rail transit enables them to travel farther than by bus in congested areas). The older systems in New York, Chicago, Boston, Philadelphia, and Cleveland generally have more closely spaced stations, and the vehicles are controlled

manually by motormen in response to cab or wayside signals. The new systems in San Francisco, Atlanta, Washington, D.C., Baltimore, and Miami have computer-aided control systems. Stations are farther apart, and passengers ride farther at faster speeds.

4. *Light rail transit* involves streetcar-like vehicles that operate both on streets and on grade separated rights-of-way. Vehicles are electrically powered from overhead wires. Passengers board by step-entry from either low platforms or street level. Stations can be quite modest, as in Pittsburgh, New Orleans, and Cleveland or elaborate, as in Buffalo. Fares are normally collected on the vehicle. The eight light rail systems operating in 1982 provided 1 percent of the national vehicle hours of service and carried almost 2 percent of the passengers. Streetcars were the predominant transit mode before 1920, when almost every city had a privately operated system. They are again becoming popular: San Diego opened a new system in 1981, Buffalo in 1985, and Portland in 1986. When rights-of-way along abandoned railroads are available, these systems are cheaper to construct than heavy rail. However, when the rights-of-way must be purchased, and tracks and stations constructed, light rail is not significantly cheaper than heavy rail.

5. *Trolleybuses* with electrical power drawn from overhead cables are comparatively rare in America. Unlike light rail, they have not enjoyed a revival, and they make a significant contribution to transit only in San Francisco, Philadelphia, Boston, Seattle, and Dayton, Ohio. This is somewhat surprising, as trolleybuses offer several advantages for congested central cities: they are lower and easier to enter than buses, they accelerate quickly, and they do not pollute the air.

6. *Commuter rail service* is provided on railroad rights-of-way with diesel-hauled or electrically powered trains. Generally there are one or two stations in the central business district (CBD), and fares are collected by conductors. Service is usually operated by commercial railroads and by Amtrak under contract to metropolitan transit agencies. Exceptions are New York and Philadelphia, where commuter rail is operated by both the transportation agency and Amtrak. Most of the equipment and stations are old, and their

use is governed by railroad procedures. Commuter rail plays an important role in Boston, New York, Philadelphia, Pittsburgh, Washington, D.C., Chicago, and San Francisco. In 1982, 285 million passengers (equivalent to almost 4 percent of the nation's transit trips) traveled by commuter rail. It would appear that passengers travel much farther (an average of twenty-five miles per trip) on commuter rail than on heavy rail or on bus; this statistic reflects the concentration of commuter rail service around New York City, to which people commute long distances from Connecticut, the Hudson Valley, and Long Island. Statistics for commuter rail are not as complete as those reported for other modes so they are shown to the right of Table 4 and are not included in the totals column.

America's public transit is provided by a fleet of about 56,000 buses, 820 trolleybuses, 9,600 rapid rail cars, 1,100 light rail cars, 4,400 commuter rail cars, 300 commuter rail locomotives, and 2,000 paratransit vehicles. Excluding commuter rail, 132 million vehicle hours of revenue service were provided and 7,667 million passenger trips were made in 1982. Commuter rail increased the total by 285 million trips. For all 343 agencies, this represents about 26 million trips on an average weekday, made by approximately 10 million people.

Geography of Transit

Transit service is geographically widespread. All metropolitan areas, most small cities, and many rural areas have some form of public transit. However, service is neither provided nor consumed uniformly: 85 percent is found in the twenty largest cities with 49 percent of the total population of the United States. Forty-one percent is consumed in the New York-New Jersey urbanized area, and another 11 percent in Chicago. An additional 33 percent is utilized by the next eighteen largest urban markets. Transit serves a variety of trip purposes in these big cities. Elsewhere transit is primarily used for the journey to and from work; in the off-peak hours it is used mostly by women, senior citizens, and students.

Although transit use increased between 1970 and 1982, the proportion of all trips made by transit compared to total trips actually declined from 3.7 to 3.2 percent. Both automobile ownership and travel increased during the 1970s, and transit suffered from the competition. Transit enjoys no monopoly in urban travel. The overwhelming growth in "automobility," together with vigorous competition from taxicabs, has meant that, although transit ridership has increased, its share of urban travel has declined. Whereas 17.5 percent of the households in the United States did not own an automobile in 1970, that proportion had declined to 15.9 percent in 1980. The cost of purchasing an automobile increased at only half the rate of the consumer price index over the decade, meaning that the real cost of an automobile declined. More American households could afford to purchase automobiles in 1980 than in 1970, and they were using them instead of transit, despite the real increase in gasoline prices.

Even for the journey to work, a market segment in which transit enjoys advantages over the auto, transit use has declined (Fulton, 1983). Significant declines occurred in the Northeast, and these were not offset by the increases in the West and South. The majority of cities with a million or more residents increased the number of workers using transit, but small increases in the majority did not offset the loss of almost 600,000 regular users between 1970 and 1980 in the Northeast.

A variety of cultural processes explain transit's changing role in urban transportation. These include increasing competition from the automobile, dispersal of work throughout metropolitan areas, and governmental investment in highways. Yet there are markets in which transit remains successful. These need to be examined as a prerequisite to any discussion of the spatial distribution of transit. Work trips still account for 59 percent of all weekday transit trips. This is down from 70 percent in 1970, because trips to suburban job sites have been lost to automobiles. However, the proportion of transit trips from the suburbs to the CBD has increased in most areas, with the exception of Northeastern cities, where it has declined slightly. In San Francisco, for example, these trips have increased from 48 to 53 percent and in Houston from 13 to 15 percent. Transit succeeded in maintaining its share of CBD trips, and with the continuing increase in CBD office growth, this market is likely to grow.

Another important market segment consists of college and high school student travel. Fourteen percent of all transit trips are school related, a circumstance that can cause operational problems when school and commuter travel coincide. American transit operators cannot influence their environment as operators can in some foreign countries. For example, in Poona, India, operators refuse to grant passes to students unless schools reschedule their hours to avoid peak travel demand. One of the consequences of accepting governmental assistance in America is that it virtually precludes the imposition of travel restraints.

Medical and shopping-related trips account for 11 percent of transit travel. Since transit is not convenient for this type of travel, it is used primarily by persons from low-income or autoless households. Often these are the same. Seventy-one percent of all trips were made by persons from households with an income of less than $20,000 per year in 1982, and 40 percent with an income of less than $10,000. Many of these trips originated from homes with women as heads of household. This, in part, accounts for the fact that 62 percent of riders are women. Women's use of transit has declined as more women have joined the work force. In 1970 only 43 percent of the women over sixteen years of age were working outside the home, and many homemakers used transit in the midday hours for shopping and social purposes (Giuliano, 1979). By 1980, 52 percent of these women were working, thereby decreasing the demand for midday transit travel.

Large transit markets exist for work trips to the CBD, as well as to schools and colleges. Another transit market exists for travel by persons from low-income households. This suggests that the greatest market potential for transit is to be found in high-density neighborhoods populated by low-income individuals and students and along radial corridors connecting the suburbs with the CBD or other commercial megacenters. Pushkarev and Zupan (1977) summarize this argument in *Public Transit and Land Use Policy*. Graphs in their publication indicate that transit usage increases sharply above a density of seven dwelling units per acre. This density occurs in older suburban areas constructed before 1960 and is occurring again as lower-density, inner-city suburbs are undergoing rejuvenation. Older, single-family homes are being replaced with condominiums and apartments, which increase density to levels that can sustain fixed-route transit.

Relationships between nonresidential floor space (a surrogate for employment) in the CBD and demand for transit are described by Pushkarev and Zupan (1977). Where the CBD has less than 20 million square feet of nonresidential space, the bus mode is most suitable. Above 20 million, light rail becomes a feasible alternative, and above 50 million rapid rail should be considered in any plans for future development.

The interrelationship between transit, population density, and employment must be considered when evaluating scenarios for strategic management. At successively higher levels of population density and employment, transit can afford to operate more frequent service over longer periods of the day, with faster, higher-capacity modes. Other factors such as the relative travel-time ratio between public transit and the automobile and the availability and cost of parking in the CBD also come into play. These relationships are known, and considerable effort can be saved when they are considered strategically.

Typology of Bus Transit

Classifying transit agencies into groups helps analysts understand variations between transit agencies and the strategic opportunities available to each type of agency. It also helps management evaluate the performance of an agency by reference to its peers. Rail systems can be classified as heavy, light, or commuter. However, there are so few systems in each category that a further division serves little purpose other than to differentiate new systems (completed since 1970) from old systems. By comparison, there are considerable differences among the 311 motor bus systems. My colleagues and I have developed a typology for bus transit for our research on transit performance (Fielding and others, 1984). Cluster analysis techniques were used to differentiate bus transit systems into twelve groups, each distinctive in nature and composed of agencies with similar operating characteristics. Only bus systems or the bus divisions of multimodal agencies were included in the typology.

Characteristics used to create the typology were size (the number of vehicles required for peak service), peak-to-base operating ratio, and average operating speed (Figure 3). Both size and peak-to-base demand are useful predictors of the cost of producing service. Average speed distinguishes between suburban and small-city systems (fast) and central city systems (slow).

For descriptive purposes it is useful to reduce the number of groups from twelve to five categories on the basis of size. The regional transit systems in cities such as New York, Chicago, Los Angeles, Cleveland, and St. Louis (groups 11 and 12) are large, costly systems that provide almost half the nation's bus service and recover between 40 and 60 percent of their operating costs from fares. Groups 9 and 10 are similar to each other in size but differentiated in terms of speed. These include slower systems in older cities such as Milwaukee and New Orleans (group 10) and faster systems in new and expanding areas such as San Diego, Salt Lake City, and Houston (group 9). Systems in group 8 are distinctive in terms of their emphasis on peak-period service. They are usually fast, commuter-oriented systems and represent a wide range of size categories. Groups 5, 6, and 7 are typical midsize bus operations with between 50 and 150 peak vehicles. These are the most efficient systems. The remaining systems (groups 1, 2, 3, and 4) are small, with fewer than 50 vehicles. There are some exceptions to the size criterion in the last two categories because the small- and medium-sized systems operate under a range of speed and peak-to-base characteristics.

This classification was created to help managers evaluate the costs and performance of their agencies in comparison with other systems operating under similar conditions, but it is also useful for evaluating strategic options. For example, an agency in peer group 8—a group of high-speed, peak-service, commuter-oriented systems—might compare its costs per revenue hour and find that they are substantially higher than the peer-group mean. If the cause of this higher cost is determined to be inefficient use of labor, then the agency could evaluate such strategic options as increasing part-time labor or contracting for service with private operators. Both options will probably require approval by employee representatives, and the comparative data on cost and labor efficiency will be

Figure 3. Peer-Group Typology for Bus Transit.

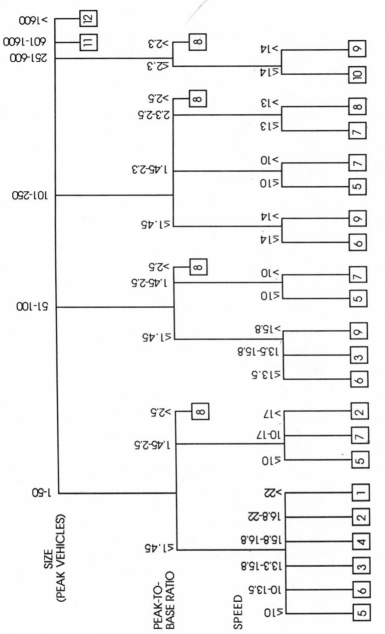

Transit systems can be classified into twelve peer groups based on size, peak-to-base service demand, and average speed.

Source: Fielding and others, 1984.

useful in negotiations. In subsequent chapters, the reader will be referred back to these peer groups when budgeting, labor, and marketing are discussed. The value of the typology for strategic management can be seen by observing the cost per hour for transit between 1980 and 1984 (Figure 4). The national average cost per revenue vehicle hours is not representative. The larger systems (groups 9, 10, 11, and 12) are the most expensive, whereas the midsize systems are the least expensive (groups 5, 6, and 7). A U-shaped cost curve is illustrated by Figure 4, which indicates that diseconomies of scale exist in transit; smaller and midsized agencies are more cost efficient than large agencies. Information of this nature is important when evaluating strategic opportunities for agencies of different size and operating characteristics.

Strategic Management

As described in Chapter One, strategic management is a systems approach to public administration. Decisions on what an organization should do in the future are based on external and internal analysis and the expectations of constituencies *(situation assessment).* These are integrated with estimates of the financial resources available *(fiscal planning);* determinations of who will do what and how it will be accomplished *(management* of labor, service planning, marketing and community relations); and the monitoring of ongoing activities *(performance evaluation)* (Figure 2).

Strategic management is more than strategic planning. It goes beyond the analysis and evaluation of strategic options. It involves deploying resources to achieve goals on the basis of plans and scenarios and uses performance evaluation both as a control mechanism and as a stimulus for revision. For transit, strategic management means analyzing possibilities and capabilities, defining the market and the relative competitive advantage of transit over the automobile, deciding where the best opportunities for growth exist, recognizing the constraints on growth, and appraising relationships between external events and future prospects. Strategic management involves developing a vision of what the future might be but does not require waiting until an ideal plan is developed. Instead, satisfactory plans or targets of

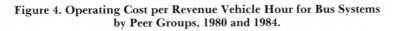

Figure 4. Operating Cost per Revenue Vehicle Hour for Bus Systems
by Peer Groups, 1980 and 1984.

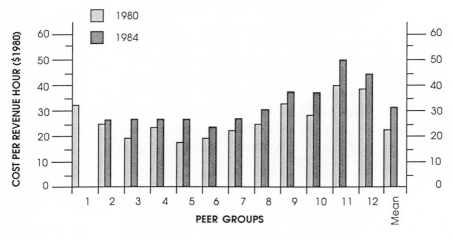

The U-shaped cost curve is more apparent in 1980 than in 1984.
Source: U.S. Department of Transportation, 1982, 1986.

opportunities are selected and then modified in response to feedback
and changing circumstances.

The idea of strategic management is not new to transportation. As illustrated by Table 1, the Short-Range Transportation
Plan (SRTP) and the Transportation Improvement Plan (TIP),
required by the U.S. Department of Transportation since July 17,
1975, rely on a similar cycle of analysis. However, few agencies have
utilized this approach. Both managers and transit directors have
become so involved in day-to-day operating decisions that they do
not have time to assess the strategic health of their agencies. They
are not able to monitor constituency and community expectations
or to spend sufficient time with employees determining how these
expectations might be met with funds from different sources.
Federal agencies have exacerbated the problem by accepting
incomplete plans and fiscal programs.

Orange County Transit District (OCTD). This transit
district in southern California forms an exception. When the agency

moved to its new headquarters in 1976, the board members recognized that it was time to begin thinking strategically about the future. The district had developed a bus system, but the board also wanted to reserve funds for the planning and construction of a rapid transit system. The board asked management to assess the performance of its bus system in comparison with peer-group agencies and to forecast future funding needs. Recent cost increases for bus operators had alarmed board members because these costs might jeopardize the district's ability to develop rail rapid transit. The following goals were promulgated by the board and used by staff to establish future plans (Orange County Transit District, 1977).

1. To serve the people of Orange County by providing public transportation that is convenient, effective, safe, and efficient
2. To respond to the transportation needs of the transit dependent, such as senior citizens, youths, and handicapped persons who cannot afford private transportation
3. To provide a convenient and effective alternative to the automobile to reduce traffic congestion, conserve energy, and contribute to cleaner air
4. To provide leadership in transit planning while cooperating with local and regional jurisdictions to assure coordinated and compatible transportation and land use plans
5. To provide a blend of transportation modes that address the existing and future needs of a growing and dynamic residential and business community
6. To balance the need for public transportation with the needs of the nonriding, taxpaying public by providing transit service that is responsive to the demand, cost effective, and productive.

Management used the board's goals to develop a transit management cycle, which integrated all the steps in strategic management into the annual budget cycle. In aggregate, the goals created a mission that has since shaped OCTD's management philosophy and actions. The transit management cycle, which took effect over the course of four years, consists of several steps. Managers express the six goals as tangible objectives that employees can achieve within specified time limits. In developing these objectives, managers consult employee groups in an effort to refine the purposes and to ensure that all departments understand the objectives and how employees might contribute to their achievement. For example, management initially proposed as an effectiveness objective that ridership be increased from thirty to thirty-five passengers per revenue vehicle hour over five years. Employees suggested that demand-responsive service be excluded and fares be held constant. The final objective stated that ridership would be increased on fixed-route service from thirty to thirty-five passengers per revenue vehicle hour within five years, assuming no real change in fares.

Alternative transit scenarios were developed to achieve this objective. One scenario suggested replacement of several commuter express routes that had low ridership with van and car pools. This required establishment of a ride-sharing division, so the costs as well as the benefits had to be evaluated.

Organization of a ride-sharing department also had financial consequences because different sources of government assistance were available for this activity. A financial cash-flow model is used for this analysis, which is programmed to illustrate how revenues from local, state, and federal sources will change given different assumptions about the economy and/or policy changes. Estimates of fare revenue are also calculated on the assumption that fares will increase proportionately with the cost-of-living index (there will be no real change in fare revenues). Total available financial resources determine the level of service that OCTD can provide while still reserving funds for future rapid transit developments. A separate model is used to estimate operating costs for different scenarios as a function of changes in labor and fuel inputs.

The most cost-effective scenario becomes the strategic plan presented in the SRTP. When integrated with the TIP, the SRTP describes the operating and capital expenses of the scenario, budgets them, and shows where the funds will come from. The critical element—the TIP—is considered the strategic budget, because it demonstrates how funds will be allocated on an annual basis to accomplish a task over three to five years.

After the board of directors adopt the budget (in the form of the SRTP/TIP), it is management's responsibility to implement the proposed service program through functional departments. For OCTD the SRTP/TIP has provided a common design connecting all sectors of the organization, and it can be used for this purpose by any transit agency. It specifies how employees and divisions must work together to achieve annual service objectives within budget constraints. Communication between departments is facilitated, thereby reducing independent conflicts.

Emphasis shifts from strategic planning to strategic management following adoption of a budget. Although the entire process is called strategic management, the strategic emphasis is more apparent during implementation. Funds are allocated to departments to achieve objectives. Monitoring performance against these objectives is essential.

At OCTD, monthly reports show how labor costs and passenger revenues relate to projected costs and revenues. Quarterly reports summarize the fiscal information and present performance measures pertinent to the first three goals: (1) safe operation is monitored by accident statistics per vehicle mile; (2) effectiveness objectives are tracked by measures of service reliability and ridership by seniors, youth, and persons with disabilities; and (3) penetration of new markets is reported as an indicator that OCTD is addressing existing and future needs.

The OCTD plan is flexible. Changes can be recommended to the board each quarter, and the entire plan is revised annually. Eight months before the annual budget must be adopted, revision of the SRTP/TIP begins. Accomplishments are reviewed, anticipated changes in costs and revenues are calculated, and alternative service strategies (scenarios) are evaluated. Year two of the plan becomes the basis for the forthcoming year's budget, and fiscal estimates are calculated for a new fifth year. New processes, new formats, and improved techniques of monitoring are examined annually. The performance of other agencies in OCTD's peer group is also reviewed. Such comparison keeps the planning process fresh and challenging to all participants.

Other Examples. Several other agencies have initiated strategic management. The benefits achieved by the Utah Transit Authority have been described by Klein (1985). Meyer (1983) presents cases covering the Canadian Air Transportation Administration, the Pennsylvania Department of Transportation, the Port Authority of New York and New Jersey, and the Toronto Transit Commission. Methods used in the Canadian studies will be particularly helpful to American transit managers, as they show what is possible when policy is not ambiguous.

The *Strategic Plan, 1984-1986* published by the Montreal Urban Community Transit Commission (MUCTC) (1984) is a classic case study that should be on every transit manager's bookshelf. The plan details the goals, objectives, and action plans for a three-year horizon with a provision for annual updates. The commission recognizes that it has an excellent reputation for its skilled transit planning and operations but wants to make further improvements. Emphasis in the plan is also given to marketing and consumer relations, as well as to employee morale and satisfaction.

The commission realizes that it cannot establish objectives without reference to its environment. A number of important factors were and are beyond its control: the economic situation, costs related to the automobile, transit financial assistance rules. In view of an expected decrease in subsidies from the government of Quebec, MUCTC did not plan any expansion of service during the 1984–1986 period. Rather, it adopted the following five goals that acknowledged financial reality but emphasized the maintenance of service standards while devoting special efforts to marketing and employee development (Montreal Urban Transportation Commission, 1984, p. 31):

1. To develop, quickly and in coordination, all aspects of its activities related to the marketing of its services and to customer relations
2. To gradually improve the quality of its urban transit network (metro-bus-trains) with a view to giving better service to users, while keeping cost increases at a minimum
3. To continue the implementation of policies and programs covering all aspects of human resources management, with the

prime purpose of increasing employee motivation and job satisfaction

4. To ensure that the commission's installations, equipment, and vehicles remain attractive and efficient

5. To continue to improve administrative efficiency in all its departments.

Like OCTD, MUCTC views the strategic plan as part of the annual management cycle. In addition to the plan itself, the main components of this cycle are:

- The budget, which details the allocation of resources in accordance with the plan
- Control and revision during the year
- Evaluation of results, which may lead to revision of objectives for the next year.

Strategic Management: The Public Agency's Environment

The nature of public agencies furnishes a unique context for strategic management. Entire books have been written on strategic management, and courses on the subject are taught in most business schools, but the distinctive attributes of the public sector are seldom explained. Ring and Perry (1985) conclude that several contextual differences distinguish management in the public sector from that in the private. They recommend that the following constraints and consequences be acknowledged:

1. Interest groups are diverse and unstable, so that management needs to maintain flexibility and coordinate competing interests. Ambiguity in policy can be an asset in this respect.

2. Employees of public agencies are protected from political influence by civil service codes and union affiliation and need not share the same objectives as management and the policy board. This is less likely to occur in private organizations where effectiveness of the firm relates directly to salaries and job security.

3. The tenure of public officials is relatively short, imposing a near-term outlook that may lead to a few in-office accomplishments but not necessarily to transportation improvement.

Strategic management in the public sector can be extremely difficult. It is certainly more time consuming than private-sector management because success depends on the skillful use of influence rather than authority. Local customs, state and federal regulations, civil service protection, and labor agreements all serve to constrain authority. Achieving agreement on strategic management plans requires frequent meetings between transit managers and employees, the public, and representatives of other agencies. The MUCTC plan took more than a year to develop and was introduced gradually over two years. The OCTD plan was implemented over four years. Because strategic plans must be adopted cooperatively by employee groups, development and maintenance of good working relationships with others are essential. Especially helpful is the capacity to convince those adversely affected by policy change that they are being treated fairly; otherwise any unhappy group can obstruct progress and render an executive manager impotent.

Sufficient time must be allowed for employee participation. Various approaches are possible. A consultative approach was used by OCTD in which tentative decisions were made by managers before they asked for employee input. In Minneapolis-St. Paul, the employees of the Twin Cities' Metropolitan Transit Commission were more involved; they determined what actions were needed to improve service reliability and then left management to formulate policies to implement employee suggestions.

These constraints do not preclude strategic management, but they do require more time than most agencies allocate to the SRTP/TIP process. They demand that greater attention be given to possibilities suggested by the analysis of similar agencies and a realistic assessment of internal capabilities before goals and plans are developed to satisfy the expectations of different constituencies.

Strategic Management in Perspective. It is easy to confuse strategic planning with strategic management because the latter incorporates the former. Strategic planning is the evaluation of alternative scenarios to accomplish goals and objectives. Selection of scenarios is followed by budget development (sometimes called strategic budgeting to distinguish it from the annual budget), management of implementation, and performance monitoring. The entire process is called strategic management—a continuing three-to-five-year process implemented through the annual budget. Strategic management not only provides for the evaluation of options, but it can also build the basis for cooperation. Competition rather than cooperation between departments prevails in public agencies because common objectives have not been formulated and shared. The planning process assures that regular, organized time is given to thinking strategically about an agency's mission amid changing expectations. Rather than allowing an agency to become overwhelmed by internal conflict, strategic management forces articulation and appraisal of assumptions about the provision of transit. It also provides an opportunity to build a consensus about central objectives within an agency and to evaluate programs, plans, and budgets in reference to these objectives.

A note of caution is warranted. Strategic management is not universally applicable. In some agencies the press of operating deficits is so overwhelming that sufficient time is not available for "strategic thinking." Such agencies require action planning or scanning rather than strategic planning. In other agencies, external politics do not allow the fiscal certainty needed to evaluate alternative plans and budgets. Transit agencies are so dependent on governmental agencies for most of their operating support that, if one or more of these agencies is unwilling to provide some assurance about forthcoming funding, strategic management will not be productive. All that a resource-dependent agency can do is to wait for the decision and then allocate expenditures wisely. Jacksonville, Florida, and Nashville, Tennessee, provide examples of superbly managed transit agencies that are so dependent on the year-to-year grants from local government that it has not been prudent for them to devote staff effort to strategic management.

Emergency Planning. SRTP/TIP requirements can guide emergency short-term planning that, if implemented, can form a foundation for future comprehensive strategic management. A case in point is the Port Authority of Allegheny County (PATH), which provides transit service in Pittsburgh and has faced serious problems in recent years. The city's population has declined, the CBD has deteriorated as employers have left for the suburbs, and both ridership and revenue have declined. Internally, management has faced well-organized bargaining units whose rights are protected by state and federal regulations.

To cope with these problems, management tried various ploys between 1981 and 1985: it delayed filling vacancies, hired at entry-level salaries, imposed a nonunion salary freeze, postponed maintenance, and used office automation to reduce staff requirements. It also reduced costs across a wide range of service, removing more than one million miles of bus service between 1980 and 1985 and scaling down the number of peak-period vehicles from 810 to 758.

Unfortunately, PATH made its service reductions without revealing to employees and the community that the reductions were part of a three-to-five year plan to adjust service to anticipated revenues. Neither the community, which had been accustomed to high levels of transit service, nor the labor unions understood the need for service reduction. PATH was accused of mismanagement, and the county commissioners and the commonwealth of Pennsylvania initiated reviews of the transit agency with the intention of reorganizing it.

Emergency planning based on the SRTP/TIP guidelines kept PATH intact. It originated in a study completed with the assistance of the Pittsburgh Chamber of Commerce and several "loaned" executives experienced in corporate planning. When situation assessment revealed that there was not enough time to develop a comprehensive plan, the executives proposed four key short-term objectives:

1. Since sound financial planning was of the essence, PATH should immediately hire a financial manager to develop a general financial management capacity for the agency. This

would enable PATH to forecast revenues and costs without having to hold up planning while waiting for annual funding decisions to be made by the county commissioners.

2. A dedicated funding source needed to be found or created to underwrite PATH operations.

3. PATH needed to gain control over labor costs and work rules through changes in the enabling legislation.

4. Service reliability had to be improved.

All these proposals were consistent with steps outlined in the federal SRTP/TIP requirements. Three of the objectives have already been accomplished. A financial manager was hired who developed the needed financial capability. New legislation was passed in June 1986 that has permitted management to improve its control over labor costs, and the results of improved service reliability are already apparent. The number of bus passengers per revenue vehicle hour has risen from a low of thirty-four in 1982 and 1983 to thirty-eight in 1986, and the ratio of fares to operating cost has increased from 41 to 45 percent. Because the objectives were reasonable and measurable, and because staff assisted in formulating the strategic plan on which the objectives are based, managers are psychologically committed to PATH's success. Morale is high, and interdepartmental cooperation is now evident in an organization whose future was once in jeopardy.

Transit management is not impossible. Although transit management has been described as a high-risk, rapid-turnover, "burnout" type of job, it need not be so. Reasonable goals for transit can be established that are consonant with the historical and political situation and consistent with the achievements of peer-group agencies. The management challenge is to formulate objectives, appraise and deploy resources, and evaluate how well objectives are being met. Subsequent chapters explain in detail how to accomplish these stages of strategic management.

4

Measuring and Monitoring Transit Performance

"We never do anything much about a problem until we learn to measure it." Moynihan (1978, p. 12) used these words in discussing the economics of regional growth, but they apply equally well to public transit, for transit managers are able to surmount certain problems today only because of the modern statistical and accounting techniques available to them. Particularly important for strategic management in transit are the measuring and monitoring of performance; without such evaluation, managers are merely supervising operations.

This chapter looks within the transit agency to explain three general performance concepts, to explore the construction of indicators to monitor performance, and to discuss how the use of these indicators applies to strategic management. Most of the discussion is drawn from my own research. Three ideas prevail throughout:

1. Only a few indicators are needed to monitor the important dimensions of transit performance.
2. Efficiency indicators, effectiveness indicators, and overall indicators are the most helpful for strategic management.
3. Improving performance is management's responsibility. External agencies may require performance to be monitored and may even designate indicators for its measurement, but improvements must be left to internal managers.

A small set of diagnostic indicators that track an agency's performance over time, as well as compare it with that of its peers, can be as useful for transit management as the Dunn and Bradstreet industry norms are for private firms. These indicators may not capture every activity of an agency, but they do indicate progress in the key areas discussed below.

Public transit agencies formerly gauged their success by the number of riders rather than their costs. Privately owned transit agencies also gauged success by ridership—but only because their fares reflected marginal costs. Input costs—labor, fuel, and equipment—were relatively stable, and costs were controlled by cutting service on routes where revenue fell below marginal costs. However, marginal cost pricing was abandoned when government subsidies became available. Many transit authorities lowered fares and expanded routes while paying little attention to the cost of producing service. Meanwhile, the industry has continued to assess performance in terms of ridership.

A more balanced assessment of transit performance can be achieved by using service input, output, and consumption figures to measure three important dimensions of transit operations: efficiency, effectiveness, and overall performance. *Efficiency* describes how well factors such as labor, equipment, facilities, and fuel are used to produce outputs as represented by vehicle hours or miles of service. *Effectiveness* measures the consumption of transit output as well as the impact of transit on societal goals, such as reducing traffic congestion. *Overall* indicators integrate efficiency and effectiveness measures, as when costs of service inputs are related to consumption. Cost per passenger and the ratio of revenue to the cost of producing service are overall measures. *Cost efficiency, service effectiveness,* and *cost effectiveness* are the terms used to describe the three dimensions of transit performance presented in Figure 5.

The concepts of efficiency and effectiveness can be confusing. Economists prefer to define efficiency as maximizing net benefits, that is, maximizing the value of output minus its cost. Net revenue per passenger, per hour, or per mile measures transit efficiency in this sense. It is represented by the cost-effectiveness dimension in Figure 5. This definition is difficult to use in public transit because

Figure 5. Framework for Transit Performance Concepts.

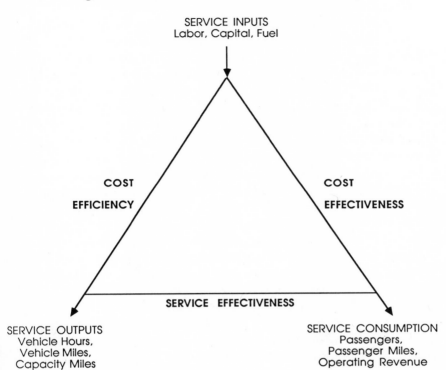

Performance in transit can be conceptualized as input, output, and consumption dimensions. Measures can be developed for each dimension. Cost efficiency is the relationship between input and output. Service effectiveness measures the consumption of service outputs, and cost effectiveness measures the relationship between the cost of producing service and consumption.

it is impossible to define "value of output" solely in terms of revenue when transit is expected to achieve many different objectives. For example, transit agencies are required to charge the elderly and those with disabilities half the normal fare during midday hours. Efficiency as used here is what economists would call "production efficiency," meaning the resources used to produce output. Effectiveness is "distribution efficiency," which means the utilization of output to accomplish goals. I am thus using the terms *efficiency* and *effectiveness* with the broad connotations preferred by public administrators.

Drucker (1973) describes efficiency as "doing things right" and effectiveness as "doing the right things." These are phrases that roughly capture the spirit of the two concepts. Efficiency is clearly under the control of transit management, which can be held accountable for performance. Effectiveness is more difficult to evaluate, because management can "do the right things" and still not have a successful operation. For example, it is possible to produce reliable service and deploy it in the right area at the right time, but find that consumers simply choose not to use it.

Failure to distinguish efficiency from effectiveness can create problems. A formula recommended to allocate operating assistance for the Delaware Valley failed in part because it confused efficiency with effectiveness (Pierce and others, 1976). The proposal recommended that assistance for the twenty-two operators in Pennsylvania and New Jersey be based on demand (annual revenue passenger miles), supply (annual revenue seat miles), and what was mistakenly labeled efficiency (ratio of annual revenue passenger miles to annual revenue seat miles, multiplied by annual passengers). This is a measure of what proportion of seated capacity is used, which was entangled with annual passengers to produce a meaningless indicator. The formula was rejected by the governors of the two states because it was too complicated. Simple allocation formulas, which would have been both administratively practical and supportive of improved performance, could have been worked out if the concepts of efficiency and effectiveness had been kept separate.

Numerous transit-performance studies have used the concepts of efficiency, effectiveness, and cost effectiveness. Analysts have debated at length whether efficiency should be considered a more important measure of operations success than effectiveness, but uncertainty remains. Transit operators prefer to use effectiveness measures expressed in terms of passenger statistics, whereas federal, state, and local agencies have generally given more attention to efficiency measures. The U.S. General Accounting Office (1981) has criticized the emphasis that Congress has given to service consumption and population when allocating federal operating assistances. The office has recommended that service supply measures such as revenue hours of service be used as incentives to produce more transit output per unit of operating cost. At the state level, California, New York, and Pennsylvania have mandated that transit agencies be audited for efficiency as well as for effectiveness as a condition for receiving state operating assistance (Miller, 1979). The political tide is evidently turning in favor of efficiency as a respectable gauge of transit operations, but there is still considerable opposition to this approach among transit managers.

Transit Performance Analysis

Availability of a national report that accumulates transit industry financial results by uniform categories has assisted performance analysis. The Urban Mass Transportation Act was amended in 1974 to include Section 15, which requires a uniform system of accounts and records as well as a uniform system for reporting. UMTA used the results of a previous industry study (Project FARE) to issue regulations in 1977 that require annual submission of reports by all agencies desiring federal operating assistance. The first figures based on the 1978–79 fiscal year were released in 1981. Subsequent annual reports have been appearing about two years after the close of each fiscal year.

Using the Section 15 annual reports, transit managers can easily calculate performance measures for cost efficiency, service effectiveness, and cost effectiveness. Section 15 data permit not only the tracking over time of a single agency's performance but also the comparison of peer-group transit agencies in a given year. Using performance indicators derived from Section 15 data, management can monitor performance either after each pay period or every quarter and implement corrective action when necessary. Section 15 data provide the basis for the kind of control over operations that the strategic approach to transit management requires.

Statistics and the Performance Measures. Three types of statistics from the Section 15 data are used to calculate transit performance indicators: service input, service output, and service consumption statistics. Together, they can be used to monitor the costs of producing and utilizing service.

1. *Service Input.* This is the quantity of resources expended to produce transit service, expressed in either monetary or nonmonetary terms. Examples of service input statistics include operating cost (dollars expended for operations, maintenance, and administration), employee hours (total, operating, maintenance, or administration), capital investment (number of vehicles or peak vehicle requirement), and energy utilization (fuel cost or volume).

2. *Service Output.* This is the quantity of service produced by a transit operator, expressed in nonmonetary terms. Examples of this type of statistic include vehicle hours (total and revenue hours), vehicle miles (total and revenue miles), capacity miles (total and revenue capacity miles), service reliability (miles between mechanical failure), and service safety (number of accidents).

3. *Service Consumption.* The amount of service used by the public may be expressed in either monetary or nonmonetary terms. Examples include passengers (total, revenue, and special groups), passenger miles, and operating revenue (total and passenger).

The three categories of statistics yield three types of performance measures: cost efficiency, service effectiveness, and cost effectiveness. A wide range of performance measures can be derived from these statistics. Holec, Schwager, and Fandialan (1980) used forty-seven for Michigan. For my own research, forty-eight performance measures were identified that can be calculated from Section 15 data.

Reduction of Performance Measures. Although the list of feasible measures is large, many of these are only useful for individual departments. For overall assessment, a small, representative set is required. Statistical analysis has been used to reduce my list of forty-eight performance measures to seven groups of measures representative of the performance concepts of efficiency, effectiveness, and the combination of the two (Fielding, Babitsky, and Brenner, 1985). One "marker variable" or indicator was chosen from each group. Alternative indicators were also identified that could be used equally well for assessing performance (Table 5).

Each indicator is expressed so that higher scores are better than lower. For example, revenue hours (or part thereof) per dollar of cost is used rather than cost per revenue hour. This change may be difficult to become accustomed to, but it aids comprehension because improving performance is represented by increasing numbers. This is a tremendous advantage when tracking the performance of an agency over several years, comparing the performance of one agency against peer systems, or presenting results to elected officials who are unfamiliar with transit terminology.

In selecting performance measures, consideration must be given to the availability and reliability of the data. Financial statistics are the most reliable. Passenger statistics, particularly passenger miles of travel, are the least reliable. Controllability is another consideration; it is to the advantage of transit managers to evaluate those aspects of operations that are under their control. Generally, system assets (fixed facilities) and the system environment (the service area and its characteristics) are more or less fixed and cannot be altered by the manager in the *short run,* whereas service input and output can be controlled to a greater degree. Management has greatest control over service output (supply), since service input can be adjusted to provide whatever level of output is desired, although system assets, especially vehicles, may become a limiting factor if managers attempt to make more than marginal increases in service.

Using Performance Measures for Management

Performance indicators can measure an agency's progress toward organizational objectives. Distinguishing between inputs, outputs, and consumption of service is advisable so that factors affecting the results can be analyzed. When overall indicators are required for administrative purposes or public relations, individual measures can be combined to provide cost-effectiveness ratios.

Table 5. Recommended Marker Variables for Dimensions of Transit Performance.

Performance Dimension	Recommended	Good Alternative
Cost Efficiency	RVH/OEXP—Revenue vehicle hour per operating expense	TVM/OEXP—Total vehicle miles per operating expense
Service Utilization	TPAS/RVH—Unlinked passenger trips per revenue vehicle hour	TPAS/RVM—Unlinked passenger trips per revenue vehicle mile
Revenue Generation	CORV/OEXP—Corrected operating revenue per operating expense	REV/OSUB—Operating revenue per operating subsidy
Labor Efficiency	TVH/EMP—Total vehicle hours per total employees	REV/OEMP—Revenue vehicle hours per operating employee
Vehicle Efficiency	TVM/PVEH—Total vehicle miles per peak vehicle	TVH/PVEH—Total vehicle hours per peak vehicle
Maintenance Efficiency	TVM/MNT—Total vehicle miles per maintenance employee	TVM/MEXP—Total vehicle miles per maintenance expense
Safety	TVM/CACC—Total vehicle miles per collision accident	TVM/$C&L—Total vehicle miles per dollar collision and liability expense

Source: Fielding and others, 1984.

However, the key to successful administrative use of performance indicators is to keep the list small and easily understood.

The Washington Metropolitan Area Transit Authority (WMATA) uses performance measures to report the quarterly accomplishments of both bus and rail operations. Fifty-five measures are reported for bus operations, and 124 have been suggested as rail measures. More data are assembled by WMATA than can be used for management purposes. Reduction is needed if the measures are to be useful. BART in San Francisco adequately summarizes progress by using twenty-two indicators, displayed as one table and twelve graphs. Each graph illustrates changes in performance over three years and provides management with a means of assessing performance against adopted objectives (Figure 6). Special attention is given to indicators of labor efficiency, such as the amount of paid sick leave, because management can control these costs if they deviate from the desired standard.

The Jacksonville Transportation Agency in Florida not only monitors its own performance but also checks it against the performance of other operators in the same peer group. Jacksonville belongs to a group of medium-sized, comparatively fast systems with a peak-to-base ratio greater than 2.5 (peer group 8). Section 15 data are used to calculate average peer-group performance for the recommended "marker" variables listed in Table 5. The peer-group mean for each indicator is represented as 0.0 on Figure 7, and the performance of Jacksonville is represented in reference to this datum. Jacksonville is clearly a superior transit agency. It is generally above the mean on all nine indicators and has an outstanding safety record. The only reason for management's concern is the decline in ridership (unlinked passenger trips per revenue vehicle hour) in 1983, and the below-norm performance on labor efficiency (TVH/EMP) this same year.

The Southern California Rapid Transit District (SCRTD) in Los Angeles uses performance monitoring strategically. One of its goals is to deliver safe service, which is monitored by measuring the number of collision accidents per vehicle mile each month. During the first half of 1986 these exceeded the standard of 4.2 accidents per 100,000 miles and, in comparison with the performance of its peer agencies in New York and Chicago, SCRTD was found to be the

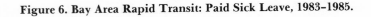

Figure 6. Bay Area Rapid Transit: Paid Sick Leave, 1983–1985.

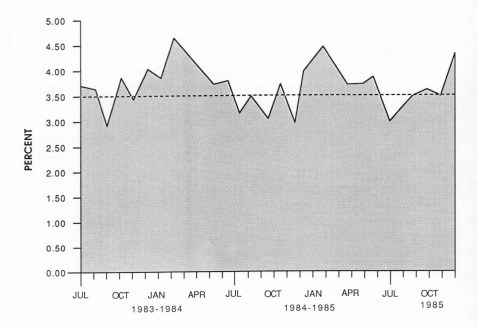

One of the twenty-two indicators reported quarterly, which tracks whether management is achieving the absenteeism standard of 3.5 percent (9.1 days per year) established as a goal. Actual levels have been slightly above.
      Source: Bay Area Rapid Transit District, 1986.

least safe operator. Analytical studies suggested that the negative
performance could, in part, be explained by the speed differential
between buses and automobiles operating on arterial highways in
Los Angeles. The Santa Monica Municipal Bus Line also had more
accidents than its peer group because it suffered from the same
environmental hazards. However, the performance of SCRTD was
poor and was steadily declining.

      An action plan was developed to improve safety. This
involved changes in recruitment procedures (checking driving
records and testing for alcoholism and drug use), training (more on-
the-road training and reclassifications of instructors), regular
monitoring of employee records (including off-the-job behavior),

Figure 7. Jacksonville Performance Review Summary and Comparison.

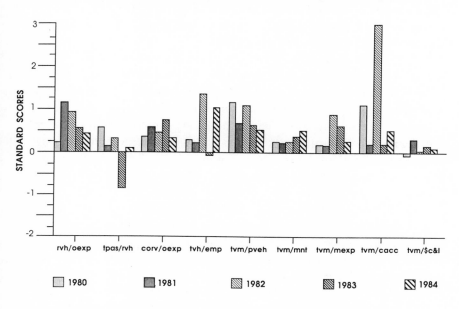

Seven performance dimensions are shown using nine indicators. Annual change is indicated by standard score as well as comparison with the peer-group mean represented by zero.

Source: U.S. Department of Transportation, 1982, 1983, 1986.

and prompt suspension of coach operators considered to be unsafe. Although the action program cost $1.4 million annually, it was estimated to have saved $3.6 million annually through decreased collision and liability expenses.

Analysis of Transit Efficiency. As earlier noted, efficiency in public transit generally refers to how well labor, vehicles, and fuel are used to produce service. Capital investment in equipment and facilities is normally regarded as a nonrecoverable cost in the United States. If this should change with the increased "privatization" of transit, depreciation schedules could be used to incorporate replacement cost. Labor efficiency can be separately calculated using operating, maintenance, and administrative categories. Maintenance efficiency is more difficult to measure: labor is the predominant cost, but parts, supplies, and lubricants are also used and can be collectively measured by vehicle miles per maintenance expense. Overall cost efficiency is measured by either hours or miles of service as a ratio to operating expense.

Hours of service provide a more reliable index of transit output than miles, because operating conditions affect the latter. Buses operating on congested city streets will travel more slowly, covering fewer miles in the same amount of time, than those using arterial streets or freeways. Service hours are preferred because labor is the most costly input, and relationships can be calculated in pay hours for different categories of labor. Miles of service are more appropriate when one is assessing maintenance efficiency and safety.

Capital costs or depreciation are eliminated from most studies of American transit because up to 80 percent of the capital investment in vehicles and facilities is financed with federal subsidies. Even when depreciation is taken into account, the choice of an appropriate rate is always questionable. But straight-line depreciation over twelve years, plus the current rate of inflation, can guide this choice for public agencies.

Labor Efficiency. Labor overshadows all other costs, representing about 75 percent of the cost of producing transit when fringe benefits are included. Driver salaries and benefits alone account for almost half of operating costs. Until very recently the labor portion of transit operating costs had been increasing faster than the general inflation rate because of generous salary and fringe benefit settlements and the additional labor required to offset declining productivity. Between 1970 and 1980, the cost of providing a vehicle mile of public transit increased 52.9 percent from $1.89 to $2.89 (in constant 1980 dollars). Increased labor expenses accounted for 43.3 percent of the increase. Pickrell (1983) has broken this down into 25.3 percent for increased compensation and 18 percent for additional labor to offset declining labor productivity. During the same 1970–1980 period, labor productivity measured in vehicle miles per employee decreased by 17.3 percent from 13,646 to 11,287 vehicle miles per employee. During a period of expanding service, these declines in labor efficiency went unnoticed. Had performance indicators been used to monitor what was occuring, management could have used this information when negotiating new contracts with employee unions.

The ratio of vehicle service hours to pay hours or to employees is the most useful measure of labor efficiency. Service hours are obtained from operating schedules and pay hours from the payroll. Employees are calculated on the basis of 2,080 hours of work per annum, so as to incorporate overtime work and vacations. These figures can be calculated systemwide, for operating divisions or for different employee groups. Service hours per pay hour provide an especially useful figure for analyzing whether management uses drivers efficiently by minimizing overtime and maximizing the proportion of paid time that drivers spend operating vehicles. It also serves as a financial review of actual pay hours against budgeted pay hours and is one of the most useful strategic pieces of information that managers can obtain after each pay period.

Labor efficiency varies considerably between agencies. These variations may result from different labor-contract provisions or from different operating practices; some agencies, for example, hire more employees to cover for absences or deploy a larger ratio of peak-to-base service. Labor-contract provisions and operating practices are all under the control of management, however, and can be altered if productivity is monitored.

It is difficult to obtain reliable service-hour-to-pay-hour statistics for purposes of comparing several transit agencies since these are not published in Section 15 reports. For making such comparisons or for determining labor requirements, however, it is reasonable to utilize vehicle hours per employee as a measure. Alternatively, one can resort to revenue vehicle hours per operating expense or labor expense.

When analyzing the labor efficiency of administrative and maintenance employees, the ratio of service hours to pay hours is not so useful as it is for drivers. However, calculations based on the number of administrative and/or maintenance employees per peak vehicle is helpful. Section 15 reports contain statistics on the number of employees by employment category, as well as by the number of vehicles required for peak service. Number of employees per peak vehicle is a useful indicator of overall labor efficiency, which is easily calculated from Section 15 data. Peak-vehicle requirement rather than the number of active vehicles is preferred as a measure of size. Since many transit systems maintain reserve fleets as a contingency against future shortages of petroleum and sudden increases in demand for transit, statistics on active vehicles are misleading.

Vehicle Efficiency. Utilization of transit vehicles can be measured either in miles or in hours. Normally, miles are used because they relate easily to maintenance requirements. In performance analysis, however, vehicle service hours provide a good alternative. Either peak vehicles or active vehicles can be used as the denominator, depending on operating policy. A low value on the ratio between vehicle miles and peak vehicles could mean that an operator is overcapitalized. However, if it is operating policy to offer substantial peak-period service, then vehicles will be underutilized during the midday.

Efficient use of vehicles seldom receives careful attention in American transit. Agencies do not include as an operating cost depreciation on vehicles and facilities purchased with federal capital assistance. Federal officials carefully scrutinize requests for additional vehicles and new facilities, but once a capital grant is approved, funds need be repaid only if the vehicle and facilities are sold or withdrawn from use before their useful life is over. Tye (1973) has shown that this policy leads to overcapitalization and the early retirement of vehicles. Now federal agencies are analyzing the "spare ratio" (the relationship between peak vehicle requirements and active vehicles) and requiring agencies to justify purchase of new vehicles when they already have more than 20 percent over peak vehicle requirments.

Fuel Efficiency. Variation in fuel consumption depends on changes in the operating environment, different vehicle sizes, and the number of air-conditioned vehicles. Although fuel constitutes less than 10 percent of the operating cost per vehicle hour, management must take these factors into account when evaluating proposed changes in equipment. Variations in lubricant use can be explained by vehicle age and quality of maintenance. In a 1981 management study for the Metropolitan Transportation Authority in New York City, lubricant use was found to vary with maintenance performance by depots. Poor maintenance associated with high lubricant use was found to impair service reliability seriously. A lack of buses, due to poor maintenance, accounted for a missed-trip rate of as high as 30 percent for some depots.

Maintenance Efficiency. Although it is frequently overlooked in performance evaluation, economy can be achieved in maintenance expense. The numerator for maintenance measures is usually miles rather than hours, because miles relate more closely to maintenance requirements. Inventories of spare parts, along with decisions as to what and where maintenance will be performed and whether some maintenance will be subcontracted to private firms, can have substantial effects on cost.

The amount of time needed to perform various maintenance functions is represented by the number of maintenance employees required. The transit industry is moving gradually in the direction of setting maintenance work standards. This will help agencies to define maintenance jobs and establish time and accuracy standards for each task. Time-series data for each agency are needed to establish standards, whereas comparisons with other similar agencies help management determine whether work standards need revision.

Since quality of maintenance affects service reliability, an overall indicator is frequently used to measure the number of road calls made per million miles to report mechanical failures. However, this measure is meaningful only to the agency in which the data are collected. Comparative data are unreliable because there is no accepted definition of "road calls." Frequent failures while vehicles are in service indicate substandard preventative maintenance, and this measure should be monitored by each maintenance manager.

Overall Cost Efficiency. Output per dollar of cost can be measured by taking the ratio of service output, measured in hours or miles, to cost (Table 5). Since wages are the principal cost in transit agencies, separate cost evaluations for drivers, maintenance, and administrative employees are helpful for performance studies.

Costs per unit of output also provide the basis for the development of cost models that allow overall costs to be apportioned to miles and hours and vehicles. Cost models are essential for analyzing the costs of proposed service changes or for comparing investments in different types of service. They can also be used for analyzing the costs of similar service provided by different operators. Cost allocation models are especially useful for estimating the cost of proposed changes and are discussed as a budgetary technique in the next chapter.

Measuring Service Effectiveness

Statistics on transit effectiveness are less reliable than statistics on efficiency. Utilization of service is difficult to measure accurately. Passengers get on and off vehicles and pay different fares. In bus operations, vehicles seldom run on the same route all day, so farebox revenue does not provide a reliable estimate of utilization by route. Most transit agencies calculate passenger usage by multiplying daily fare revenue by a passenger index derived from periodic on-board surveys that count pass users, reduced fare and transfer passengers, and nonpaying children (Smith, 1985). Rail rapid transit and demand-responsive transit can provide more accurate reports on passengers because they can count entering and departing passengers. For these two modes, the most accurate assessment of utilization is provided by farebox revenue.

Transit managers have far less control over the utilization of service than they have over its supply. Fares and quality of service do influence utilization, but the comparative time and price of auto travel, changes in disposable income, and the weather are also influential. Because transit managers cannot control many of the factors affecting utilization, performance analysis for strategic management purposes should rest on efficiency measures. Utilization of service should not be neglected, but these measures can seldom detect changes that are easily correctable. Overreliance on passenger statistics as an indicator of performance is one reason why costs escalated during the 1970s. Additional passengers were gained, especially during the peak travel periods, but the marginal cost for these additional passengers far exceeded the additional revenue, so that transit became much more expensive. Most policy makers were not aware of these higher, peak-period costs when they encouraged transit as an alternative to automobile commuting.

Utilization of Service. Consumption of service is measured by passenger trips or passenger miles, both of which present problems of definition and measurement. Passenger trips can be counted as linked or unlinked trips. A *linked trip* is counted as a single journey from origin to destination, regardless of transfers. This is the measure ordinarily used in transportation forecasting. For public information, however, transit agencies normally report *unlinked trips.* Each boarding is counted as a new trip, so that a traveler who transfers between three vehicles while commuting to work is counted as three passengers. With this method of counting, transit systems that operate a grid network of routes with timed transfers will appear to have more riders than similar systems operating radial networks.

The same difficulty arises when demand-responsive transit is compared with fixed-route transit. The former transports passengers from origin to destination without transfer, whereas the latter can have a transfer rate of between 25 and 35 percent. The apparently higher utilization rate of fixed-route transit has been used inappropriately when making comparisons between the two modes operating within the same transit agency. Linked trips should be used for comparisons between modes and between areas.

Passenger miles are computed according to the distance each passenger travels. One passenger traveling ten miles is the equivalent of five traveling two miles. But difficulties arise when using this statistic. First, the cost to the transit agency occurs at boarding. Distance traveled does not add to costs unless the vehicle is overcrowded. Second, calculating distance traveled is difficult even when a transit agency has zonal fares. A sampling method was developed for use in reporting statistics to the federal government, but it is costly for transit agencies to implement. Third, the recommended method fails to provide data useful for service planning (Attanucci, Burns, and Wilson, 1981).

Passenger miles are employed as a measure of utilization because they are analogous to the measures used by airlines and the ton miles used by railroads and trucking companies. When passenger miles are compared with seat miles or vehicle capacity miles, a measure of capacity produced to capacity consumed is established. But this creates another problem: should capacity miles be measured only on the basis of seating capacity, or should they include standing capacity?

Either vehicle hours or vehicle miles can be used as the denominator in ratio measures of service utilization. Vehicle miles are the most frequently used, although vehicle hours provide a more uniform measure when speed varies. Unlinked passenger trips are the most reliable statistic from the Section 15 data and are preferred as the numerator for comparative studies. With improved reliability, the passenger-mile statistic could be used as the numerator.

Revenue Generation. Problems arise in classifying revenue, and the definitions provided with the Section 15 chart of accounts should be followed for maximum comparability. Passenger revenue includes farebox receipts, pass sales, and auxiliary income. Advertising revenues and leasing fees are counted as operating revenues, not as passenger revenues. Problems also arise over classification of financial assistance provided by local agencies as compensation for low fares. For example, the City of Commerce, California, charges no fare, and Seattle offers free central city trips. City agencies cover the costs in both cases, but the funds are not counted as farebox revenue. Section 15 classifies these as local assistance, but as a result Commerce and Seattle have lower-than-expected passenger revenue. Such variations can make between-system comparisons of revenue misleading. Disaggregation of revenue by mode is another problem; only total revenue is reported in the Section 15 statistics, and researchers must disaggregate the revenue according to the number of passengers carried by each mode.

Operating Safety. Deciding whether safety is an efficiency or effectiveness indicator is difficult. Operating safety is related to the way in which service is provided, but it also influences consumption. I prefer to classify it as an effectiveness indicator and measure it in terms of miles between collision accidents or miles per dollar of collision and liability expense. Information for both indicators is reported in the Section 15 annual report. Collision accidents are reported more reliably than total accidents, which include many minor injuries reported by passengers.

Collision and liability expense summarizes in dollars the total payments made for property and liability insurance, as well as payments made to settle claims against the agency and money spent repairing damaged vehicles. Variations from year to year should be expected for this indicator because claims may take several years to settle. However, it provides the best overall indicator of operating safety.

Public Assistance. The public assistance performance measures are not so useful to management as they are to the agencies that monitor the use of state and federal transit funds. They provide a way to assess equity in the distribution of funds, as well as the efficiency of assistance in terms of vehicle hours produced or effectiveness in terms of passengers carried. The formula for distributing federal operating assistance has been the object of frequent criticism. Until 1982, each urbanized area received a proportion of the total transit subsidy based on population and population density. This resulted in a distribution of funds that was unrelated to need. For example, in 1976, urban areas with less than 200,000 people averaged a subsidy per passenger of twenty-five cents, whereas the largest urban areas (one million people and over), where transit was essential, received only six cents per passenger. Since 1982, a more complicated formula has been used that reduces the magnitude of this discrepancy.

Allocation of capital assistance is also inequitable. Seventy-five percent of all federal capital funds as of 1983 had been allocated to ten cities that comprised only 40 percent of the nation's population. All ten have rail systems either in operation or under construction. That political influence is at work is also evident in cities with all-bus systems. The highest per-capita allocation for cities without rail systems between 1965 and 1976 was made to Seattle. On the basis of its 1970 population, Seattle received $90 per capita, whereas the average for nonrail cities was $19.63 (Briggs,

1980). Expansion of the Seattle bus system was aided by influential members of Congress representing Seattle. This political intercession enabled Seattle to obtain far more than its fair share of discretionary capital grants.

Use of performance measures as well as population criteria would permit an allocation of funding that was more commensurate with need. The U.S. General Accounting Office (1981) suggested to Congress the addition of two performance measures to the funding formula: (1) revenue seat hours of service produced and (2) criteria measuring transit availability. However, Congress could not reach consensus on this formula and in 1982 chose a complicated formula for Section 9 block grants: 46 percent was allocated in proportion to vehicle miles, 11 percent according to route miles, 7 percent in proportion to passenger miles times passenger miles per dollar of operating cost, and 36 percent on the old basis, in proportion to population and population density. The only merit of this formula was that it preserved the status quo. It also serves as an additional reminder of how much the political process affects transit funding.

Social Effectiveness. These measures indicate how well transit service is utilized by the intended beneficiaries. Federal legislation has required that special attention be given to the transit dependent, a requirement that UMTA has implemented through planning regulations. Applicants for federal assistance must identify concentrations of elderly and low-income households, as well as those without automobiles, and indicate both the level and quality of service provided. Revenue vehicle hours per census tract is an indicator that can be used to compare the level of service provided to transit-dependent areas. Frequency and accessibility of service, along with number of passengers per elderly and autoless households, are other helpful effectiveness measures.

Market penetration can be measured by passengers per household within one-quarter mile of transit routes or stations. Another useful measure is the number of households within one-quarter mile of transit routes or stations that use transit frequently, occasionally, or never. Unfortunately, Section 15 does not require transit operators to estimate population within the one-quarter mile service zone, so analysts cannot compute these important market penetration statistics for the nation's transit agencies. However, these are measures that metropolitan planning agencies and transit operators should maintain.

Measuring Cost Effectiveness

Overall measures of performance are popular with governmental agencies that monitor transit. For management, it is more helpful to determine changes in production and consumption separately rather than use measures that integrate both but obscure where change is occurring. Cost per passenger is a commonly used measure that carries little meaning. Knowing how costs are changing or whether the number of passengers is increasing or decreasing helps management to determine corrective action, but cost per passenger confuses the issue. If both costs and numbers of passengers were increasing, a public agency could be going bankrupt and the ratio would hint of no problem. If a single overall cost-effectiveness measure is required, then operating deficit per passenger or subsidy per passenger is preferable. These measures approximate what economists consider to be minimization of cost or economic efficiency. A more positive measure is the additional trips per dollar of net cost.

Cost-effectiveness and cost-benefit ratios are too often used in transit for the wrong purpose. They are useful for comparing service proposals designed to achieve similar trip purposes with similar modes. They are not useful for comparison of fixed rail and bus transit or for comparison of express and local bus service. Public policy is better served when costs and benefits are expressed separately by measures of cost efficiency and service utilization. When they are not, excessive costs can easily be obscured by ridership adjustment or omission of certain costs. Wachs (1982) has explained the ethical problem created in transportation planning by underestimating costs for rapid transit and overestimating ridership in order to produce a favorable cost-effectiveness ratio. This misrepresentation would be less likely to occur if decision makers required the costs of producing service and the amount of service consumed to be stated separately.

The ratio of operating revenue to operating cost is another mixed measure that is popular with governmental agencies. The California Transportation Development Act was amended in 1979 to require all recipients of state financial assistance to achieve a 20 percent ratio for general transit and 10 percent for special social service transportation. Although legislators had considerable difficulty in defining eligible costs and revenues, the ratio has nevertheless served a useful purpose by requiring a threshold of passenger support for new service. The purpose was to limit increases in operating deficits, but operators have been creative in finding new revenues and reclassifying some costs so as to exclude them from the ratio. Better policy could have been achieved had the state used deficit per passenger as the threshold for performance.

In recognition of its widespread administrative use, operating revenue per dollar of operating cost is included here as one of the recommended indicators. But these statistics should be interpreted with caution because of the policy differences between agencies. Both fare and subsidy policies influence the ratio. Within each peer group there is substantial variation, and this indicator is of little use in comparative studies. Nevertheless, it is useful for administrative agencies seeking to specify minimum levels of operating funds needed from local sources.

Administrative Uses of Performance Measures

Managerial use of performance measures has been emphasized in the preceding sections, but performance measures are also helpful to administrative agencies responsible for the allocation of public assistance to transit agencies. Administrative use of cost-effectiveness measures was earlier disparaged. However, positive use of performance measures for administrative purposes deserves attention, so that the monitoring of transit performance may be improved for administrative as well as operating purposes. As transit has become increasingly dependent on federal, state, and regional agencies, reviews of accomplishments have been legislatively mandated. Performance measures can be used as an aid in auditing, comparing peer groups, and allocating assistance. However, the earlier admonition about responsibility warrants repeating: performance is management's responsibility. Government agencies can insist that performance be measured and ensure that controls are in place, but only management can use the results to implement changes. Far too much effort is devoted by regional and state agencies to conducting performance reviews whose recommendations are ignored by the operating agencies. Their efforts would be more effective if they required that performance be monitored using a prescribed set of indicators and then determined whether the data are in fact being collected and used for performance monitoring.

Performance Reviews. Government agencies administering financial assistance require performance reviews to determine whether or not grants are improving the performance of transit systems. Financial audits do not reveal this information: they ascertain whether funds are being used according to appropriations and whether or not the financial procedures provide security in cash management and accountability in the use of public money.

Many states, along with the federal government, require transit agencies to report performance as a condition of receiving financial assistance. Legislators have introduced these requirements out of concern over rising transit costs that threaten to grow higher still as influential constituencies lobby for additional support. They have mandated uniform reporting of expenditures and achievement, and some states, such as California, New York, and Pennsylvania, have required administrative agencies to analyze the results. Unfortunately, most performance review programs are too complex, require submission of too many items, and provide inadequate legislative guidance on evaluation objectives. The best require measurement of only a few items representing the efficiency and effectiveness dimensions.

In its 1979 amendment of the Transportation Development Act, the California legislature required performance reporting in exchange for operating assistance. Every three years a performance review must be performed by the regional transportation agency designated in the legislation. Changes in performance must be described, analyzed, and reported in terms of the following measures:

- Operating cost per passenger
- Operating cost per vehicle service hour
- Passengers per vehicle service hour
- Passengers per vehicle service mile
- Vehicle service hours per employee.

A performance committee established by each regional transportation agency reviews the results. Members represent transit operators, labor leaders, and transit users. The legislature was attempting to structure a process whereby spokespersons for these groups could discuss the results of the performance review and suggest ways of improving performance in a neutral forum. Performance committees were a compromise; legislators desired a tough performance monitoring program, but management and labor refused. The proposal to confer on a regular basis was a compromise that the legislature accepted as a way to initiate a process designed to improve performance.

In New York, performance reviews were also established by the state legislature as a reaction to transit deficits. Before the State Department of Transportation may allocate transit assistance to an agency, it must judge the agency's operations to be economical and efficient. Operators within the New York metropolitan area are excluded. Findings of economy and efficiency are based on seven indicators grouped into efficiency, effectiveness, and economy categories.

In Michigan, performance auditing of transit agencies began because of a state requirement that each department and agency demonstrate its efficiency and effectiveness. To meet the requirements, the Bureau of Urban and Public Transportation in 1978 selected a methodology that analyzed the dispersion of individual agency data in relation to the average indicator values for a peer group. The procedure was tested on mid-sized transit agencies to illustrate how attention could be focused on specific transit agencies whose performance was well above or well below average.

Section 15 reports were used to compute forty-seven performance indicators. The mean, range, and standard deviation for each indicator were calculated. Agencies were then compared on each indicator, and those with values more than one standard deviation above and below the mean were identified. It was also proposed that change in the indicator over time be recorded for each agency and adjusted for expected change. For example, the cost per vehicle mile was matched against the consumer price index to see whether operating costs per mile were increasing at a greater or lesser rate.

Michigan used more indicators than were necessary. A smaller number of indicators representing the efficiency and effectiveness dimensions would have reduced the amount of data collected, provided more easily understandable results, and still fulfilled the legislative requirement. Use of miles rather than hours as the denominator in several of the indicators also distorted the results. Operators complained that because of operating conditions that varied from agency to agency, measures using service miles did not allow for comparisons of agency performance. Use of service hours would have been more equitable.

The Surface Transportation Assistance Act of 1982 required the secretary of transportation to conduct triennial reviews of transit agencies receiving UMTA grants. UMTA, mindful of the experience of states such as Michigan, has implemented the requirement cautiously. Agencies are reviewed to determine whether they are complying with the federal regulations governing use of grants. At the same time, UMTA regional officials analyze the efficiency and effectiveness of each agency over a three- or four-year time period and examine its achievements against the achievements of peer systems. The Irvine Performance Evaluation Method is used for this purpose. The indicators described in Table 5 are used to summarize performance by each agency and to review this against the performance of peer groups defined by the typology in Figure 3. Between 110 and 125 agencies are reviewed annually on the basis of Section 15 data from the previous three years. The purpose is to identify aspects of superior and inferior performance for each agency and to examine these against requests for federal assistance.

Peer-Group Comparisons. Almost all transit managers compare their agencies against others that they consider to be peers. Administrative agencies have tried to replicate the process in order to assess performance, but until Section 15 data became available, this was a weak evaluation strategy. Operators disputed the accuracy of statistics and showed how differing operating environments easily accounted for variations. Section 15 reports have improved matters by presenting statistics in a uniform format so that the methods of comparative evaluation described in Chapter Three can be used with confidence.

The East-West Gateway Coordinating Council in St. Louis used the Section 15 data from seven similar systems to evaluate the performance of Bi-State Transit in 1982. Thirteen performance indicators were chosen representing different dimensions of performance. Mean performance was computed, and the Bi-State statistics were compared against this mean for 1979 and 1980. Unfortunately, miles rather than service hours were used as the denominator for six ratio indicators. Since Bi-State ranked no higher than fifth out of seven on these six ratios, the use of miles as a basis of peer-group comparisons was criticized. Bi-State's performance was higher when measured using revenue hours or peak vehicles as the denominator.

Allocation of Operating Assistance. Incentive-based funding for transit is an appealing administrative concept, but its implementation has been opposed by transit operators. Ideally, management should be rewarded for improving efficiency, but such systems are difficult to design. For example, subsidies based on vehicle miles or seat miles have been proposed, but they encourage agencies to operate vehicles so as to accumulate miles regardless of a service's usefulness.

Pennsylvania has done more than any other state to develop an equitable system for allocating subsidies that provide adequate funds, as well as incentives for improved performance. Pennsylvania began subsidizing transit operations in 1968 and revised the assistance formula in 1980 to provide for continuation of service and an incentive for improved performance. Allocation is determined by threshold requirements as well as by formula. Each system is required to achieve a farebox-to-operating-cost ratio of at least 40 percent. Additionally, systems are not to permit operating costs per hour to increase at a rate greater than that computed from the consumer price index and an index of transit labor costs. Miller

(1980) illustrates the method with a transit system whose annual cost was $10 million. If the allowable cost increase were 8 percent, then the next year's allocation for the same vehicle service hours could increase to $10.8 million. However, if costs increased to $11.2 million, the $400,000 deficit would become a local responsibility.

The required farebox recovery ratio is also assumed to apply in the calculation of the deficit. Using the previous example, if a system projected costs of $10.8 million, then operating revenue would have to be at least $4.32 million (40 percent). Any shortfall would have to be borne locally, since the eligible deficit would be $6.48 million. The federal operating subsidy is deducted from the allowable deficit. Hence, subtracting a $1.48 million federal allocation leaves an operating deficit of $5 million. The commonwealth of Pennsylvania would contribute between 66.66 and 75 percent of this amount. The 8.33 percent difference is the performance incentive—worth about $410,000 in the example cited above.

Pennsylvania works out a performance incentive using four measures: cost per hour, revenue per hour, ridership per hour, and the revenue-to-expense ratio. Each receives equal weight. To receive the incentive payment for the first three measures, a system must maintain or improve its performance in relation to that of the previous year. For example, to meet the cost-per-hour test, a system's cost cannot increase at a rate greater than the average of the consumer price index and the transit labor cost index for the urbanized area. In the case of revenue per hour and ridership per hour, a system must maintain the same level or increase it. The revenue-to-expense (cost) ratio is determined annually by the commonwealth. Forty-five percent was required in 1978, 40 percent in 1980.

By combining need with performance incentives, Pennsylvania has developed a relatively simple framework for allocating operating assistance that may discourage the rate of cost increase. The incentive seems to work best for the smaller systems: twenty-eight of the thirty-one agencies achieved at least one incentive payment, and four earned the entire 8.33 percent incentive allowance. The framework is equitable in that it allocates more funds to the larger metropolitan areas (although for these areas, the penalties do not provide the same incentives to control costs as they do for the smaller urbanized areas). The framework is also administratively practical. It allows transit managers to predict their funding allocation with sufficient accuracy and timeliness to meet budgetary requirements. Because hours rather than miles are used as the measure of service produced, problems associated with comparability between areas are diminished. Finally, the emphasis on efficiency rather than on effectiveness shows that legislators recognize the urgent necessity for cost control in transit and are willing to reward efforts to achieve it.

Effectiveness of Measuring Performance

A systems approach to transit has been emphasized because it identifies production as well as consumption attributes. Most management studies have given too much emphasis to consumption and have neglected operating costs. More attention must be paid to the costs of transit inputs and their efficient use in producing output expressed as vehicle hours or miles of service. Ridership as a measure of effectiveness should not be neglected, but it should be placed in a more reasonable perspective. A simple triangular model of cost efficiency, service effectiveness, and cost effectiveness was designed to help specify the dimensions of transit production. Measures of transit performance have been described for each dimension and examples provided on how measures could be devised for performance reviews, peer-group comparison, and the allocation of transit-operating assistance.

This chapter has emphasized cost efficiency because, in a period of fiscal austerity, an appropriate goal for transit managers is to allocate labor, capital, and fuel in a manner that will maximize the amount of transit output for the same or a declining level of public assistance.

During the 1970s, transit expansion occurred amid a confusing and often contradictory policy environment in which governing boards seemed to have a clear idea neither of goals nor of how transit could be used to accomplish diverse objectives. The simple triangular model presented in this chapter should bring some order to this situation: it identifies the dimensions of transit production and consumption and indicates how performance can be measured. It also illuminates how dependent transit agencies have become on governmental support. Given this dependence, a transit agency's budget for the current year, as well as its anticipated budget for future years, becomes the pivot about which service is planned to accomplish objectives. Performance measures can be used to determine whether funds allocated and services provided are in fact accomplishing these objectives.

5

Effective Budgeting
and Financing
for Public Transit

People often think of budgeting as a dull subject best left to accounting experts. But a budget is in fact a crucial document. In Wildavsky's words, a budget is "a series of goals with price tags attached" (1964, p. 5). It translates a transit agency's goals into action, integrating labor and capital with available financial resources and organizing them into service provision. Budgets authorize programs and provide financial data for evaluating performance with the measures described in Chapter Four. They are also highly political weapons that permit elected and appointed decision makers to punish opponents and reward supporters.

This chapter defines budgeting's many functions and opportunities by means of a conceptual approach to the process. With the intent of convincing the reader that budgeting's role is pivotal, I will describe different types of budgets, summarize revenue sources, and explain how to forecast costs and revenues, allocate costs, and analyze operational efficiency.

The central importance of budgeting to strategic management cannot be overstated. For example, since funding is seldom sufficient to fulfill all expectations, preparation of the annual budget frequently leads to intraagency bickering. This competition can help clarify relative contributions by different departments to agency goals, and the skillful manager will turn it to his or her advantage. Guiding the budget through its preparation, comparing the relative contribution of departments to agency goals, eliciting approval from the legislative authority, and then auditing expenditures to ensure goal attainment are the most important activities in which transit managers can engage. Those who control the budgetary process dominate policy implementation because they select objectives, determine priorities, and monitor progress. Those who control the budget in effect control the agency.

Budgets in Transit Organizations

Budgets for transit organizations are less controversial than those for city governments because, in the former case, there are fewer interests competing for available funds. Nevertheless, transit budgets are created in a political environment. Employee labor unions attempt to influence expenditures, while transit patrons protest fare increases. Yet it is the professional and managerial employees who have the greatest effect on transit budgeting. Final budgets generally reflect their estimation of what financial resources are likely to be available and what transit service should be offered.

Elected and appointed officials serving on policy boards tend to have minimal influence on transit budgets. Although they approve the budget, board members seldom have the time or knowledge to propose changes beyond increasing or decreasing categories of expenditure or adjusting salaries for inflation. They rarely analyze staff decisions on type and frequency of service (which represent 75 to 80 percent of the budget) to determine whether the agency could achieve the same objectives at lower cost. This state of affairs is acceptable to staff members, since they tend to prefer a "professional" approach, free of interference from their policy board. Strategies that prevent policy boards from understanding budgets are common; one such strategy is to make small changes to previous (already approved) budgets. Although it may suit the purpose of transit professionals, exclusion of the policy board from genuine participation in financial allocation is unwise, as it can insulate the agency from the community it serves. A preferred strategy is to involve the board in the development of the

short-range Transportation Improvement Plan (TIP), from which
the annual budget is developed. The policy board is usually well
suited for the task of evaluating alternative scenarios for future
development.

   Satisfying External Requirements. External funding agencies actually possess more influence than do local policy boards.
Transit agencies' financial dependence on federal, state, and other
local agencies allows these external agencies to influence operating
policies and procedures by imposing eligibility requirements for
funding. As an example, the seven transit operating affiliates of the
New York Metropolitan Transportation Authority (MTA) receive
operating assistance from twelve separate funding programs to
cover approximately 49 percent of operating costs in 1981. Each
program requires the MTA to certify in advance that it is complying
with applicable state or federal requirements. Although the amount
of external funding for MTA is larger than for most transit agencies,
the variety of governmental assistance programs—and with them
the variety of requirements—is typical. These requirements,
including affirmative action plans, equality of service to minority
population areas, and full accessibility for persons with disabilities
have changed transit authorities into "resource-dependent"
agencies (Pfeffer and Salancik, 1978).

   Block grants for capital and operating assistance approved by
the Surface Transportation Assistance Act of 1982 removed some
regulations, but others have remained. Section 13(c) of the Urban
Mass Transportation Act, for example, obliges the secretary of labor
to certify that the funded agency agrees to "protect individual
employees against a worsening of their positions with respect to
their employment" that might result from federal funds provided to
offset the costs of operations, capital investment, or demonstration
programs.

   Department of Labor rules governing this requirement have
forced transit agencies to negotiate agreements with employee labor
unions before they can obtain the funding due them. The overall
effect has been to perpetuate obsolete work practices and to preclude
modernization programs that would reduce labor costs. Labor
unions can wring concessions from management that they have

been unable to obtain during labor negotiations solely by refusing to sign the Section 13(c) agreement. Transit managers with millions of dollars worth of capital equipment and operating assistance in the balance are in a weak position to bargain. For example, in order to gain federal funding to complete the subway system in San Francisco, BART agreed in 1969 to accept employees from private and public transit systems whose work opportunities might be adversely affected by BART operations. At first each employee group worked under its own labor contract. As a result of arbitration in 1973, however, BART had to create a new contract merging the most advantageous clauses from each of the former contracts. This outcome accelerated BART's labor costs in its initial years and resulted in labor-management friction that further added to the stress caused by BART's technical difficulties.

A more obvious and costly constraint imposed on American transit was that agencies make public transit vehicles fully accessible to wheelchair patrons. The requirement has a federal legislative history dating back to 1968, with enforcement legislation passed in 1973 (Fielding, 1982). Section 504 of the Rehabilitation Act of 1973 specified that "no otherwise qualified handicapped individual . . . shall, solely by reason of his handicap, be excluded from the participation in, be denied the benefits of, or be subjected to discrimination under any program or activity receiving federal financial assistance" (Public Law 93-113 87 Statute 355).

Regulations implementing Section 504 were published in 1979 and remained in force until 1981. During the two years in which the regulations were in force, transit agencies acted bizarrely. They bought buses equipped with lifts, each at an additional capital cost of $12,000 and with annual maintenance costs ranging from $500 to $4,015. These lifts reduced seating capacity and increased energy consumption. Furthermore, the majority of persons with disabilities refused to use the lift-equipped buses because the lifts were unreliable, the buses did not go where they desired to travel, and they were unwilling to endure the embarrassment of delaying other bus patrons.

Agency requirements are not always detrimental. The federal requirement that each transit agency prepare a three-to-five-year transportation plan (SRTP) that identifies priorities for transportation improvement, including estimates of costs and revenue (TIP), has been helpful to fiscal management. The SRTP/TIP provides a method for integrating cost estimates with forecasts of revenues (Table 1). It is also an excellent way to involve policy boards in the selection of development scenarios, which they can evaluate both in terms of an area's needs and agency goals and in terms of the funding likely to be available. By the time an uninvolved policy board receives an annual budget, the agency is already committed to operating service initiated in previous years, and the board can make only minor changes. This is not the case with the SRTP/TIP. Here the board is evaluating options for the future, and its choices on what service will be operated, where, and by whom can influence future operating policy. Such decisions are then implemented gradually over several years as part of the annual budget. Conceptualizing the budget process in this way—as the annual element of a continuing effort to improve transit—captures the very essence of managing strategically: such an approach subordinates the allocation of resources to the achievement of a desired transit scenario.

   Budget Process. The budget process in transit agencies is typically quite straightforward (Figure 8), with incremental decreases and increases in previous budgets generally determining the annual budget. These changes are influenced by the cost of inputs, increases in service proposed in the SRTP, and anticipated revenues from fares and external sources.
   Budget preparation should be a top-down rather than a bottom-up process. Preparation begins with the executive staff's review of the assumptions and scenarios of the SRTP/TIP against projected revenues and costs. The chief executive or controller next instructs the departments on the details of their individual budget preparation; these instructions normally include the following elements:

- A budget calendar
- Allowable cost increases for labor (salaries, wages, and fringe benefits) and other items
- A format for departmental requests

Figure 8. Annual Budget Cycle.

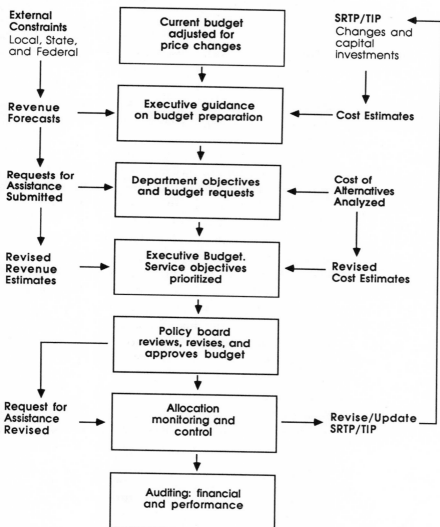

Budgets are developed by incremental changes from previous budgets. The link to the SRTP/TIP requirement is essential for strategic management.

- Work load and labor efficiency expectations
- A forecast of the agency's financial status for the approaching fiscal year.

Responsibility for preparing budgets should rest with departmental managers, although the controller can provide assistance where needed. Once managers have completed their budgets, the general manager and executive staff conduct department-by-department reviews to ensure compliance with instructions, to consider special departmental requests, and to assign service priorities. The general manager then submits the budget to the policy board for review, revision, and approval. The policy board's approval of the budget initiates an allocation, control, and monitoring cycle. Funding requests must be submitted to local, state, and federal agencies. With completion of the annual budget, work begins on updating the SRTP/TIP for the next cycle.

Control and monitoring ensure that budget overruns do not occur and that expenditures are achieving service objectives. Monthly reports summarize the agency's expenditures and revenues, which are then compared with budget appropriations and estimates. Quarterly reports combine financial data with output by presenting the hours and miles of service produced from expenditure of funds for labor, fuel, and other items. The question of whether the agency achieved its service objectives is also addressed. Details of patronage and farebox revenue also appear in the quarterly performance reports.

Audits can take two forms: financial and performance. Financial audits determine whether a transit agency has accounted for its revenues according to generally accepted practices, and whether it is spending funds for approved purposes. Performance audits serve a broader function, that of determining whether a transit agency is complying with regulations promulgated by local, state, and federal agencies. These regulations typically concern such matters as highway safety, pollution control, accessibility for those with disabilities, and achievement of revenue-to-cost ratios. California, for example, requires all transit systems receiving state funding to be audited for performance every three years. Reports must include assessments of the efficiency, effectiveness, and cost effectiveness of each agency.

Although the SRTP/TIP process makes budget preparation systematic, many agencies have not adopted it. For some agencies, funding from external sources, especially local, is so uncertain that they cannot forecast revenue with precision. Therefore they must plan and operate one year at a time. They accept the current funding level as the base and develop next year's service plan in response to increases or decreases in local funds.

Types of Budgets

Budgets serve different functions within a single organization. Three types of budgets are generally used by transit agencies: line item, lump sum, and program. Line-item budgets predominate, and even though policy makers may approve program or lump-sum budgets, the agency will itemize expenditures at the operational level. Program budgets, for example, are often used for long-term planning and are then converted to line-item budgets for annual programming purposes.

Transit agencies using line-item budgets determine activities on the basis of funding, by allocating resources in set amounts by object or function. Many agencies use the Uniform Financial Accounting and Reporting Elements (FARE) adopted in 1973 by federal agencies to comply with Section 15 of the Urban Mass Transportation Act. Accounts are itemized under the following categories: labor, fringe benefits, services, materials and supplies, utilities, casualty and liability costs, taxes, and promotion. Use of these categories reduces the burden of reporting to federal and state agencies. Annual budgets can then be reported in three columns for actual expenditure in the previous year, estimated current-year expenditure, and projected expenditure for the forthcoming year.

Line-item budgets can be overly restrictive and inflexible. For example, the budget may allocate funds for maintenance salaries, materials, and supplies but not allow the maintenance manager to exceed the allotment for any line item without policy approval. This approach often precludes internal economizing; for example, a manager might be prevented from making a new-parts purchase that would reduce labor costs. It may also prompt year-end extravagance as managers attempt to spend all funds in each line item.

Lump-sum budgets are less restrictive. An agency assigns a single sum of money to each of several functions—for example, to vehicle operations, vehicle maintenance, nonvehicle maintenance, and general administration—and the function manager allocates funds to specific expense categories. The Section 15 chart of accounts defines each function. Although this type of budget allows managers greater flexibility, the agency's top management must base budget preparation on viable plans and must closely scrutinize and control all actions taken within each function. Private transit firms commonly use lump-sum budgets. Their managers are rewarded for operating within budget and thereby contributing to profitability.

Program or performance budgets are based on a predetermined amount of work. They are rarely used in public transit agencies except for work that is performed under contract. For example, a governmental agency may contract with a private entity to supply a designated number of hours of peak-hour service or specialized service for persons with disabilities. A program budget designates the amount and quality of work that is expected. In the case of contracting for service, management decides on the levels of service and allows the governing board to select the contractor. Program budgets indicate not only what is to be accomplished but also what it will cost. They can also specify penalties to be imposed if the work is not accomplished. For example, in San Mateo County, California, private operators receive a lump sum each month to produce a specified number of hours of service for persons with disabilities. If service reliability falls below a prescribed level, the contractor is penalized by reduced payments.

Budgeting Strategies

Three different strategies are used to construct budgets: incremental, zero-based, and cross-functional analysis.

Incremental Strategy. This involves adjusting line-item amounts in response to proposed changes in service, performance, or revenue. If service is to be increased, then item amounts for the additional service expenses and revenues are increased. If better maintenance performance is desired, then line-item amounts for maintenance are increased. And if revenues from external sources change, service can be adjusted accordingly. Incremental changes in budgets normally represent changes in available funds. Policy boards prefer incremental budgets with expenses shown by object class. Agencies can use the Section 15 chart of accounts to show expenditures by function and class in three columns. The requested appropriations appear alongside the previous year's allocation and the current or amended allocation.

Zero-Based Budgeting. Transit agencies employ zero-based strategies when they need to appraise the effectiveness of different programs after a period of service expansion. The usefulness of this type of budgeting depends on how well the agency has developed objectives that can be specified in budgetary terms. The term *zero-based* is a misnomer, since programs are seldom reduced to zero. Usually budgets are prepared at 90, 100, and 110 percent of previous levels and then analyzed in terms of how marginal changes will affect service objectives. In most instances, it is a question of marginal rather than zero-based analysis.

Zero-based budgeting was developed to permit electronics firms to control expenditures on different products, some of which quickly became technically outmoded (Pyhrr, 1977). The approach can be useful to transit agencies during a period of consolidation when serious questions must be asked about the functions performed by the agency. The steps are as follows:

1. Identify decision units (these are usually programs in a transit agency).
2. Analyze each decision unit.
3. Evaluate and prioritize the functions of each decision unit that is to be included in the budget request. The consequences for agency goals of not funding various functions, or of increasing or decreasing funding for various functions, are then examined.

4. Prepare budgets reflecting decisions made about each function
    and decision unit.

The first two steps involve a management process, the third a
planning process, and the fourth a budgetary one. However, using
the budget to initiate periodic performance reviews of units or
programs shows that the budgetary process is in fact the nucleus of
strategic management.

Decision units in transit agencies can be as general as vehicle
operations or as specific as park-and-ride operations, depending on
the magnitude of the budget. A two-staged process of evaluation is
conducted for each unit. First, management should consider
different ways of performing the same function. Then, the potential
effects of increased and decreased funding for each function should
be evaluated. For example, a transit agency operating park-and-ride
express service from suburbs to central city (a function in
operations) might analyze the cost and effectiveness of this service
as provided by different agents—by the agency itself, by private contractors, or by organized car pools and van pools. Once the supplier
has been selected, management must decide whether to curtail,
expand, or continue the current level of funding.

When the Public Works Department of San Diego County (a
"decision unit") used a zero-based budget approach in 1980 to
determine how it would operate fixed-route transit (a "function")
in the northern part of the county, it considered four alternatives:

1. Do nothing and allow other communities to use the state and
    federal funds available to the area.
2. Operate the service itself.
3. Contract with the local transit agency.
4. Solicit bids from private contractors.

After eliminating the first two alternatives, the county
solicited bids to operate the service. The local transit agency bid
$3.65 per revenue mile, whereas the lowest private contractor bid
$2.25. The transit agency offered to supply professional operators
and coordination with service in the city of San Diego, but its high
labor costs offset these advantages. The county chose the private

contractor because it could provide more hours of service for the funds available, but the county also wanted to make sure that the service would be reliable and safe. Therefore, the county negotiated a contract that rewarded or penalized the private company according to its performance against standards for on-time service, cleanliness, and maintenance of vehicles.

The disadvantage of zero-based budgeting is that it impedes analysis of alternative ways of performing a function. The provision of transit service in northern San Diego County, for example, could be analyzed more easily before it was contracted out. Once service had begun, specification of costs and effectiveness would become much more difficult. For example, should the overhead for county supervision, financial management, and county lobbying in Sacramento and Washington, D.C., be charged to the private operator or not? Transit agencies are running up against these kinds of cost allocation problems as they attempt route refinement studies and consider alternative ways of providing services. Success with zero-based budgeting depends on the abilities of the managers involved and on their willingness to subject their operations to impartial scrutiny.

Cross-Functional Analysis. This method of analysis is zero-based budgeting at the micro level. This approach permits examination of costs shared by organizational units that might otherwise go unquestioned in budget analysis. For example, a proposal to change the maintenance inspection program from every 9,000 to every 6,000 vehicle miles will improve service reliability. The change, however, will affect not only maintenance but also operations and administration. The question is whether the improvement in service quality, which should reduce costs for on-the-road repairs, towing, and supervision, will outweigh the costs that will be borne for more frequent inspections and preventative maintenance. Cross-functional analysis permits management to study the relevant cost ratios before proceeding with a proposed change.

Budgeting strategies should encourage this type of comparative analysis. The financial impact of a proposal on each function must be examined and then summarized. Some data will be difficult to collect; for such activities as service recovery time and handling of customer complaints, costs will have to be estimated because quantitative estimates will probably not be available. However, the advantage of cross-functional analysis is that it provides a formal assessment of alternative methods and procedures that involve several decision units.

Budgets and Strategic Management. Budget preparation and review are demanding activities in any public agency. They compel a reevaluation of objectives as well as a careful review of the methods used to produce service within the constraints of available funds. If budgeting is to be a smooth process, the cooperation of the entire managerial and supervisorial staff must be obtained. Too often upper management fails to apprise supervisors of the role of the budgets in unifying diverse activities and gives them few opportunities to participate in budget preparation. Supervisors are cautioned against exceeding budgetary allocations and then punished with funding cuts when they economize.

Operating budgets should be flexible documents based on a range of cost estimates that are revised throughout the annual cycle. Integration of the annual budget with the three-to-five-year budget forecasts required for the SRTP/TIP also reduces controversy, because it allows operating supervisors to see annual changes as part of an organizational plan for service improvement. Tension lessens when employees realize that budgets are part of a strategic management process in which different objectives can be realized over time.

Forecasting Financial Resources

Forecasting revenues is an initial step in financial planning (Figure 8). This information is combined with the current budget and planned service changes to guide the preparation of capital and operating budgets. Varying assumptions are used to estimate the amounts, sources, timing, stability, and constraints of income streams in the short and long term. The objective is to develop a framework for estimating future revenue under different assumptions. This section focuses on forecasting the amount of operating revenue and of local, state, and federal assistance that will be available to an agency. It is important to incorporate into forecasting the effects of possible future interest rates and inflation rates on investments and borrowing; these topics are adequately covered by Cheng (1982), however, and will not be addressed here.

Operating Revenue. Passenger revenue accounts for an average of 39 percent of total transit income, with additional operating revenues coming from advertising and charter bus operations. Passenger revenue is the most reliable source of funding and should allow an agency to take an informed approach to designing annual and short-range budgets. However, only in rare instances do transit agencies project when and in what amounts operating revenue will be available beyond the one-year horizon. The few forecasts that have been compiled have been based mostly on simplistic methods that provide only "ballpark" estimates of anticipated revenues. For example, it was reported in 1982 that "Houston does not worry about fare increases inducing ridership losses. Revenues are forecast by multiplying the forecasted ridership by the average transit fare. Ridership forecasts are based upon planned bus hours of service assuming a constant ridership per service hour" (Anagnostoupolous and others, 1982, p. 43). The effects of planned changes in fare policy and service are thus not taken into account in the estimation of future revenue. Nashville, Tennessee, uses a similar method but assumes that ridership will decline .33 percent for every 1 percent increase in fare—an industry axiom developed in 1947 by Curtin (1968) that is unreliable when used without disaggregation by trip type and reference to the socioeconomic characteristics of riders. Use of the Curtin axiom provides a simple estimate of what may happen when fares are raised, but more comprehensive and useful models have been developed that incorporate changes in several variables.

Better forecasts of passenger revenue can be derived from an aggregate transit-demand model which projects the number of transit trips that patrons will make in the region served. The analyst then disaggregates the results by trip type and fare elasticity in order to forecast ridership and revenue impacts. Aggregate demand models assume that an identifiable set of economic and demographic variables influences the level of ridership on specific routes or in a given area. A linear regression model can be calibrated from time-series data (usually monthly statistics over three to five years) to establish the positive and negative effects of such variables as characteristics of the transit service, demography, and number of workdays in the time period. Seattle Metro uses a model calibrated on workdays per quarter, employment in the region, and gasoline prices in order to forecast ridership. Price elasticities are then applied to type of rider (market segment) in order to estimate revenue under different fare policies.

A better example is provided by Button and Navin (1983) in their work for the Greater Vancouver Regional District, British Columbia. An aggregate ridership equation was developed in which monthly ridership was positively related to increases in family income, population increase, and number of working and weekend days and negatively related to fare increases, availability of autos, and such seasonal factors as school and university vacations. The authors estimated future values for the eight variables in the model to forecast aggregate ridership.

Although Button and Navin found that changing economic and demographic conditions exerted the strongest effect on aggregate ridership for purposes of financial forecasting, they recommended that ridership be stratified by time of day, length of journey, purpose of trip, and type of user in order to obtain better estimates of both ridership and revenue. On-board survey data were used for stratification. A fare-elasticity matrix, based on studies reported in Table 6, was combined with the stratification of aggregate ridership forecasts to produce estimates of fare revenue.

Button and Navin explain that a fare-elasticity matrix is used to forecast fare revenues when there is a dearth of reliable statistical data. But if the transit agency has consistently maintained fare, service, and ridership data, planners can calculate elasticities of demand from these records rather than adopting elasticities from other areas. Jacksonville, Florida, has used this method to calculate both fare and service elasticities, which are then used to project revenue changes resulting from increases in cash fares and in prices of prepaid passes. Here is another area where performance monitoring helps an agency to manage strategically. Changes in ridership after

Table 6. Summary of Fare Elasticities.

Aggregate	Elasticity Mean/Standard Deviation[a]	Number of Cases
Type of Fare Change		
Fare increase	−0.34 ± 0.11	14
Fare decrease	−0.37 ± 0.11	9
City Size		
Populations > 1 million	−0.24 ± 0.10	19
Populations 500,000 to 1 million	−0.30 ± 0.12	11
Populations < 500,000	−0.35 ± 0.12	14
Disaggregate		
Transit Mode		
Bus	−0.35 ± 0.14	12
Rapid Rail	−0.17 ± 0.05	10
Commuter Rail	−0.31	1
Time Period		
Peak	−0.17 ± 0.09	5
Off-peak	−0.40 ± 0.26	5
All hours	−0.29 ± 0.19	5
Trip purpose		
Work	−0.10 ± 0.04	6
School	<−0.19 to 0.44	3
Shop	−0.23 ± 0.06	5
Trip Length (bus)		
< 1.3 miles	−0.52 ± 0.11	3
> 1.3 miles	−0.21 ± 0.15	3
Route Type		
CBD Oriented	−0.40 ± 0.04	3
Non CBD Oriented	−0.62 ± 0.09	3
Systemwide	−0.55 ± 0.08	3

[a]Standard deviation when available
Source: Adapted from Mayworm, Lago, and McEnroe, 1980; Webster and Bly, 1980.

previous fare increases are used to predict the effect of fare increases on current riders.

Another method uses fare revenue as the dependent variable and attempts to estimate future revenue directly from a regression model. This approach is appropriate when an agency lacks data on ridership by fare group but has adequate records on how revenue has changed with changes in fares. Numerous independent variables have been tested, but the significant variables are similar to those used to predict aggregate ridership—monthly variations in workdays, seasonal travel demand, and real gasoline prices. Wang and Skinner (1984) have summarized these studies and have confirmed that increasing fares leads to decreased ridership but increased revenue and that there is some switch to transit as gasoline prices increase.

Transit agencies employ a variety of methods to forecast ridership—methods that can be modified to provide estimates of future passenger revenue under different assumptions. Multisystems, Inc. (1982) reviewed different approaches to route-level-demand modeling and concluded that the most commonly used methods were too simplistic and provided only very general results. Some of these approaches are discussed as planning procedures in Chapter Eight. Agencies with staff who can use these models should adapt them to local circumstances.

Opportunities to increase revenue ought to be investigated in all forecasts. In this respect, the experience of Canadian operators can help suggest strategies. Canadian transit operators have always set higher fares than their American counterparts and made use of variable charges to reflect the additional cost of providing long-distance and peak-period service. American agencies, in contrast, have been encouraged to keep fares low and uniform. The Toronto Transit Commission, for example, achieves a revenue-to-cost ratio of 70 percent by increasing fares in proportion to operating costs for different types of service.

Failure to adjust fares to reflect costs has led to inequitable outcomes in the United States. Correcting these inequities provides opportunities to increase revenues. Cervero (1981) has shown that inner-city residents traveling less than two miles pay ten to twelve times as much per mile as does the average user, and that suburban (and presumably more affluent) commuters pay less than the average user. The practical outcome of such policies is that inner-city workers commuting to downtown on crowded buses receive a subsidy of about ten cents per trip, whereas more affluent suburban residents who commute to downtown on more comfortable express buses are subsidized to the tune of about $3 per trip. This kind of disparity is fairly common; inequality is likely to occur where inner-city trips are short and fares are not varied by distance to reflect the marginal cost of longer trips from the suburbs. Hodge (1986), however, has argued that this disparity is not unfair in that suburban areas yield more governmental support for transit.

Opportunities exist for increasing revenues through fare policy in the two markets in which transit has an advantage over the automobile: in the older, low-income neighborhoods where trips are short and demand remains constant all day, and along congested corridors from the suburbs to the central city during peak hours. Distance-based fares with rates charged to reflect marginal cost per mile can keep fares low for short trips by center-city residents as well as require suburban residents to pay a fairer share for longer express trips. Peak-hour surcharges also increase revenue and are easier to implement than distance-based fares. They have the additional advantage of discouraging transit use when systems are overcrowded. Forecasting revenues provides the financial analyst with opportunities to explore such fares within the framework of strategic management.

Local, State, and Federal Assistance. Estimating future governmental assistance is an easier task than forecasting operating revenue. If assistance is budgeted annually, as it is in Boston and Nashville, Tennessee, projections can be based on past experience. Projected increases are normally based on anticipated inflation adjustments, with government allocations added for new services and capital programs. Of the $5.3 billion provided for operating assistance in 1984, local governments contributed 50 percent, state agencies 33 percent, and federal agencies 17 percent. Where local and state assistance are derived from a sales tax dedicated to transportation, as in California, estimates are based upon projected taxable sales. For all areas outside of New York City, the state of New York bases allocations on service-provided and service-consumed criteria, which can be predicted by the agency. Using these various sources of information, fiscal planners can derive

revenue estimates for both dedicated and non-dedicated funding
sources. However, it is prudent to make both high and low
estimates. Projections are normally made over three to five years.
Beyond five years, forecasts are unreliable because policy changes
that might jeopardize funding cannot be anticipated that far ahead.

Federal assistance has been less predictable than local and
state assistance. Apportionments are determined by formulas
inserted by Congress into transportation legislation. Allocations for
the duration of the legislative commitment (normally three years)
can be calculated. However, Congress can change the amount of its
commitment each year when appropriating funds. Therefore
assumptions must be made about both the size of the appropriation
and the restrictions or additions that Congress might add.

Formula grants under Sections 5 and 9 of the Urban Mass
Transportation Act provide the majority of assistance. However,
agencies also claim assistance under the other sections described in
Table 7. There is also some discretion in using Section 9 funds for
capital projects in addition to the discretionary funds available
under Section 3. A transit agency that can forecast financial
requirements three to five years in advance is better placed
strategically to maximize federal assistance by applying for funds
under different sections. Success in federal "grantsmanship"
requires both fiscal planning and knowledge on how different
categories of funds might be used.

Because transit agencies depend on external governmental
assistance, a great deal of effort is devoted to forecasting future
revenue streams under varying scenarios. The conditions most
likely to influence local and state assistance can be specified and
programmed as a spread-sheet to yield results under differing
conditions; federal assistance is forecast in a similar manner,
although this exercise entails more difficulties. Projections of
governmental assistance are then merged with estimated operating
revenues to predict revenue streams. In addition, constraints on
spending, such as restriction of funds to capital or planning
projects, must be specified. Results of the forecast can then be
matched against projected operating costs and capital requirements
to determine the amount of service an agency can afford to provide.

Table 7. Urban Mass Transportation Act by Section and Expenditure
for Fiscal Year 1984.

Section	Type of Program	$Million
3	Capital improvement grants provide up to 80 percent of cost of new equipment, property acquisition, construction, and modernization.	$1,063
5	Operating assistance grants cover up to 50 percent of operating deficits involved in providing transit service and 80 percent of cost for annual routine bus and related equipment replacement.	302
6	Research, development, and demonstration projects are funded on a contract or grant basis for studies, tests, demonstrations of new methods, equipment, technology, and systems.	29
8	Planning and technical studies grants to public agencies provide 80 percent of cost of transportation planning, engineering surveys, designing and evaluation of urban transportation projects.	46
9	Formula grants (capital and operating) for rehabilitation, replacement, construction, and modernization of rolling stock. Apportioned to urbanized areas by population, population density, service, and ridership.	1,798
9a	Formula grants (capital) operate in the same way as Section 9 grants; however, funds come from the Mass Transit Account of the Highway Trust Fund.	92
10	Managerial training grants provide fellowships for advanced training of personnel employed in managerial, technical, and professional positions in the urban transportation field.	1
11	University research and training grants are available to public and private nonprofit institutions of higher learning to assist in establishing or carrying out comprehensive research in transportation.	2
16(b)(2)	Capital assistance grants to support transit for elderly and handicapped riders provide funds to nonprofit organizations for transit services where existing services are not available, insufficient, or inappropriate for elderly and handicapped persons. Section 3 funds are also available for this purpose.	33
Total		$3,366

Source: U.S. Department of Transportation, 1985.

Forecasting Operating Costs

Because transit agencies have far more control over operating costs than over revenues, forecasting costs is less problematical. Service levels are fairly uniform throughout the year with some seasonal variation to accommodate Christmas shopping and the holiday schedules of schools and universities. Costs can be forecast on the basis of previous costs and modified by executive guidance in these areas:

- Number of service hours
- Projected changes in labor costs, including costs associated with fringe benefits
- Estimated cost inflation for fuel and materials used to produce and maintain service.

Development of a budget is an iterative process. Costs associated with producing a proposed level of service are calculated from past costs modified by present cost assumptions. Managers explore different means of accomplishing each activity to find ways of reducing costs with special attention given to labor requirements, which account for about 75 percent of cost. Cherwony, Gleichman, and Porter (1981) have summarized various procedures that are available to forecast operating costs. The simplest are *single-unit cost methods* that forecast costs by incrementing the current cost for miles or hours of services. *Cost allocation methods* disaggregate unit costs into variables such as hours, miles, and peak vehicles and then increment each. *Cost build-up methods* can estimate future labor costs more accurately than cost allocation methods. These methods disaggregate service hours depending on the type and seniority of operators assigned to individual routes. Cost build-up methods are more appropriate for route costing than for systemwide forecasting and will be discussed as a planning technique in Chapter Eight. *Avoidable cost methods* are used when assessing the potential for private subcontracting. Only the costs "avoided" through subcontracting are included. For example, advertising expenses and the cost of complying with planning and reporting requirements (for which the agency remains responsible) are excluded from both private and public costs for purposes of comparison. Each costing procedure requires judgment in allocating cost to different variables and skill in projecting these costs when forecasting. Methods should be chosen according to the importance of the task and the time available. The three-variable procedure, in which costs are fully allocated to hours, miles, and peak vehicles, is the most frequently used method.

Cost Allocation Methods. Data for the calculation of cost models can be obtained from current operating statistics or from the Section 15 report prepared by the agency. By calculating the relative efficiency with which operating labor is used during different portions of the day, analysts can further disaggregate these data to differentiate between the cost of peak service and the cost of base service. Use of cost allocation models for forecasting requires estimation of future operating levels by service type and projection of changes in factor prices for the variables used in the model. After this, cost estimates can be developed for subsequent years according to the amount and type of service planned. Most transit systems have well-defined operating plans, even though they seldom project accurate estimates of their future costs. Cost allocation models provide agencies with a method for estimating these costs that is more accurate than simply incrementing cost per mile or hour according to inflation indexes.

Three types of cost allocation models are useful for analyzing the cost of proposed changes: fully allocated cost models, fixed and variable cost models, and temporal variation models. The latter two are variations of the first. All three use annual, budgeted costs for factor inputs and allocate these to service output measures such as vehicle miles, service hours, and number of vehicles required.

Fully Allocated Cost Models. Cost allocation models are based on the concept that the cost of producing service is a function of a few service output variables such as vehicle miles, hours, and number of peak-period vehicles. As a means of arriving at the unit cost for each variable, transit costs are allocated to one or more output variables, summed, and then divided by the quantity of the variable used (Table 8). A common form of cost allocation model is:

$$UC = Uh(VH) + Um(VM) + Uv(PV)$$

where:

UC = Unit cost of route, route segments, or type of service
Uh = Unit cost associated with hours
VH = Vehicle hours required
Um = Unit costs associated with miles
VM = Vehicle miles required
Uv = Unit cost associated with vehicles
PV = Peak vehicles required

As additions or deletions to service require changes in hours, miles, and peak vehicles, costs can be estimated for planned changes. Many transit systems use property-specific variables in their cost allocation models. Some include riders as a fourth variable (Chicago and Cincinnati), whereas SCRTD in Los Angeles has a pullout factor that captures the vehicle-servicing costs of placing an additional vehicle into service.

Fully allocated cost models take their name from the fact that all system-operating cost items are based on the output variables. Consequently, the sum of costs for all routes will equal total operating costs for the system. Annual costs are normally used to estimate coefficients, although it is possible to use monthly or pay-period costs.

Fixed and Variable Cost Models. Fixed and variable cost allocation models differ from fully allocated models in their treatment of overhead costs such as advertising and vehicle depreciation that do not vary directly with the amount of service produced. This approach is useful when management is considering small changes to service that may require use of another peak vehicle but that will not cause increased administrative costs or additional building maintenance. Assigning a full peak-vehicle share of cost ($10,000 to $15,000 annually) to such small changes

Table 8. Fully Allocated Approach for Expense Assignment.

Function and Expense Object Class[a]	Vehicle Hours	Vehicle Miles	Peak Vehicles
501 Labor			
010 Vehicle operations	X		
041 Vehicle maintenance		X	
042 Nonvehicle maintenance			X
160 General administration			X
502 Fringe Benefits			
010 Vehicle operations	X		
041 Vehicle maintenance		X	
042 Nonvehicle maintenance			X
160 General administration			X
503 Services			X
504 Materials and Supplies			
010 Vehicle operations		X	
041 Vehicle maintenance		X	
042 Nonvehicle maintenance		X	
160 General administration			X
505 Utilities			X
506 Casualty and Liability Costs		X	
507 Taxes			
010 Vehicle operations	X		
041 Vehicle maintenance		X	
042 Nonvehicle maintenance			X
160 General administration			X
508 Purchased Transportation		X	
509 Miscellaneous Expenses			X
510 Expense Transfers			X
511–516 Total Reconciling Items			X

[a]Section 15 Reporting System, Level R
Source: Adapted from Cherwony, Gleichman, and Porter, 1981.

would unfairly penalize the proposal. Use of only variable costs is more appropriate.

Fixed and variable cost models modify the fully allocated approach illustrated in Table 8 by classifying each expense object as fixed, semivariable, or variable. Classification of cost items is subjective; analysts assign costs differently, and thereby produce different results. Variable costs generally include operator, fuel, and maintenance items. Management supervision, supervision of operations and maintenance, advertising, and vehicle depreciation are semivariable costs. General administration, buildings, and utilities are classified as fixed costs.

Calculation of the unit cost output for each combination follows the same steps as does the fully allocated approach. The expense items in each column are summed and divided by the relevant service output statistic. Rather than producing a single-unit cost per vehicle hour, the fixed and variable cost model produces three different types of service cost: variable-hour unit cost, semivariable-hour unit cost, and fixed-hour unit cost. Analysts can then choose the most appropriate costs to use when forecasting the results of different service changes.

If costs are disaggregated into fixed and variable categories, operating changes can be evaluated when private companies bid to offer public transit. UMTA has been urging public agencies to allow private companies to operate portions of regional service under contract to and subsidized by the public agencies. The question arises as to how fixed costs should be allocated to the private contractor when comparing public and private costs. Here the concept of *avoidable cost* has proved useful; avoidable costs are the fixed and variable costs that the public agency will avoid by not operating a service. This amount is compared with the price that the private firm is willing to bid. Fixed costs such as depreciation on vehicles are calculated in one of two ways: either the public agency supplies the vehicles, or public agencies are charged straight-line depreciation over twelve years for buses purchased with state and federal funds. The aim is to keep both sides nearly equal for cost accounting purposes.

Appraisals of minor service changes also benefit from disaggregating overhead costs. When assessing peak-hour express bus service, analysts assign excessive overhead costs to peak service if they do not disaggregate. Analysts can decide whether to assign fixed and semivariable cost to peak vehicles according to the magnitude of the proposed change. When only one or two buses are added, it is probably not appropriate to include fixed costs.

Temporal Variation Models. Peak-hour transit service is more costly to produce than midday (base) service because labor agreements prevent management from adjusting the workday to coincide with peak demand. More overtime must be paid to employees, and it is difficult to use the coach operators during the midday because there are fewer buses in operation. When part-time drivers are permitted under the labor contract, the cost of peak-hour service is reduced but additional fringe benefits are incurred. As a result, average as well as marginal costs of providing peak-hour services are significantly higher than all-day services. Under the fully allocated cost model, the unit cost for vehicle hours obscures these differences, but adjustments can be made for temporal variations in labor efficiency.

Temporal variation models are cost allocation models that focus on the time-period variations in labor efficiency. Only the cost for coach operators is affected. Nondriver cost items are assigned to miles and peak vehicles. Managers can analyze operator labor cost by calculating the ratio between pay hours and service hours for different periods of the day, days of the week, and types of work. Generally, the pay-hour-to-service-hour ratio is higher for peak periods: more employee hours are required to produce an hour of service during peak periods because of inefficiencies caused by contract restrictions.

Labor efficiency is established by calculating indicators for the peak and the base period. These are generally derived from an audit of a sample month's data on vehicle hours and pay hours during the peak and base period. For the Twin Cities' Metropolitan Commission, labor efficiency for the base was estimated by Cherwony and Mundle (1978) at 1.14 and for the peak at 1.31, for a relative labor efficiency of 1.15. The ratio of peak to base service was 1.03. The resulting modification to the fully allocated cost model for the Twin Cities was:

Fully Allocated: $UC = 9.90H + 0.31M + 1{,}353V$
Peak: $UC_p = 10.57H + 0.31M + 7{,}353V$
Base: $UC_b = 9.20H + 0.31M$

where:

UC = Unit cost
H = Vehicle hours

M = Vehicle miles
V = Peak vehicles

All fixed costs in this example are allocated to peak vehicles, so that routes operated only in the peak hour are expensive. Differentiation into fixed and semivariable overhead would reduce the allocation. Mileage costs remain unchanged; temporal variation is a function of the amount of peak service offered and of relative labor efficiency.

Cost Models in Perspective. Numerous agency-specific models can be categorized as cost allocation, fixed and variable cost, or temporal variation models. Whatever form they take, cost allocation models are essential tools. It is only by building models of cost structure that transit managers can make informed decisions about changes in service, pricing, and future costs.

The cost of producing transit service did not receive much attention during the 1970s, when transit service was expanding under the impetus of surplus funds. However, given the current, more austere financial conditions, transit agencies must carefully appraise existing services and seek operating efficiencies. Cost allocation is a relatively quick, simple, and appropriate method for estimating expenses that vary in a consistent manner with the scale of service changes. It is a planning technique that is essential for budgeting and forecasting. The fully allocated model is the easiest to calibrate and use, but variable cost and temporal variation models are appropriate when proposed changes can be more accurately assessed with these methods. Care must be taken in calculating and forecasting personnel expenses in each model. Personnel costs are of such magnitude that even slight errors in estimates will produce considerable differences in total operating costs.

Coordinated Fiscal Strategy

The conceptual approach to finance and budgeting encompasses much more than the simple compilation of the annual budget. Rather, it integrates forecasts of available revenue with the estimated costs of proposed changes in service and the annualized costs of capital investments. The transit agency governing board can then provide guidance on proposed service and investment programs well in advance of annual budget development, so that community preferences can also play their part in the budgetary process.

Opportunities to implement the conceptual approach already exist. Providing a structure is the federal requirement that each metropolitan area, as a condition of financial assistance, develop a Short-Range Transportation Plan (SRTP). One part of the SRTP, the Transportation Improvement Program (TIP), is a staged, three-to-five-year program of transportation improvement projects consistent with the short-range plan. A program in this context is the same as a budget for which both an annual element and a five-year estimate must be prepared. The TIP must be updated annually or biannually to indicate priorities and must include realistic estimates of total costs and revenues for the program period.

A transit planning or coordinating agency exists in every urban area for the purpose of organizing and overseeing transit affairs. Referred to as a metropolitan planning organization (MPO), this agency is responsible for compiling the SRTP for its metropolitan area in cooperation with the institutions furnishing the region's transit service. Normally, each transit agency prepares a separate SRTP that it then submits to the MPO for synthesis with the rest. Federal legislation also requires that the MPO develop goals for each agency and that proposals for capital investments include an analysis of alternative investments that would accomplish the same ends. Special attention must be given to various transportation alternatives that would utilize existing resources and facilities more efficiently rather than create new facilities and services.

The federal SRTP/TIP process with its annual update was designed to implement the same kind of fiscal planning strategy that is proposed in this chapter. However, the performance-monitoring step was omitted from the regulations because opposition from the transit industry made federal agencies unwilling to require performance assessment. This reluctance has abated since passage of the Surface Transportation Act of 1982. Triennial reviews of each agency are now required that determine compliance with federal regulations and assess performance using Section 15 data.

All the elements for the conceptual approach to budgeting are available to transit agencies. It is therefore surprising that they are not used as a coordinated strategy. Again, this lapse reflects transit management's insistence on measuring performance in terms of numbers of passengers. More attention is now given to efficient service production, but in any list of agency goals this will fall below the goal of providing effective transit service. However, if transit is to survive in medium-sized urban areas, its managers must above all else emphasize the goal of efficiency. Otherwise, transit will not survive to be effective.

6

Improving Labor Efficiency

If transit managers are to gain control over spiraling costs, they must improve labor efficiency and reduce the rate at which wages have been increasing. Twenty-one percent more employees were required to produce 2 percent less transit service in 1980 than in 1960, and wages increased much faster than the consumer price index. To increase efficiency, transit agencies will have to improve labor-management relations, since the most important opportunities for progress will involve adjustments to work rules and labor practices. Recent contract settlements are encouraging; the average increase per paid hour allowed by contracts signed in 1983, 1984, and 1985 was less than 1 percent above the consumer price index, while labor productivity has declined by less than one-half percent over five years.

Trends in labor productivity are presented in this chapter in order to demonstrate the magnitude of the inefficiency problem, why it has occurred, and how progress toward the more efficient use of labor might be monitored. Transit unions and their organizations are described, and their contribution to service provision is emphasized. Labor contracts and negotiation strategies and agreements, including Section 13(c) agreements are described in the following chapter. Considerable descriptive information is provided in both chapters, because many managers are unfamiliar with the conduct of labor relations. Chapter Seven concludes with examples of how productivity might be improved.

Trends in Labor Productivity

Opinions vary as to whether labor productivity in transit has increased or decreased over the past two decades. The consensus is that it has decreased. Even those who have reported increases have shown that the rate of increase is far below that achieved by the nonfarm economy as a whole. Several reasons account for this decline. First, when public agencies took control of failing private companies, they were obligated to continue previously negotiated work-rule concessions. Second, more administrative personnel have been hired to oversee compliance with federal and state regulations. And third, organized labor used its political muscle to obtain more favorable working conditions during the early 1970s when governmental assistance was plentiful.

Estimates of labor productivity in transit differ because of the measures used. Meyer and Gomez-Ibanez (1977) used both number of passengers and vehicle miles as indicators for total factor productivity to show that the former declined at an annual rate of 1.2 percent between 1948 and 1970 and that the latter rose at a rate of 0.6 percent. Both are weak measures of labor productivity, as the authors acknowledge. Patronage measures consumption, not production, and the increase in vehicle miles produced reflected expansion of routes into suburban areas while service was being reduced in central cities. Neither statistic provides a reliable measure of transit productivity. Pickrell (1983) provides more reliable measures. He estimates that the cost of operating a vehicle mile of transit service grew in real terms from $1.89 to $2.89 between 1970 and 1980. Increases in labor compensation and declining productivity accounted for 43 percent of the change, with 18 percent due to the decline in productivity.

Labor productivity should be measured in terms of vehicle hours of service produced rather than in vehicle miles, because the vehicle hours figure is not distorted by the shift of service to suburban locations. Unfortunately, vehicle miles must be used in order to compare productivity rates over time because data on vehicle hours are not available. A rate of declining productivity similar to that observed by Pickrell can be observed in the statistics in Table 2. An additional 32,900 employees in 1980 operated 47.8

million fewer vehicle miles of service than in 1960, a compounded rate of decline of approximately 1 percent annually. The negative effects of declining labor productivity on transit performance can be gauged by comparison with an average labor productivity increase of 2.2 percent in the nonfarm sector of the American economy over the same period. Lest this be interpreted as merely a failure of public enterprise, one should also note Kendrick's (1973) observation that productivity in private transit was declining at a similar rate before the public takeover of failing private firms in the late 1960s.

Declining productivity is not unique to American transit. Canadian transit has experienced a similar decline of approximately 1 percent per annum in contrast to commercial and manufacturing productivity, which has increased by more than 3 percent (Sage Management Consultants, 1978). The causes are the same: work rules that restrict management's ability to utilize labor efficiently and increased peak-hour service. More than half the operating labor in Canadian transit is required for only two to three hours during the morning rush hours and for three to four hours in the afternoon. In addition, the spread between the morning and afternoon rush periods has been increasing beyond the maximum workday specified in labor contracts. Additional operators must be employed at the same time that there are fewer opportunities to use them effectively during the remainder of their work shift. Consequently, Canadian transit employed 20 percent more drivers in 1976 to operate the same number of vehicle hours as in 1962.

Since 1979 Section 15 data have provided more reliable statistics on transit productivity in the United States than existed previously. The results are encouraging. Between 1980 and 1984, labor productivity when measured by revenue hours operated per employee has declined by only 0.46 percent (Figure 9). The most efficient groups (those with more hours per employee) are small and medium-sized systems with peak-to-base ratios less than 2.5. These agencies are able to schedule service so as to utilize their labor force efficiently. The least labor-efficient agencies are those systems in peer groups 11 and 12. These include the large regional systems in major metropolitan areas, where system size, together with the demand for additional peak-period service, explains the difficulty of using labor efficiently.

Figure 9. Labor Efficiency by Peer Group.

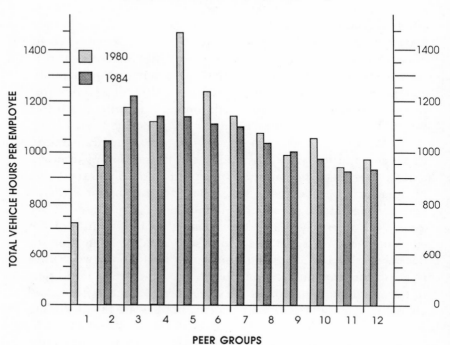

Slight differences in labor efficiency, measured in annual vehicle hours per employee, have a substantial influence on operating cost. A full-time employee works
the equivalent of 2,080 hours per annum. The national average was 1,110 in 1980
and 1,070 in 1984. The most labor efficient are groups 3, 4, 5, 6, and 7.

Source: U.S. Department of Transportation, 1982, 1986.

Size and Labor Efficiency

The inverse relationship between size and labor efficiency is
apparent in both Figures 4 and 9. Nevertheless, readers are
cautioned against using the reported diseconomy of scale as
justification for trying to increase efficiency by reducing the size of
agencies. If the size of an agency were reduced, or some services were
eliminated, there might not be an immediate rise in labor efficiency
because most labor relations are governed by negotiated contracts.
Changes would come only through attrition. What Figure 9 does

indicate is that transit labor unions in large systems (peer groups 10, 11, and 12) have been more successful in negotiating work-rule agreements that require less operating work and more benefits than have unions in small and medium-sized systems. Diseconomies of scale are a function of the relatively greater power of organized labor in larger transit systems. This becomes apparent when the labor efficiency of a large metropolitan agency is compared with that of smaller agencies within the same area. In number of pay hours required to produce a vehicle hour of service, smaller agencies are between 30 and 40 percent more labor efficient. The reason for this difference lies in work rules and labor force deployment. For example, it was estimated that in 1982 SCRTD in Los Angeles (1,870 peak vehicles) required 154 minutes of paid time to produce each revenue hour of service, whereas within the same county the Long Beach Public Transit Agency (119 peak vehicles) required only 105 minutes and Santa Monica Municipal Bus Line (93 peak vehicles) only 113 minutes.

Organized labor holds a strategic advantage in large transit systems. A prolonged work stoppage is devastating to commerce in the metropolitan center, and the additional automobile traffic is unacceptable to all commuters. Business leaders and elected officials urge management to make concessions rather than risk a strike or to settle it quickly if one does occur. The pressure to concede to labor overwhelms management, despite the fact that it knows all too well the effects of work-rule concessions on productivity.

Another advantage for labor unions is their political power. Employees contribute to union-sponsored political-action committees in order to ensure the election of officials sympathetic to union policies. The larger the union, the more responsive elected officials are to its needs and desires. One result is that labor representatives enjoy many contacts with board members who are elected officials.

The complexity of a large transit operation is another reason for its higher costs. Large metropolitan transit agencies serve both central cities, with demand concentrated into peak workday hours, and suburban areas. It is difficult and more costly to schedule labor to accommodate service peaks while simultaneously providing a basic level of transit to a dispersed service area. When service is focused in one community, as it is for most municipal operators, changes in service to accommodate additional demand are more easily implemented.

Transit Work Environment

Work and compensation for more than 80 percent of transit employees are governed by labor agreements. One must appreciate the work environment in order to understand why antagonistic attitudes prevail between management and employees and even between different employee groups:

1. There are few opportunities for drivers to gain promotions, eliminating an important incentive for conscientious work.
2. Operations, maintenance, planning, scheduling, marketing, and other departments function independently and have traditionally resisted information sharing.
3. Operating a bus is not only one of the most controlled, but also one of the most autonomous, blue-collar occupations. Street supervisors rigidly enforce operating schedules, but operators have considerable freedom in customer relations.
4. Drivers represent the transit organization to the clientele. They take the brunt of the public's dissatisfaction with company policies, yet they have no real voice in policy formulation. This impotence produces negative attitudes toward management and operator stress.
5. The job environment of mechanics is quite different from that of drivers. There are promotion opportunities within the maintenance division as well as attractive outside employment opportunities for diesel mechanics. In addition, they have more control over work schedules and seldom have contact with the riding public. As a consequence, mechanics and drivers want different employment conditions.

The difficult working conditions for drivers, the conflicting interests of employee groups, and the fact that salary expectations have been enhanced by governmental spending for transit all contribute to an antagonistic relationship between drivers and management and between drivers and other employees. Work stoppages are fairly common in the largest agencies, and grievance hearings are a weekly occurrence. Management and labor representatives seldom cooperate for the benefit of the transit-riding public. And to make the situation worse, operators, mechanics, and clerical employees are frequently represented by competing unions.

Labor Costs

Attempts to improve the efficiency of transit service must focus on labor utilization, because even small savings in labor costs can have highly beneficial effects on total costs. This does not mean that improvements in vehicle technology, marketing, and service deployment are unimportant; rather, it suggests that proposed changes should be viewed from the perspective of reducing labor costs as well as improving service, comfort, and convenience. Employee salaries, wages, and fringe benefits account for 74 percent of transit operating costs (Table 9). Only a small proportion, about 7 percent of operating costs, is paid to executive, professional, and supervisory employees. The remainder represents payments to skilled and semiskilled employees.

Although hourly rates paid to transit employees may appear high, they are not substantially different from manufacturing wages paid in the major metropolitan areas, and they were less than wages paid to drivers employed by Greyhound and Trailways in 1982. Precise comparisons are difficult to make because of the way in which wages are computed and adjusted for cost-of-living changes. The median wage rate for the forty public systems with the highest top operator wage in January 1982 was $10.92 an hour, whereas average hourly manufacturing wages in 1982 were $9.04. A typical Greyhound operator, paid on the basis of revenue mileage this same year, was estimated to have earned $13.96 an hour.

Common Misapprehensions. Transit labor costs have been exaggerated by unfair comparison of large public transit agencies with small private transit firms. Peterson, Davis, and Walker (1986) concluded from a sample of eight large cities that the total compensation paid to public transit bus drivers was 28 percent higher than that paid to unionized private-sector drivers and 91

Table 9. Transit Operating Cost by Mode, 1982.

Code	Expense Object Class	Motor Bus	Rapid Rail	Other[a]	Joint[b]	All Modes
501	Labor					
501.01	Operator's salaries and wages	$31.5	$9.8	$25.9	$3.8	$23.6
501.02	Other salaries and wages	18.7	41	24.3	38.6	26.1
502	Fringe benefits	23.1	29.3	17.4	21.8	24.4
503	Services	3.2	1.9	2.8	12.6	3.6
504	Materials and supplies					
504.01	Fuels and lubricants	10.1	0.1	4.9	1.6	6.6
504.02	Tires and tubes	1.0	0.0	0.0	0.3	0.6
504.99	Other materials and supplies	6.8	6.5	5.5	7.6	6.8
505	Utilities	1.0	10.9	3.7	5.3	4.0
506	Casualty and liability costs	2.3	0.6	1.2	11.8	2.5
507	Taxes	0.4	0.0	0.0	0.1	0.3
508	Purchased Transportation	1.6	0.4	11.3	0.0	1.6
509	Miscellaneous expense	0.7	0.2	0.0	2.1	0.7
510	Expense transfers	(0.3)	(0.5)	2.3	(0.5)	(0.7)
	Total	100%	100%	100%	100%	100%
	Total operation expenses (millions)	$4,509.60	$1,794.10	$271.40	$546.80	$7,122.00
	Reconciling items (millions)	0	0	0	0	170.10
	Total expenses including reconciling items	$4,509.60	$1,794.10	$271.40	$546.80	$7,292.10
	Systems reporting	311	9	169	64	336

aStreetcar, trolleybus, demand response, and other modes
bOperating expenditures for multimodal systems that cannot be assigned directly to a particular mode
Source: U.S. Department of Transportation, 1983.

percent higher than that paid to nonunion drivers in the sample. Had they chosen data from small public operators in these cities, they would still have found that public compensation was higher but that the difference was smaller. For example, they compared wages and benefits paid by the Chicago Transit Authority (which operates 2,300 buses) with those paid to unionized drivers for private bus lines in Chicago (with between 51 and 71 buses). The comparison should have been made between the private companies and the small transit agencies in the Chicago urbanized area that operate express service.

The base wage rate for transit operators can be misleading. In addition to the base rate, operators receive premium pay for time worked in excess of contractual agreements, as well as penalty payments when work is spread out or split between different periods of the day. These payments are intended to compensate employees for the undesirable aspects of transit work. Collectively, they are referred to as *work rules*. Employee representatives negotiate for these rules under the labor contract, and management seeks to deploy service in such a manner as to avoid payment of premiums and benefits. However, management cannot eliminate premiums and benefits entirely, and operators can anticipate receiving bonus pay if they choose to work additional hours or pick blocks of work involving split shifts or excess hours. For example, Tri-County Metropolitan Transportation District (Tri-Met) in Portland paid coach operators $12.74 an hour in 1985, and an employee could thus expect to earn $26,500 annually. However, many full-time operators earned $3,000 and $10,000 a year above that figure because of overtime and work-rule bonuses.

Fringe benefits, including insurance and employer-paid pensions, sick leave, and vacation benefits, add to labor costs. In fact, these constitute 24.4 percent of total operating costs for all modes. The obligation to furnish these benefits is specified in the labor agreement, and management has had difficulty in controlling their increase. For example, each contract specifies the number of paid days off permitted for sick leave. If employees regard these as a benefit to be used whether or not they are sick, as about one-third of employees are prone to do, then costs are increased. Medical claims increase and additional employees have to be hired, or other employees have to be paid overtime to cover for the missing employees.

Monitoring Labor Costs. Although labor costs represent the greater part of total operating cost, most agencies have not established methods for gathering and analyzing statistics to monitor either labor cost or the efficiency of labor utilization. In a study of absenteeism in California, Perry and Angle (1980) reported that none of the twenty-four agencies surveyed had a systematic method for gathering and analyzing information on employee absenteeism even though absenteeism increased operating labor costs by 12.5 percent. Information on health care and pension costs is more readily available but is seldom analyzed for its role in labor costs. For example, Perry and Angle also found that the amount of sick leave claimed was positively correlated with the amount provided by the labor contract. Employees seemed to consider sick leave as a benefit to be used as holiday time rather than as insurance against illness, even when a medical certificate was required for eligibility.

Techniques for improving data collection are provided in UMTA Section 15 guidelines. Section 15 data must be collected in standardized form and reported annually to UMTA. If compiled quarterly, or even more frequently for wage-related data, these statistics can be used to monitor costs. Chapter Four presented a data-gathering model and suggested that total vehicle hours per employee be used as an aggregate indicator of labor efficiency, but the following measures might also be used:

- Revenue vehicle hours per operating employee hour
- Total vehicle miles per maintenance, support, and servicing personnel
- Peak vehicles per maintenance, support, and servicing personnel
- Days absent per operating employee
- Days lost on workmens compensation per employee group.

Monitoring employee performance will assist management in labor negotiations. In an effort to reduce absenteeism among drivers and mechanics, Tri-Met in Portland had until 1985 been offering a day off with pay for each seventeen weeks an employee had perfect attendance. An employee who missed no days could enjoy three additional holidays per year. This was estimated to cost the agency $135,000 annually. By monitoring absenteeism, Tri-Met discovered that the small number of employees who accounted for most absenteeism simply ignored the incentive. Therefore the agency was giving paid days off to workers who had always maintained good attendance records. The program was not working as intended, and Tri-Met used this information in 1985 when negotiating for changes in benefits.

Transit Labor Unions

Almost all transit agencies with more than fifty vehicles have collective bargaining contracts with one or more unions. Although a wide range of national unions (which are called "international" because of their Canadian affiliates) and local unions are involved, three dominate the industry: the Amalgamated Transit Union (ATU), the Transport Workers Union (TWU), and the United Transportation Union (UTU). In transit, ATU predominates with 79 percent of the contracts and 94,000 members. TWU has far fewer contracts, but because of its leadership in New York, Philadelphia, Miami, and San Francisco, it represents 85,000 employees. The UTU has its origins in the railroad industry. With 121,000 members, it is numerically much larger than the other two unions, but few of its members are employed in public transit.

Undesirable work schedules, the repetitive nature of transit work, the desire for job security, and the need for grievance procedures have all facilitated a high level of employee allegiance to organized labor. The tradition began with the railroad unions founded in the 1860s and 1870s and was carried over to the street railways of the early 1900s and the omnibuses of the 1920s and 1930s. In sum, American urban transit has a tradition of more than a century of organized, frequently militant, union action that influences contemporary attitudes (Luna, 1971).

The extremely adversarial relations that exist between management and organized labor surprise foreign observers and those familiar with labor relations in other public agencies. As suggested above, both the militant history of the industry and the nature of transit work have led to the conflict. Because punctuality and reliability are essential in transit, transit employees are penalized for tardiness or erratic performance that would not be punished in other industries. American workers resent this kind of control, especially when traffic congestion, adverse weather, or cantankerous passengers may be responsible for the problem. Whereas on-time performance is still a matter of pride for transport workers in Europe and Japan, pressure to attain that goal has come to be resented by American workers. Although organized labor agrees with management that operating on schedule is important, workers express hostility toward management because supervisors rather than labor representatives enforce compliance with work schedules.

International unions control bargaining at the local level. This puts management at a disadvantage because it generally cannot match the skills and knowledge of negotiators provided by the international affiliate. Also, international representatives seek pattern bargaining; that is, they pattern compensation and work-rule requests to correspond not so much to local conditions as to precedents that union negotiators have established in other cities. Union negotiators are reluctant to concede points at one agency that might be detrimental to negotiations in another agency. Management and governing boards, however, react negatively to pattern bargaining. They are responsible to local constituencies and believe that wages, benefits, and work rules for transit employees should be consistent with those prevailing locally. International representatives are unyielding on this issue, and this irritant is a frequent cause for delays, impasses, and strikes. Perry, Angle, and Pittel (1979) suggest that unions should develop regional expertise in order to speed up negotiations, improve the sophistication of local labor officials, and reduce the tendency of managers to overreact in the presence of international officials.

The media make labor negotiations in transit appear purely political. Rather than reporting on the months of negotiations leading up to a final contract, the media tend to focus on the later, more political, stages. *BLEEPING* has been suggested by Kheel

(1978) as a term to describe public-sector collective bargaining in its final stages. It comes from BLEEP, the acronym for bargaining, lobbying, electioneering, extorting, and politicking. Collective bargaining resolves the majority of work-related issues. But lobbying, electioneering, extorting, and politicking are used by both management and labor to gain the attention of the elected officials who can help resolve the economic issues. Often the threat of a work stoppage is required to place transit on the civic agenda. Thus BLEEPING makes labor negotiations in public transit far more visible than labor negotiations in private transportation agencies.

Increasing labor efficiency is the key to the strategic management of a transit agency. Careful studies of past performance, monitoring of current performance, and evaluation of strategies for improving future performance ought to be at the forefront of every managerial initiative. Unfortunately, the distribution of governmental assistance has not encouraged this approach. Assistance has been allocated to cover deficits and has emphasized the achievements of social and environmental objectives rather than economical provision of service. In some respects, labor unions have encouraged this orientation by emphasizing the public service benefits achieved by transit while skillfully negotiating increased benefits for the employees. Although management has welcomed the political support supplied by organized labor, it has only recently begun to negotiate contracts and monitor labor performance in a manner that preserves a greater share of the benefits for patrons in terms of improved service.

7

Developing Labor Contracts

The labor contract establishes roles for labor and management within each agency. Management of course does not "own" labor as it owns vehicles, equipment, and facilities. Rather managers must negotiate with employees or their representatives for the right to utilize employee labor under prescribed circumstances. Contracts are normally negotiated for two or three years and are continued if neither party gives notice of its desire to renegotiate the agreement. Each contract contains clauses pertaining to wages and benefits, work rules, scheduling of work, and vacation time, as well as sick and special leave, employee obligations, and sanctions. Walton and McKersie (1965) divide bargaining into four subtasks that can be used to describe what happens in transit:

1. *Distributive bargaining* establishes wage rates and fringe benefits. Labor seeks to maximize benefits for employees, whereas management wishes to restrict or reduce wages and benefits in order to maintain or increase service. When resources were plentiful in the early 1970s, bargaining was amicable because the interests of both parties could be satisfied. Now that resources are limited, negotiations are acrimonious.

2. *Integrative bargaining* achieves objectives that require joint decision making. For example, work rules govern the scheduling of individual routes into "blocks" or "runs." The manner in which operators choose a block of work, the hours they work, and their days off must be negotiated. Management aims for changes that will allow more efficient use of labor for a

proposed service schedule, whereas labor tries to preserve jobs and reduce the negative attributes of transit work.

3. *Attitude restructuring* involves bargaining over workplace behavior. Attendance policies, on-time reporting, dress codes, and procedures for service operation are carefully negotiated because supervisors hold employees accountable for these provisions. An example is the incentive bonus for perfect attendance in Portland that was discussed earlier. Relatively minor items in attitude and procedure may be controversial, as when employees want to wear union identification badges or have the payroll department deduct their union fees.

4. *Intraorganizational bargaining* assumes importance when employee aspirations conflict. Employees in any one union usually have differing opinions about how bargaining should proceed, and it is essential that union representatives be allowed sufficient time to reconcile intragroup differences that develop over the course of negotiations. Breaks allowing each team to caucus often delay negotiations for weeks, but they are necessary because the final proposal must be voted on by employees before it becomes a contract.

Becoming skilled at these diverse processes is a challenge for management's negotiating team. Not only must an equitable contract be negotiated and a work stoppage avoided, but the attitudes and feelings of employees must also be considered. After the contract is settled, the employees represent the agency to the public. If they are alienated by the contract, then both the clientele and the corporate image will suffer.

Wage Rates. Hourly rates of pay for different classes of employees are normally the most controversial issue in every contract. During the 1970s wage gains within the industry exceeded increases in both the cost of living and wage gains achieved by other municipal and manufacturing employees. Two factors accounted for wage increases. First, there was the practice of establishing wages near parity with other transit agencies so that wage increases in one agency soon "rippled" across the industry. Second, the cost-of-living adjustments (COLAs) granted in the 1960s became prodigiously expensive during periods of accelerated inflation. An example from the Massachusetts Bay Transportation Authority (MBTA) in Boston illustrates how wage rates increased and why they have now leveled off. In 1981 the top operator hourly rate of $11.05 at MBTA was one of the two highest rates in the nation. It had increased by 130 percent between 1971 and 1981 because employees had been granted a full COLA increase every quarter. This was far more than that achieved by Boston police and fire fighters, and it created animosity among municipal employees and dissension in the state legislature.

Boston's Carmen's Union had been a leader in improving wages and benefits for transit workers, but its very success alienated its political supporters. Legislation was passed by the commonwealth of Massachussetts in 1980 that removed several of labor's traditional "rights." Management was given the authority to terminate the COLA and greater power over work assignments. As a result of this backlash, Boston MBTA employees lost their COLA and went without a salary adjustment for four years, falling from first to ninth in the nation in terms of top operator pay rates.

Work Rules. Most labor agreements contain detailed procedures governing job security, the handling of grievances, selection of work, duration of the workday, holidays, and the functions to be performed by different categories of employees. Managers trying to improve efficiency find that work rules tend to be very restrictive. Union leaders are reluctant to alter these rules and demand that management provide economic rewards before employees give up any provision that protects the size of the work force. Listed below in question form are some of the issues involved in work rules. Examples of how they apply in the MBTA are shown in parentheses:

1. What is a normal day's work before overtime must be paid? (Eight hours and five minutes with overtime at 150 percent of the base wage.)
2. How much paid time is allowed for report time at the beginning of the shift? (Ten minutes, and all straight shifts must provide a paid meal break of at least twenty minutes.)

3. What is the normal work week? (Five days of eight hours each.)
4. What are the operator's responsibilities? (To abide by the rules and regulations published by the authority governing the operations of its business and the conduct of its employees.)
5. Who can move vehicles? (Only operating employees or operators assigned to yard work.)
6. What tasks can "cover employees" perform while they are waiting to be called for work missed by scheduled employees? (Only scheduled work for which no operator is available or additional runs.)
7. Where do drivers take over an existing run? (Only at the depot or at a supervised terminal. If the point of relief differs from the starting point, drivers must be paid for travel time.)

Scheduling Work. Transit service is affected by clauses in the labor contract that control management's ability to schedule employees to match demand. Management bargains for changes that will permit more efficient utilization of labor, whereas union representatives wish to make work less demanding and to obtain premium payments for undesirable work.

Rostering is the term used in many contracts to refer to the scheduling of drivers to "blocks" of work or "runs." Connecting trips on different routes into blocks of work can reduce the need for "layovers" and "recovery times" between trips. However, contracts usually state that insofar as it is practicable, blocks will be confined to one transit route with recovery time allowed between trips. This is an advantage for patrons because drivers become knowledgeable about the route; but unless headways are adjusted to suit varying running times, labor utilization is less efficient than assigning trips on different routes.

Employees prefer straight shifts with a paid meal break and no midday layoff; for such a stint they receive approximately eight hours' pay. Many contracts specify the proportion of these "straight runs" (Figure 10). However, the peaked nature of transit demand means that all operators cannot be scheduled efficiently using straight shifts. Therefore, management attempts to set up "split shifts" in which the employee is given an unpaid break during the day. The employee is paid for the hours worked (normally eight

Figure 10. Service Demand Profile and Operator Work Assignment.

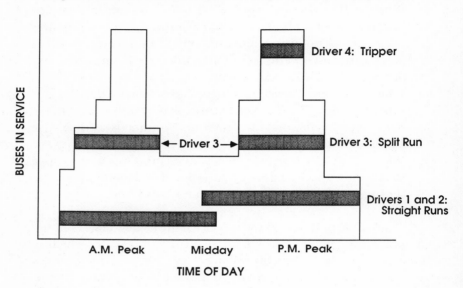

Work shifts are frequently called runs and may include work on different routes. Drivers can choose straight runs, split runs, or trippers based upon seniority.

hours) and a given spread-time penalty bonus if the day "spreads over" more than the number of hours (eleven, twelve, or thirteen) designated by the contract.

Part-time employment is one solution that has gained in popularity among transit managers trying to schedule service to match demand. Part-time employees can be scheduled to operate "trippers"—runs that are required only in the morning or afternoon peak times. This practice has been vehemently opposed by organized labor because it reduces the opportunity for overtime and penalty payments.

The use of part-time operators can increase labor efficiency because fewer pay hours are needed to operate scheduled service. In addition, part-time operators normally receive a lower wage and fewer benefits than do full-time operators. However, these potential savings can be canceled out by "givebacks" in wages and fringe benefits exchanged for union approval of part-time employment.

Chomitz, Giuliano, and Lave (1985) recommend that careful analysis of peak-to-base service demand and work rules precede any attempt to bargain for changes in the labor contract, because these will determine the potential economic benefits. An agency with a high peak-to-base demand and tight work rules causing a high pay-to-platform (less efficient) labor utilization will benefit more from part-time labor than will an agency with a low (more efficient) pay-to-platform ratio. Even a small wage increase to recompense employees for agreeing to accept the use of part-time drivers can have cumulative effects that will soon swamp the positive results from the changes in work rules.

Boston is one city that has benefited from part-time labor. In 1982 the MBTA began to hire part-time people, primarily for the bus division, at an hourly rate of 70 percent of the top operator rate. They received none of the fringe benefits available to full-time employees except for free transportation, a uniform allowance, and the mandated retirement benefits. It has been estimated that the use of part-time employees by the MBTA has reduced annual operating cost by $5.6 million (Attanucci, Wilson, and Vozzolo, 1984). The MBTA contract now permits 15 percent of all operators to be part time. Part-timers may work up to six hours daily, without spread-time penalties. Unlike most transit agencies, the MBTA did not have to bargain with labor for this provision because it was imposed by the Massachusetts legislature in 1980 as an "inherent management right."

Using part-time operators is but one of many ways to improve labor efficiency. Increasing the "spread time" of shifts, using regular employees on biddable extra work, guaranteeing operators forty hours of work each week rather than eight hours each day, and improving the scheduling of operators who cover for absent employees are all more acceptable to unions than is the use of part-time labor. In 1977, Seattle Metro became the first large agency to win the right to employ part-time operators. The innovation spread rapidly, and by 1983, 92 percent of the nation's transit agencies had obtained a part-time operator provision. But many agencies did not realize economic benefits from this provision because their managements had failed to analyze the long-term costs of the concessions they made when negotiating for the right to use part-time operators.

Transit labor negotiations consume a great deal of time and energy. Both management and labor spend months preparing for negotiations and then bargaining over the contract. Elected officials are also involved because the consequences of the agreement will be apparent to their constituents in the form of higher fares and the funding that local agencies will be asked to contribute. Although contract provisions are fairly standard, each contains language specific to the agency. Again, while unions practice pattern bargaining, separate agreements must be reached with each agency. When labor and management have reached agreement, each side must then convince its supporters of the fairness of the contract.

Negotiations and the Contract

It is important for managers to prepare strategies well in advance of contract negotiations. Labor unions have several advantages: their interests are narrower than those of transit agencies, and they receive professional assistance from staff in their international organizations. But transit managers can also use certain resources to their advantage; for example, they can collect comparable performance data and estimate the costs and benefits of potential labor-related changes. Furthermore, management can estimate the agency's ability to pay for concessions and determine whether or not fare increases will be required to cover projected labor costs.

Management has begun to take a more aggressive stance in labor negotiations and to seek reductions in benefits and changes in work rules. As already noted, Seattle Metro obtained the right in 1977 to hire up to one-half of its operating employees on a part-time basis, and this concession has spread throughout the industry. Attempts to reduce COLAs began shortly thereafter. In 1979 both San Francisco's BART and Chicago's Transit Authority endured strikes in order to win reductions in cost-of-living increase clauses. Each had decided that it was worth enduring a strike to achieve this goal. San Diego Transit eliminated its cost-of-living clause entirely and in two years fell from having one of the highest operator wage rates to thirtieth in the nation. In each instance, changes were achieved by agencies that were well prepared for labor negotiations. Management presented union representatives with demands rather than merely responding to their requests.

Negotiation Strategies for Management. Preparations for negotiations should begin at least twelve months before expiration of a contract. A management negotiating team should be created to review both grievances filed during the expiring labor agreement and current labor practices in the industry. This phase should produce a list of changes sought by management. Costs should be determined for each change so that management knows what each penny of increase or decrease will mean in terms of cost per service hour. The ability to estimate the cost to the agency of proposed changes in the labor contract before negotiations is a real advantage. Such preparation facilitates negotiations because the cost of adjustments to work rules, wages, and benefits can be quickly calculated during the negotiation process. The American Public Transit Association (1983) has published a transit managers' handbook called *Preparing for Negotiations, Implementing the Contract, and Contract Administration.* It is an excellent primer that expands the brief outline proposed in this section.

About sixty days before the expiration of the current contract, union representatives request negotiations for a new contract. The union usually makes the first proposals because management presumably could continue to operate under the existing contract. In subsequent meetings, and only after analysts have evaluated the effects of union proposals on cost per service hour, management presents its proposed changes.

Negotiations usually occur in two phases. In the first, all nonwage-related issues such as posting of notices, access to facilities, shift changes, and uniforms are considered. Then the second, more controversial stage of *distributive bargaining* over wages and benefits commences. In reviewing the cost and service consequences of the initial union proposal, management should respond with information gathered about costs and benefits from peer-group agencies and from comparable local industries. The objective of this feedback is to encourage union representatives to revise their proposals or reveal their objectives. If they decline to do so, then management can present counterproposals. These must respond to the issues presented by the union and include both the benefits to the employee and the costs to the agency. Psychology is important in the "game-playing" of union negotiations; the counteroffer should be conservative, and the union's reaction carefully studied.

Both sides submit subsequent proposals that fine tune the initial proposal and permit eventual agreement. It is during this exchange that the value of the previously developed costing model becomes apparent. The cost of each labor counteroffer can be estimated quickly and evaluated against the desired outcome. Seattle Metro has a sophisticated labor-costing methodology. Management knows precisely what each economic proposal will cost the agency and how far it deviates from its desired objectives. As a result of superior labor negotiations, along with the efficient use of labor resources between contract negotiations, Seattle has been able to control cost increases despite a peak-to-base service demand of almost three to one.

When the parties agree to an individual issue, contract language should be initialed immediately following agreement. But approval of all items should be reserved until there is agreement on the total package. Consideration for *intraorganizational bargaining* by union representatives is important. They have to persuade their membership to approve the package, otherwise there is no agreement. Frequently management can counter wage demands by proposing to increase wages gradually throughout the term of the contract. Rather than accepting a fifty-cent hourly increase proposed by the union for the first year, management might offer to raise wages by this amount in the form of quarterly increments made over the year. In this manner, the union achieves the desired increase, and the agency averts the full blow of the increase by raising wages in quarterly increments of ten and fifteen cents.

When negotiators reach agreement, the governing board and union membership must approve the proposed contract. It is essential for management to keep the contents of the contract confidential until the union membership has voted, since media analysis of the proposal can provoke divisions within the union.

Helping union leaders to explain new benefits to their members is important. Before union approval, managers should advise their immediate staff of the content of the proposed agreement so that they can respond to employee questions. This is a delicate stage in the process. Although unions have been described as more cohesive than management, there are frequently differences of opinion between younger members who want higher wages and older members who are more interested in benefits, especially pension-related ones.

Interpreting the Contract. All employees who must translate the contract into action should be trained in contract interpretation, and management should encourage them to ask for help in deciphering cryptic passages. They should be told not to modify any portion of the agreement, since to do so could impair future arbitration. Top management should make all decisions on interpretation and from time to time may agree with the union to alter or modify the agreement. However, it is management's responsibility to ensure that the agreement is applied.

Good union-management relations are essential in any industry. The adversarial nature of contract negotiations need not affect continuing union-management relationships. For this reason, it is often an advantage for management to hire a professional labor consultant as a counterpart to the international representative brought in by employees. Between contract negotiations, regular meetings should be held with union officials to discuss state and federal legislation and proposed changes that might affect the agency and its employees. Under no circumstances should management staff denigrate union officials. As legitimate representatives of the agency's employees, they provide a valuable service in voicing employees' desires and aspirations and should be accorded the same respect given to other elected officials.

At the Twin Cities' Metropolitan Transit Commission (MTC), management and union officials have treated each other with an honesty and respect that has noticeably improved employee attitudes toward work. Management enlisted the cooperation of union officials to improve driver attendance. Between them they have introduced a meritorious driver award program that has substantially reduced absenteeism and improved driver morale (Olsen, 1983). Union officials have also supported quality circle programs for maintenance, stock-room, and clerical employees to share information on how the tasks that they perform can improve service reliability. Although increased knowledge and attitude change were the objectives of these programs, absenteeism has also been reduced and vehicle reliability has been increased.

Grievances and Arbitration. Grievance procedures apply both to interpretations of the union contract and to protection of individual employees who feel that disciplinary actions taken against them have been unfair. The contract describes a step-by-step method for settling both types of problems and is designed so that employees need not fear agency retribution. The procedure usually consists of a series of hearings that begin at the supervisory level and proceed by appeal to the general manager. Union officials normally help employees to appeal decisions in disciplinary cases.

Arbitration provides a means of appealing grievance decisions to an independent person. But this process is so costly and time consuming that both parties usually prefer to settle disagreements through the grievance procedure. Some contracts provide only for advisory arbitration because binding arbitration can result in extreme hardship for one of the parties. However, arbitration does provide an alternative to a work stoppage when disagreements over interpretaton of the contract must be settled.

Both grievances and arbitrated disputes affect the next round of labor negotiations. Reviewing arbitrated and grievance decisions is an important first step in preparing the negotiating team, whose members must realize that arbitrated decisions set legal precedents.

Protecting Employee Interests

Organized labor agreed to support the federal capital grant and assistance program of 1964 only after Congress made the following stipulation in Section 13(c) of the Urban Mass Transportation Act:

It shall be a condition of any assistance under this Act that fair and equitable arrangements are made, as determined by the Secretary of Labor, to protect the interests of employees affected by such assistance. Such protective arrangements shall include, without being limited to, such provisions as may be necessary for (1) the preservation of rights, privileges, and benefits (under existing collective bargaining agreements or otherwise); (2) the continuation of collective bargaining rights; (3) the protection of individual employees against a worsening of their positions with respect to their employment; (4) assurances of employment to employees of acquired mass transportation systems and priority of reemployment of employees terminated or laid off; and (5) paid training or retraining programs. Such arrangements shall include provisions protecting individual employees against a worsening of their positions with respect to their employment which shall in no event provide benefits less than those established pursuant to Section 5(2)(f) of the Interstate Commerce Act of February 4, 1887 (24 Statute 379), as amended.

Section 13(c) is administered by the Department of Labor, not the Department of Transportation. Federal regulations require that before an agency can receive federal capital or operating assistance, it must negotiate and sign an agreement with relevant organized labor units. The agreement outlines methods for compensating and/or retraining employees if they are "adversely impacted" by programs resulting from federal aid. The minimum level of benefits was established by reference to a section of the Interstate Commerce Act that protects railroad employees who transferred to Amtrak.

Standard agreements governing federal funding for operating assistance and capital replacement are now negotiated with a minimum of difficulty. However, new capital projects can raise complex issues, as can proposals to use federal funds for paratransit or privately operated supplementary service. In these instances, negotiations are generally prolonged, and management frequently agrees to union demands rather than stalling capital projects.

Although several reviews of Section 13(c) have found no evidence that agencies gain funding to the detriment of their employees, nor have any employees had to be compensated for dislocation, 13(c) has provided organized labor with a bargaining advantage. Transit agency management must obtain agreement from labor before the agency can obtain federal funds for operations or capital improvements. Labor need not refuse; just by stalling, a union can place a transit agency in such a precarious financial position that management has no alternative but to withdraw plans to which the union objects. When transit was expanding during the 1970s, Section 13(c) restrained management from experimenting with new modes and innovative service plans. Although the constraints of 13(c) are more potential than real, the uncertainty surrounding them has curbed innovation.

Labor's Section 13(c) leverage is used to win points of agreement so subtle that they are seldom apparent to those not involved in the negotiations. Section 13(c) is tremendously useful to the unions. John Rowland, then president of ATU, was quoted as saying that 13(c) "is essential to us. It's our lifeblood as far as the collective bargaining process is concerned. Without 13(c), 80 to 85 percent of our settlements that we now settle through collective bargaining would never be settled" (Crosby, 1982, p. 17). Organized labor has worked diligently to obtain federal funds for transit. From its point of view, the federal program is designed to create jobs and provide additional funds within the system for wages and benefits. Section 13(c) has helped labor achieve these objectives.

Management of Employees

It is up to management to enforce attendance rules and to determine when, where, and (in a limited sense) by whom service will be provided. An efficient agency uses this discretion, coupled with knowledge of the contract and expected employee turnover, to develop personnel policies and service schedules that minimize the cost of providing service. Opportunities for long-term cost savings are fewer than sometimes thought, but they do exist. What is surprising is managers' lack of familiarity with key provisions of the union contract and their unwillingness to figure out how minor changes in such provisions as those governing attendance, vacation scheduling, and manpower planning can reduce costs. Improvement of productivity is management's responsibility and can be accomplished despite the constraints imposed by labor agreements.

Attendance Policy. Unscheduled absenteeism is a serious problem that cost American transit roughly $187 million in 1978. It was estimated that on the average each employee failed to show up for work or was ill for twenty-nine days per year, not counting official holidays or scheduled vacation leave (Baker and Scheuftan, 1980). Absenteeism rates in public transit were found to be three times higher than the national average for industrial employees and 50 percent higher than the rate in private-sector transportation. Not only is absenteeism costly, but it also degrades service. When there are too few extra operators (extra-board operators) to cover for unscheduled absences, buses simply do not run. Some employee absenteeism is unavoidable; employees are occasionally ill, and circumstances do arise that make it impossible for them to show up for their shifts. However, there is also evidence that much absenteeism is avoidable. For many transit employees, excessive absenteeism may be a deliberate strategy to avoid work or to obtain benefits associated with workers' compensation. To the extent that this is true, absenteeism is subject to managerial control (Long and Perry, 1985). Employees of private transit firms have better attendance records. This is a principal reason why private transit is more cost efficient.

The Washington Metropolitan Area Transit Authority (WMATA) examined absenteeism and workers' compensation claims in 1979. WMATA bus operators were out on an average of twenty workdays, which (although less than the national average of twenty-nine) cost the agency an estimated $21 million for extra-board replacements and $9 million in workers' compensation claims. A number of contributing factors were identified through group sessions with employees: no opportunity to take single days off for reasons other than illness, lack of recognition for good attendance, unpleasant interactions with passengers, and poor vehicle maintenance. Analysis of personnel records revealed that the incidence of workers' compensation claims correlates with certain times of the year (Christmas, the hunting season, and summer). It also revealed that much of the problem was caused by the excessive absenteeism of a few employees: approximately one-fourth of the employees accounted for most of the sick leave taken. Some employees were repeatedly absent because WMATA did not then have policies that deterred absenteeism.

Additional evidence of the need for absenteeism policies comes from Dalton and Perry's (1981) examination of twenty-eight Western transit agencies. They arrived at these conclusions:

1. Organizations that pay more money to employees have higher absence rates. As income increases, employees may "buy" leisure; they can afford to be absent and lose pay.
2. Organizations that do not require employees to establish proof of illness (doctor's certificate) have higher rates of absenteeism.
3. Organizations that allow for greater rates of sick leave accumulation (one and one-half days per month versus one-half day per month, for instance) have higher rates of employee absenteeism.
4. Organizations that do not reimburse earned but unused sick leave have higher rates of absenteeism.

These conclusions suggest that absenteeism is strongly related to attendance policies. The requirements necessary for such a policy are well known: a company must have a clear disciplinary policy on absenteeism, the policy must be applied fairly and consistently, and workers must be given fair warning that they face disciplinary action unless their attendance record improves. San Diego Transit established such policies in 1980 followed up by careful monitoring of personnel records. Each month an absenteeism printout for every employee is provided to supervisors and union officials. Clear policies exist, and after appropriate warnings, employees are terminated for failure to abide by them. Arbitrators asked to rule on dismissals have consistently supported the agency, even in cases where employees have had legitimate reasons for being absent.

The Milwaukee County Transit System improved attendance with individual recognition awards. By analyzing employment records, the management divided employees into three categories (Warren and Connelly, 1986):

1. Those who had very good attendance records
2. Those who were absent between two and fifteen days a year
3. Habitual offenders who missed thirty or more workdays and accounted for almost half of the hours lost each year to absenteeism.

   The main thrust of Milwaukee's program was to improve the attendance of the drivers in the second category and to recognize the loyalty of those in the first. Those in the third category were already involved in disciplinary proceedings and were considered unresponsive to incentives. A progression of incentive gifts such as free dinners and drawings for a color television were arranged on a quarterly basis. This gave operators who were genuinely sick the opportunity to start over rather than being penalized for illness during the previous quarter. Response to the program was overwhelming. During the first year, the proportion of operators in category 1 increased from 10 to 15 percent, while the percentage of operators with six to thirty absences decreased from 6.5 to 4.5 percent. Total costs for the 1985 program were slightly more than $36,000, but the agency estimated savings of at least $200,000. Careful attendance monitoring coupled with incentive awards paid off. Too often, attention is focused on employees who have the worst records and who are probably already on their way out. Managers tend to neglect satisfactory employees whose attendance can be improved with the right incentives.

   Manpower Planning. Managers continually need to estimate how many employees they will need, given planned service changes, anticipated resignations, and the projected number of replacements for employees out on vacation or sick leave. Since it addresses long-term labor needs, manpower planning differs from extra-board scheduling, which adjusts to the day-to-day variations in operator requirements. Determining the appropraite complement of operators in advance avoids crisis management and increases the reliability of service. Scheduling too few operators will result in missed trips and increased overtime. Conversely, an excess of operators will push costs over budget. The Twin Cities' Metropolitan Transit Commission (MTC) introduced an experimental program of manpower planning at one operating base in 1979 and has subsequently expanded this as it has learned how to predict seasonal requirements. The commission's objective was to increase the reliability of service without exceeding the operating budget. At the experimental base, the number of both full-time and part-time employees was increased to reduce overtime paid and to cover all trips. The number of missed trips fell from a two-week high of 128 trips to only 2 trips and the pay-hour-to-service-hour ratio declined from 1.23 to 1.19 (Smith, Kiffe, and Lee, 1980). Estimates for costs that included fringe benefits were not given. However, the program achieved its major objective of reducing missed trips without exceeding the budget for the division.

Seattle Metro uses a manpower-leveling model that predicts up to two years in advance the number of full-time and part-time operators that each division will require. This model is used to adjust service assignments to the different divisions and to cut runs to achieve optimal utilization of both full-time and part-time labor. It is based on a regression model that uses cost per service hour as the dependent variable and labor factors as independent variables. The model allows a range of employment options to be tested for each division before the work is assigned. The union contact allows Seattle Metro to hire up to 50 percent of its drivers as part-time employees, and the manpower model tests the assignment of part-time employees to different divisions to optimize their use. As service has expanded, the number of combination runs, which are available only to full-time employees, has risen by 20 percent while the "trippers"—mostly peak-hour suburban commuter runs operated by part-time employees—have increased by 170 percent.

Extra-Board Scheduling. Transit agencies employ both regular operators to provide scheduled service and extra operators to cover work assignments that are temporarily unfilled. Opportunities exist to refine manpower planning through use of the extra-board schedule. Operators who choose assignments to the extra-board are used to cover for short pieces of work ("trippers"), absences, and vacations. Some operators pick the extra-board assignment because it offers variety in work; others choose it because if management does not use the option efficiently, they will be paid for a regular shift without driving and then possibly work an extra shift at time-and-a-half pay.

Most agencies use subjective methods to determine the size of the extra-board. This frequently means that they have too many operators on hand (inefficient) or not enough (ineffective). Few agencies monitor employee indicators as carefully as MTC and Seattle Metro, and most do not know the seasonal and daily variations that are required for prudent labor management. Instead, they tend to understaff the extra-board and to rely on regular employees to work overtime in the belief that it is more economical to pay overtime than additional fringe benefits. However, absenteeism increases when employees work overtime and then take unscheduled days off. Alternative methods for extra-board scheduling are available, and MacDorman and MacDorman (1982) have estimated that a $50 million annual savings could be available to the U.S. transit industry through improved procedures for manpower planning and extra-board sizing. The San Francisco Municipal Railway saved $24,500 per day by increasing the size of the extra-board so as to limit overtime paid to regular operators.

It is almost always more efficient to cover absences with extra-board operators, unless their daily fixed fringe benefits are greater than the overtime premium paid to existing operators. For example, very short pieces of work (less than two hours) can be covered by paying overtime, whereas it should be more economical to employ additional operators to cover for runs missed by regular employees. MacDorman (1985) has developed a method to determine the least-cost arrangement for staffing to accommodate both unanticipated absenteeism and scheduled "trippers." The objective is to determine the extra-board size where the sum of the probable guaranteed pay and fixed benefits for extra-board employees equals the overtime premium that would be paid to regular employees who accept extra work. As an agency deviates from the optimal level by hiring either too many or too few extra-board operators, marginal labor costs will increase.

Potential cost savings were estimated by MacDorman for twenty-one agencies. The results indicated that many of these agencies were incurring substantial costs by employing drivers to routinely operate "trippers" as part of the extra-board. On average, these agencies were using 7 percent more operators than optimal. Contract provisions necessitate excessive employment in some agencies; in these instances, records should be compiled for use in the next round of labor negotiations. Given the magnitude of labor costs, even small economies are important.

Shedding the Peak. Peak-period operations are more costly than all-day (base) operations, because the labor and equipment used to handle the peak loads are underutilized during the remainder of the day. More than one-half of all transit trips are made in the five peak hours, forcing transit agencies to operate in a very inefficient manner. To make matters more difficult, both the time interval between the peaks and the proportion of total trips occurring during the peak are increasing. Split shifts, long workdays, biddable "trippers," and part-time labor are strategies used by managers to cover peak requirements. Labor representatives have taken a different approach by trying to maximize earnings for employees who work such undesirable schedules. As a result, Oram (1979) has calculated that peak-only service can cost two and one-half times as much as base service. Peak-hour buses do operate with higher loads, but even taking the additional revenue into account, the subsidy per passenger is higher for peak-only services.

Inefficient use of labor is the principal reason for the higher cost of peak-hour service. Various solutions have been proposed, with part-time labor preferred by transit managers. However, the arrangement sometimes referred to as load shedding provides an alternative. Load shedding reduces the amount of peak-hour service by encouraging paratransit and private providers to assume operation of the least efficient routes. Van pools and car pools are largely self-supporting. Private operators may or may not require governmental assistance when assuming commuter routes. They normally use comfortable suburban coaches designed for charter service and guarantee seating for a premium fare. In Boston, New York, and Philadephia they are largely self-supporting. In other cities such as Houston, Texas, private operators have either been granted a three-to-five-year operating subsidy or have been provided with vehicles.

Although opportunities exist for assigning some peak-hour service to private operators, privatization is no panacea. The number of express-only routes is limited, and there are few private companies in most metropolitan areas that have either the equipment or the managerial skill needed to provide regularly scheduled commuter service. And if the experience of Houston is any predictor, then those companies that do have the requisite skills and equipment will probably require public subsidies to survive.

Savings occur in two ways through the subsidization of private operators for peak-hour operations. First, reducing costs by 10 to 30 percent for service on only a few routes produces substantial savings, and, second, the existence of private providers moderates the demands of unionized workers in public agencies. But there are drawbacks to contracting: once a public agency contracts for service, Section 3(e) of the Urban Mass Transportation Act of 1964 (as amended) protects private operators from future competition from public providers should private costs exceed those of the public agency. In San Diego County, for example, public operators have been obstructed in their attempts to regain routes contracted out to private providers by Section 3(c) of the act.

Subscription bus and van pools appear better able to sustain themselves than peak-hour services operated by private companies. Transit agencies, as well as metropolitan planning agencies, are resorting to these options. The more innovative transit agencies, such as the Tidewater District in Norfolk, Virginia, and the Orange County Transit District have recognized the advantage, and are actively promoting ride sharing as a replacement for their most costly services.

Increasing peak-hour fares also encourages load shedding by discouraging noncommuting riders from using services when they are most congested. It also increases revenue because commuters have a lower price elasticity of demand. They are more likely to travel at other times rather than pay peak hour surcharges.

Nevertheless, agencies shrink from imposing peak-hour fare surcharges because of opposition from the transit dependent— especially the elderly. These people fill hearing rooms and protest any interference to their mobility, even though they could demand, and might benefit from, lower off-peak fares.

Prospects for Improving Relations with Employees

Collective bargaining is the process used both to determine the terms and conditions of employment and to preserve the dignity of work. And it is within this process that improvements in labor efficiency must be achieved. Using private providers and shedding some peak service can help, but management cannot hope to increase efficiency by relying on these exclusively. Contracts must be negotiated with consideration for the kind of service an agency desires and for the costs of deploying this service under different labor arrangements. Attention must also be given to work rules, especially those relating to duration of work and the functions performed by extra-board employees. Revisions to the operating schedule, as well as the assignment of work to divisions, ought to be considered with both the customer and the labor contract in mind. Attendance policies should be developed and monitored so as to reward reliable employees and penalize those who abuse privileges.

Linking labor negotiations with organizational objectives contributes to strategic management. The Utah Transit Authority (UTA) in Salt Lake City did this when it wished to eliminate the extra-board and place all operators on regular runs without increasing costs. UTA established a framework that allowed it to negotiate for alternative ways to eliminate the extra-board while decreasing the real cost of service, reducing avoidable accidents, improving operator attendance, and reducing voluntary turnover of operators. Management was able to conclude contract negotiations in a manner that was consistent with these goals. This approach has also enabled management to monitor performance in a way that is consistent with strategic management.

Management frequently overlooks the psychological advantages to be gained from better labor relations. For most patrons, the driver is the agency, and the driver's attitude is an important factor in turning an infrequent user into a regular rider. Unfortunately, the inflexible nature of transit work and a tradition of strong unionism tend to set employees against managers and supervisors, so that sharing of agency goals and objectives is undermined. The example from the UTA demonstrates that this situation need not continue. Significant changes were made that resulted in economies in operating cost and decreases in both voluntary turnover and customer complaints.

The transition from private to public ownership of transit agencies in the late 1960s heightened union expectations for wage increases and diminished management's authority to negotiate contracts. Uncertainty about relationships has led to more than two decades of adversarial relations between unions and management. But these attitudes have begun to change in the direction of more cooperative relations. Transit organizations are finding it less desirable to employ confrontational tactics with their work force. Instead, many have found it profitable to give employees more involvement in their jobs to increase job satisfaction. Allowing drivers to suggest changes in routes and schedules is an example. The generic name for such approaches is *organizational development*. It encompasses a potpourri of techniques to increase productive behavior in individuals, groups, or even entire organizations. For instance, management by objectives allows an employee and his supervisor to collectively set performance goals, thus giving the employee a higher stake in achieving them. Quality circles increase employee knowledge and may result in methods for improving work, such as faster ways for cleaning vehicles or better methods for replacing worn brakes. Job enrichment, to name a third technique, is a means of setting up work activities to take account of the fact that individuals must do more than just perform a task when they are at work; they wish to satisfy individual and social needs as well. Such approaches are described in the organizational development literature. Although these techniques are sometimes belittled by the more traditional practitioners of adversarial labor-management relations, they have been found useful in increasing attentiveness to customers, reducing absenteeism, cutting turnover, and increasing productivity.

8

Transit Planning:
Analyzing and Strengthening
Existing Service

Transit planners analyze different scenarios for improving service and try to identify the most beneficial strategies for accomplishing their goals. This chapter focuses on a short-range, three-to-five-year plan and on the methods and techniques useful for analyzing and strengthening existing service. Techniques used in long-range planning are not discussed since information about future opportunities and constraints is generally provided by regional planning agencies. Linked to other functions in a transit agency by its pursuit of common goals, the planning process is an important tool of strategic management.

Approaches to analysis are featured in this chapter rather than the analytical techniques themselves. Because a single chapter cannot adequately cover all the analytical techniques used by professional planners, they must be left to books devoted wholly to the subject. Approaches that will assist managers to evaluate different methods to improve transit capacity are considered under the headings of estimating demand, service supply, and managing demand. By recognizing that different methods can be used to analyze demand and supply, transit executives can improve their management of the planning function and make better use of study results.

Transit planners should analyze the benefits and costs of various transit scenarios, leaving the choice of solution to management, which must take into consideration political, financial, and administrative issues beyond the sphere of planning. Too often this distinction is overlooked; planners try to anticipate political outcomes themselves, or managers allow plans to become recommendations without considering their consequences. Planners, like fiscal and personnel specialists, are resource personnel who develop strategic options. It is management's responsibility to select the option that satisfies agency goals and recommend this to the policy board for approval.

After reviewing short-range planning practices in twelve agencies, Wilson and others (1984) identified four weaknesses of current practice that illustrate the general confusion of transit managers about the role of planning in strategic management:

1. Discrepancies exist between agency goals and the standards used to evaluate route performance.
2. Limitations are placed on feasible options, and there is a tendency to focus on problem routes and ignore satisfactory routes.
3. Adequate and reliable information on current performance of individual routes is unavailable.
4. Intraagency cooperation between planning, scheduling, and operations is poor.

Organizational problems loom large in each point cited, that is, management has not realistically confronted the need for transit service changes in light of declining governmental assistance. Patronage responses to changes in routes and fares have not been carefully monitored to generate useful information; goals have not been prioritized for route planners so that decisions made at the operations level are consistent with organizational objectives; and cooperation between departments has not been enforced. The whole approach to short-range planning is distorted by attention to problem routes. Analysis should focus on all routes, because changes along the most successful routes may be the most cost-effective ones.

Previous chapters described procedures that are applicable to the sorts of problems described by Wilson and others (1984). Setting realistic goals for transit service and analyzing routes and organizational units in terms of objectives derived from these goals are essential parts of short-range planning. Once data are gathered on routes, various techniques can be used to analyze performance, and different methods of supplying service can be considered within the constraints of the labor contract. Only the methods for estimating service demand have not been covered in previous chapters, and they deserve attention.

Estimating Service Demand

Planners forecasting transit ridership seek to establish relationships between demand; service characteristics (frequency, reliability, and price); and the characteristics of the area traversed (demographics and travel destinations). Modeling these relationships is a very complex task for the following reasons:

1. Travel is a derived demand: people travel in order to obtain the goods and services supplied at the destination.
2. The cost to the passenger for using public transit is determined not only by the fare but also by the time involved in walking to the station, waiting, and traveling.
3. Transit is provided for many purposes other than maximizing revenue so that decisions on supply are related to cost and revenue in only a very general way.
4. Relationships between demand and causal factors frequently act in both directions simultaneously. For example, the opening of a shopping center may increase demand for travel by both transit and auto, but the increased congestion may slow buses and thereby depress demand for transit.

Although demand for transit travel results from very complicated personal characteristics, models have been developed that simplify the relationships between demand and personal characteristics and enable ridership to be predicted with varying levels of reliability. Relationships are represented by a function that expresses the number of transit trips demanded for a given period in terms of a set of explanatory variables. A general formulation of the demand function is

$$Y = (X_1, \ldots, X_n)$$

where Y is the dependent variable (level of demand) and $X_1, \ldots, X_n$ are the explanatory (independent) variables. Transit agencies use different versions of this equation to predict ridership; some versions are relatively simple, one-variable models in which ridership is assumed to be a function of land use or population density, whereas others are multivariable, elegant models involving the mathematical expression of service criteria and individual traveler characteristics (Webster and Bly, 1980).

Most agencies use projected ridership as a criterion when choosing, or justifying, service improvements. Projection techniques are seldom used for route reductions, for changes in service hours and headways, or for minor reroutings. Such decisions are based on actual as opposed to potential ridership. Proposals to increase service, however, require information that is generally unavailable and must be forecasted. A recent review of models used to forecast route-level demand concluded that transit agencies prefer relatively simple models over more elegant methods (Multisystems, Inc., 1982, p. 9):

> Of the properties [agencies] that do predict ridership, most (87 percent) use technically straightforward or otherwise simple methods because they require the least time, cost, and technical sophistication. Many properties indicated that they are only interested in the potential performance of these routes in the most general terms. The precision of the ridership estimates often is less important to the property than simply *having* an assessment of the potential "success" of the new route or route change (as measured by the number of passengers it will carry or the amount of revenue it will generate). In some cases this is because routes are proposed for reasons

other than ridership potential; in others, routes are systematically implemented on a trial basis and subsequently retained or dropped based on observed ridership. In these cases ridership predictions may assist in the choice among proposed routes or may be used to identify which routes have the potential to exceed a minimum productivity standard. Once the route is in place, however, direct observation typically replaces any sort of projection as a method of evaluation.

Many agencies use more than one method to estimate service demand and to check the validity of the results. When selecting methods, managers should keep in mind the need to integrate route planning with agency goals, estimates of labor cost, and strategies for organizational cooperation. Although the elegant models may be tempting, less sophisticated methods are often better facilitators of intragency cooperation. The techniques most frequently used are described in the following subsections. Readers wanting more details should consult the report by Multisystems, Inc.

Judgmental Methods. These approaches rest on the premise that responses to previous changes in service provide the most reliable means for forecasting outcomes. This method is suitable in areas with a high level of transit service where changes in one route will lead to patronage shifts to or from adjacent routes. Forecasting such changes requires not only information about responses to previous service changes but also knowledge of service areas, traffic generators, travel patterns, and characteristics of travelers.

Accuracy in judgment can be improved in two ways. First, it can be improved by segmenting ridership by time—morning and afternoon peak periods, along with base, evening, and weekend periods—and by line segments—radial, crosstown suburban, central city and community based. Second, accuracy can be improved by using panels of experts to estimate the magnitude of change expected. A formalized "group of experts" approach, the Delphi method, was used in Pennsylvania to synthesize predictions for rural transit demand. A committee of experts was assembled to review the evidence and develop the most likely forecast by group consensus.

The Regional Transit Board for Minneapolis-St. Paul uses a hierarchical classification for segmenting routes. Each level of the hierarchy—speed, availability, frequency, and orientation—represents a key element of transit provision. Not only is the classification useful for estimating ridership by means of judgmental methods, but it can also be used for estimating the cost of supplying different types of service.

Judgmental methods are popular for a number of reasons. First, they are inexpensive because they use data and expertise that are normally readily available. Second, they can be used to analyze a broad range of planning proposals. Third, they can be used to relate route-level data with community goals for public transit. However, the method is subject to "expert" interpretation that may provide a range of opinions. Judgmental techniques are useful for ranking alternative service proposals, even though ridership response cannot be forecast precisely.

Comparative Demand Methods. These methods rely on analogy: areas with similar household characteristics and population density are expected to have similar responses to transit changes. Over time, routes in these areas should have the same ridership per mile or hour as established routes traversing comparable areas. These methods are not as dependent on the expertise of the planner as are judgmental methods. Typical neighborhoods can be described in terms of household characteristics, and ridership can be postulated by time period. The planner's task is to analyze the neighborhoods and then estimate the ridership response to the proposed service change using response rates observed elsewhere.

Many variants of the comparative demand method are used. With the most elementary method, the planner merely adapts the hourly or daily ridership of routes traversing similar neighborhoods and uses these numbers to forecast ridership for a planned route. Other methods incorporate the judgment of experienced planners who develop rules of thumb for new routes. For example, planners might estimate daily route ridership as a percentage of the population living within one-quarter mile of the bus route. The Milwaukee County Transit system uses a formula whose basic assumption is that daily ridership will be proportional to the entire population served:

$$Y = (b_1 \cdot x_1)$$

Y = Daily route ridership.

x_1 = Number of residents within one-quarter mile of the route.

b_1 = Transit response rate, which varies between 0.01 and 0.045 depending on the type of service and the community traversed.

Graphs showing the relationship between residential density and transit ridership in metropolitan areas have been widely used in transit planning. Pushkarev and Zupan (1977) discussed the appropriateness of different modes for different residential densities, with ridership forecast as a function of either dwelling units per acre or nonresidential floor space in the central business district (CBD). Sloan (1979) used density-patronage graphs to devise five transit scenarios for the suburban areas surrounding Philadelphia; from these, he forecast demand for public transit. He then evaluated several transit projects through an approach that combined management by objectives with cost-effectiveness analysis. The object was to produce a way of managing public transit more effectively and efficiently in the Philadephia region.

Technical simplicity is the reason for the popularity of comparative methods: agency analysts find them easy to use, and the results can be readily understood by board members and the general public. Transit managers must recognize the importance of the latter because of the political nature of decisions. Easily understood forecasts are essential for achieving consensus on controversial proposals.

Noncommittal Survey Methods. In this approach, analysts forecast demand by combining survey research with knowledge of the trip-generation rates of different types of households. Methods based on this approach are superior to judgmental and comparative methods in that the estimates of demand derived from simple surveys can be stated with known levels of confidence and precision. However, they are based on the responses of *potential* users and are therefore unreliable. They are also much more expensive to implement than the aforementioned techniques. These methods are primarily used to estimate the potential demand for new routes and facilities when comparative local data are not available.

Survey results can be combined with travel-demand information. Travel-demand studies have been completed for highway-planning purposes in most metropolitan areas. These studies establish trip-generation rates for households on the basis of building type (single or multiple unit), socioeconomic status, and number of automobiles owned. Travel demand is forecast by zones, with interzonal travel calculated for different trip purposes (work, social, shopping). The probability of trip makers choosing to use transit is estimated as a proportion of total trips by each trip purpose. When new transit services such as park-and-ride and express bus are proposed, survey research methods are used to estimate ridership.

A random sample of households within the originating travel zones is selected, so that interviews from a relatively small number of households yield results for the entire population with desired levels of confidence and precision. Results are then used to forecast the proportion of trips that will probably be made via the new service or facility. But this does not mean that the results are more accurate than judgmental results. Even after planners discount the propensity of respondents to claim that they will use transit more often than they actually will, predicted use normally exceeds actual use. Noncommittal survey methods, however, can provide information about transit demand in areas where there has been little operating experience. They are imprecise but nevertheless helpful to management in comparing alternative proposals.

Elasticity Methods. Certain calculations will yield the percentage change in demand (number of passengers) in relation to a percentage change in fares (price elasticity) or in service (service elasticity). They offer a relatively simple and inexpensive way of estimating response to proposed changes. Elasticity methods are helpful because they give a quick estimate of riders' sensitivity to fare and service changes, but managers should be aware of their limitations:

1. They cannot be used to estimate demand for a new route. An analyst can calculate percentage responses to change only where service already exists and there are patronage rates to work with.
2. Elasticity of demand is only valid for small changes in fares and/or service.

Ridership responses to fare changes are described as being elastic, inelastic, or of unitary elasticity. Responses are elastic when a fare change causes a proportionately greater change in ridership. If a 10 percent increase in fares leads to a 20 percent decrease in ridership, then ridership is considered to be elastic. Responses are inelastic if the ridership change is proportionately smaller than the fare change. If a 10 percent increase in fares gives rise to a 3 percent decrease in ridership, then patronage would be inelastic. Finally, responses have elasticities of unity when the proportional change in ridership is approximately equal to the proportional change in fares. In this case a 10 percent increase in fares results in roughly a 10 percent decrease in ridership.

A wide range of transit fare elasticities has been reported, with the general conclusion that transit is price inelastic. Elasticity ratios range from -0.05 to -0.87 for various types of service, with a mean of about -0.3 widely used by transit planners. This average can be misleading, however, and it is important to use an elasticity that represents a particular service type rather than the -0.3 ratio that averages many services. A number of elasticity ratios have been collected and published in Table 6 as a guide for transit agencies.

Service is also inelastic with respect to travel time, but elasticity of demand varies with time of day and type of delay (Table 10). Riders are more sensitive to travel time increases during peak hours than during the remainder of the day. They are also more sensitive to increases in out-of-vehicle time caused by a reduc-

Table 10. Level of Service Elasticities for Bus Systems.

Characteristic	Elasticity Mean/Standard Deviation[a]	Number of Cases
Headway		
Peak	-0.37 ± 0.19	3
Off peak	-0.46 ± 0.26	9
All hours	-0.47 ± 0.21	7
Vehicle Miles		
All hours	+0.63 ± 0.24	3
Peak	+0.33 ± 0.18	3[b]
Off peak	+0.63 ± 0.11	3[b]
All hours	+0.69 ± 0.31	17[b]
Total travel time		
Peak	-1.03 ± 0.13	2
All hours	-0.92 ± 0.37	2
In-vehicle time		
Peak	-0.29 ± 0.13	9
Off peak	-0.83	1
Out-of-vehicle time		
All hours (bus and rapid rail)	-0.59 ± 0.15	3[b]
Walk time		
Peak	-0.26	1[b]
Off peak	-0.14	1[b]
Wait time		
Peak (bus and rapid rail)	-0.20 ± 0.07	4[b]
Off peak (bus and rapid rail)	-0.21	1[b]
Transfer time		
Peak (bus and rapid rail)	-0.40 ± 0.18	3[b]
Number of transfers		
Off peak	-0.59	1

[a]Where available
[b]Based on nonexperimental data—time series or cross-sectional studies—rather than an actual fare or service change.
Source: Adapted from Mayworm, Lago, and McEnroe, 1980.

tion in headways or increased transfers than they are to increases in travel time when they are on board vehicles.

Several approaches are used for calculating service and fare elasticities. Grey (1975) recommends calculating the "arc" elasticity of demand for transit analysis. This is the slope of the line connecting two points on the demand curve that represents before and after ridership in response to changes in either service or fare. The "arc" elasticity for service is expressed as follows:

$$Ex = \frac{\text{percentage change in demand}}{\text{percentage change in explanatory variable}}$$

or

$$Ex = \frac{Xb}{Vb} \cdot \frac{(V^a - V^b)}{X^a - X^b}$$

Ex = elasticity of ridership with respect to change in the service variable X

V = ridership

X = level of service variable normally expressed as travel time

b and a = before and after measurements.

To provide an estimate of ridership changes for a given change in service, this equation can be rearranged as follows:

$$V^a = V^b\left[1 + Ex\left(\frac{X^a}{X_b} - 1\right)\right]$$

To forecast the effect of a fare change on ridership (price elasticity of demand), the service variable is changed to a price variable so that Ex becomes the elasticity of ridership with respect to fare change. For example if:

Ex = -0.10 for commuter trips and the present ridership (V^b) is 2,000, a fare increase from 100 to 110 cents may result in the following ridership after the fare increase:

$$V^a = 2{,}000\left[1 + (-.1)\left(\frac{110}{100} - 1\right)\right] = 1980$$

Elasticity models can be used in a wide range of applications other than in the prediction of ridership. When several elasticities are used sequentially, the effect of different factors on demand can be calculated. A high level of analytical sophistication is not required, and, given the same data, all analysts should obtain the same results. The accuracy of the calculations depends on a number of factors, including the demand for different types of transit services, the magnitude of a proposed change, and the time between before and after measurement. Transferability of the relationships shown in Tables 6 and 10 is limited; they may be useful to systems of similar size contemplating changes of similar magnitude, but each agency should calibrate models to suit its own circumstances. Careful surveying of patronage, before and after service and fare changes, is the preferred way for an agency to establish the elasticity ratios that will facilitate strategic evaluation of alternatives.

Regression Methods. Relationships between ridership and independent variables such as fares and travel time are not as simple as elasticity models make them appear. Demographic, land use, and economic variables may be changing simultaneously with changes in fares or service. Also the expected decrease or increase in ridership may not be accompanied by an equivalent change in service supplied. Regression models allow several variables that are both positively or negatively related to ridership to be considered simultaneously:

$$Y = k + b_1 x_1 + b_2 x_2 + \ldots b_n x_p$$

where:

Y = dependent variable—usually hourly ridership by route or route segment

$x_1 - x_p$ = independent variables such as number of households, autos per household, and transit service variables

$b_1 - b_n$ = factors (coefficients) that specify the rate at which the corresponding independent variable induces change in ridership

k = constant included to represent the proportion of the value of Y that does not vary with the independent variable

Independent variables normally come from one of the four groups: transit service (headway, fares, travel time, hours of service); socioeconomic factors (population, income, and auto ownership by households); land use (household and employment density); and economic indicators (availability and price of gasoline, unemployment rates, and disposable income).

The equation given above assumes a linear (additive) relationship between the explanatory variables and ridership per revenue hour. Data are collected for all travel zones in a city, to determine the explanatory variables and ridership at a particular point in time. Using this data, regression analysis produces estimates for the coefficients $(b_1 \ldots b_n)$ and an estimate for the unexplained residual (k). The result is a set of best estimates for the coefficients that satisfy statistical assumptions about the sample data. Applying the values estimated for the coefficients to data collected for the independent variables allows ridership to be predicted to a known level of confidence and precision.

Southeastern Michigan Transit Authority (SEMTA) uses two models, one developed for CBD routes and the other for non-CBD routes. They differ in that the model for CBD-oriented routes does not include variables representing population density but does include variables capturing the influence of the off-peak headway. Ridership for the non-CBD model is a function of headways and population density.

Several regression models are described in the Multisystems, Inc. (1982) review. They can be differentiated by the way in which the variables are calibrated:

1. Aggregate models are calibrated with data from statistical units and predict ridership by areas.
2. Disaggregate models are calibrated according to the characteristics of the individual or individual household and predict an individual's response to changes in variables.
3. Cross-section section models utilize data from several routes for one time period to calibrate a system-specific mode.
4. Time-series models use data gathered over several years for a specific route or route type. The model is calibrated by

analyzing ridership response to changes in service and fares during several time periods.

Regression models can provide an agency with a method for forecasting route-level ridership. Models calibrated with local data and programmed on a microcomputer can be adapted to forecast ridership for different routes and according to different assumptions about the independent variables. Regression models tend to be more difficult to apply and require a higher level of technical sophistication on the part of the analyst than do other methods of forecasting route-level ridership. They are appropriately used for major policy decisions, such as inauguration of service in new areas or route restructuring, but not for minor service changes, where elasticity models can adequately predict ridership.

Assessment. No single method is suitable for all forecasting requirements. The simplest judgmental methods are suitable for making decisions on minor route changes, whereas elasticity methods can help estimate the probable consequences of fare and service changes on existing routes. Comparative demand models are especially useful for presentation of proposals to decision makers and community groups because the analogy to familiar areas lends credibility to the results. Regression models are the most sophisticated and helpful techniques for analyzing major service changes. Their weakness is that they are unable to establish consistent relationships (coefficients) between the independent variables (explanatory variables) and ridership. There is a positive relationship between population density and transit ridership, but this does not necessarily imply causality. Accessibility to and frequency of service, rather than population density, are the causal factors.

The accuracy of the various demand-forecasting techniques is difficult to judge because few before-and-after studies have been made to test their reliability. In addition, conditions affecting demand can change between the time an analysis is completed and the date of service initiation. Judgmental and comparative demand methods are probably the most accurate when the proposed service changes are minor and restricted to relatively homogeneous areas. Noncommittal surveys are the least accurate.

Elasticity estimates provided in Tables 6 and 10 indicate a wide range of observed behavior resulting from changes in fares and service. Accuracy is probably no better than ±40 percent for fare-related changes and ±45 percent for service-related changes. Reliable projections based on elasticity should therefore provide a range of anticipated change rather than an average response. Regression techniques calibrated from an agency's own data generally predict route-level ridership more accurately than other methods. They are costly to develop and use, but this expenditure is warranted for medium-sized and large transit agencies. Regression techniques are sensitive to a variety of conditions that may cause changes in ridership.

Service Supply

Whereas many of the variables affecting service demand are beyond managerial control, service supply is largely under such control. During the 1970s, when governmental assistance was abundant, routes were extended into suburban areas, well beyond the areas traditionally served by transit. Sufficient attention was not given to analyzing either the cost of this service or the probable demand for it. To make matters worse, transit became increasingly oriented to serving the peak-period commuter whose marginal cost exceeded average cost and who was seldom required to pay a greater-than-average fare. Now that operating funds have become scarce, management has started to review all routes and service levels in terms of cost and revenues. The most successful route evaluation studies have been those that have emphasized the analysis of costs and have examined techniques of route restructuring that minimize labor cost.

Route-Costing Methods. A methodology was described in Chapter Five for allocating costs to three variables: vehicle miles, vehicle hours, and number of peak vehicles. The cost for operating each route can then be estimated by calculating the units of each variable required and multiplying this by coefficients established from systemwide financial records. However, the cost calculated is still an average based on all routes and all operating costs and thus may not accurately reflect the marginal cost of adding or deleting service on individual routes.

Operating costs can be further disaggregated at the route level by examining the labor required to operate all trips on a particular route. Labor costs vary substantially by route, depending on the number of operators required for a route and whether or not peak demands involve scheduling work shifts that incur labor penalties. Direct estimation of labor costs for individual routes by means of cost build-up methods is possible after schedules are designed and routes grouped into runs or shifts. The disadvantage of this method is the high level of effort required to apply it without computerized methods for scheduling and cutting pieces of service into runs ("runcutting").

Route Evaluation Criteria. Planners will seldom have an opportunity to design an entire network of routes. Mostly they are concerned with the evaluation of current routes and recommendations for change. A variety of performance criteria are used to identify those routes or route segments that are performing above or below desired thresholds. These criteria encompass:

- Efficiency and effectiveness (including cost per revenue hour, cost recovery, cost per passenger, and passengers per hour and trip)
- Level of service (including vehicle loads and headways, missed trips and schedule adherence, peak loads and passenger safety, bus shelter placement, transferring passengers, and public complaints)
- Route design (including bus stop spacing; route coverage; and length, duplication, and structure of routes).

American transit agencies tend to use multiple indicators of route performance. These usually address effectiveness rather than efficiency because social objectives rather than fiscal responsibility have traditionally been emphasized by these agencies. However, the more successful agencies find ways to measure both efficiency and effectiveness. London Transport, for example, has adopted a single measure (passenger miles per unit of expenditure) to quantify the contribution of route investments to the authority's objectives. Single measures, which incorporate both the cost of producing service as well as its utilization (such as passenger miles per unit of expense or net cost per passenger), simplify analysis. Using them, it is relatively easy to rank routes and establish a threshold for desirable performance. However, the question is immediately raised of whether all passengers should be treated equally. Under federal regulations, transit agencies are required to give special attention to elderly and handicapped passengers and to ensure that access to service in neighborhoods where low-income and minority households predominate is equivalent to or better than that provided in the rest of the service area.

Multiple measures of route performance have a decided advantage. Equity considerations as well as economy can be included. Also, employing multiple measures makes it much easier for staff to negotiate service changes with neighborhood groups, as different groups can perceive their own interests in the criteria used for policy decisions. A wide variety of measures can be used. As mentioned above, effectiveness measures predominate, while those measuring the cost of service tend to be less fully developed. In selecting measures, planners should ensure that efficiency measures are adequately represented and that redundancy is reduced.

Scarcity of funds for operating assistance has compelled transit managers to examine the cost of providing service on different routes. Proposed changes are compared, not only against desirable thresholds of performance but also with respect to alternative investments. For example, if an existing route is producing 1.3 passengers per dollar of net cost but dropping this route would make funds available for another route that would produce 1.5 passengers per dollar of net cost, then the alternative should be implemented even though the former route was producing above some policy threshold. In this way, standards are modified to emphasize "the best available" investments. The disadvantage of comparative investment analysis is that all passengers are regarded as similar, when this is rarely the case.

The best route evaluation measures are those that

- Consider both efficiency and effectiveness criteria
- Avoid redundancy

- Appraise routes in terms of their net cost per passenger
- Give special consideration to routes serving households without access to automobiles
- Evaluate routes with respect to the best available alternative investment of resources rather than with respect to policy standards.

Route evaluation studies that devote too much time to the "failing" routes and too little to the "successful" ones are not beneficial. Often there are more opportunities to improve the successful than the problem routes.

Methods for Service Design. Many planners have a totally inadequate picture of their current system and hence lack a basis for important service decisions. Most agencies use a "problem-centered" approach: problem routes are identified either by below-average performance on route evaluation criteria or by schedule violation or overloading. Techniques designed to identify routes that are performing satisfactorily but that could be improved are seldom used. Planners ought to consider "action-centered" approaches that seek to improve area coverage, route structure, and scheduling. The object of these approaches is to detect where labor and vehicles can be used more efficiently on existing routes (Table 11).

Wilson and others (1984) have argued persuasively for this action-centered emphasis and have developed techniques to support it. These involve collecting traditional data on service evaluation and schedule adherence and integrating them with data from route monitoring. Consideration is also given to agency goals so that service designed for special groups is not jeopardized by regarding all passengers as having the same needs. Each proposed change is analyzed in terms of its impact on both changes in operating cost based on route-specific operator and vehicle requirements and changes in ridership and revenue.

The action-centered approach to service design incorporates the solutions used in the problem-centered approach. It differs only in the methods used to detect needed changes. The former screens

Table 11. Action-Centered Approach to Service Design.

Generic Action	Favorable Route Conditions
A. Area Coverage Level	
1. Eliminate route segment	Low ridership generation on segment Vehicle savings possible from elimination Higher frequency possible from elimination
B. Route Structure Level	
1. Split route	Low productivity, uneven load profile, or long route
2. Zonal	Tapering load profile, long route, or large time differential
3. Express/Local	High ridership, tapering load profile, long route, or large time differential between local/express
C. Scheduling	
1. Increase frequency	Overcrowding, moderate rather than high ridership or even load profile
2. Decrease frequency	Low productivity and loads or headways below policy levels
3. Eliminate trips	Low ridership on trips or high cost savings from elimination
4. Increase running time	Poor schedule adherence or high loads
5. Partial deadheading	Large imbalance in passengers, large time differential in service or high frequencies

Source: Wilson and others, 1984.

all routes to look for opportunities for improvement, whereas the latter considers only routes experiencing operating problems. Planners use the action-centered approach to screen all routes against organizational objectives in order to identify a small set of routes that might have a potential for improvement by application of one or more of the generic actions listed in Table 11. Screening thus reduces the magnitude of effort in the design stage when information on running times, headways, and vehicle and labor requirements must be considered by route and route segment. The following are the principal advantages of the generic, action-centered approach to service design:

1. A wider range of criteria are used to search for routes with a potential for improvement.
2. More attention is focused on heavily used routes that provide opportunities for reducing cost and/or increasing ridership.
3. Less attention is paid to the low ridership routes. These routes are the most difficult to change as their continuance is often supported by a dedicated minority.

Route Networks. Most agencies use a combination of route networks—radial routes to speed commuter trips and grid routes to facilitate crosstown trips. A pulse schedule—where buses are scheduled to arrive and depart from transfer centers within a few minutes of each other—is a popular method for achieving coordination between the two, but it can be expensive if the cost of labor is not analyzed in the planning process.

Edmonton, Alberta, is the largest user of the pulse system. In Edmonton, routing, scheduling, and costing are done concurrently. Routes have been designed to take midday buses on a thirty-minute headway through timed-transfer locations. Route ends are extended or trimmed to make full use of buses. Peak buses are used to supplement the base system and take riders directly from major transfer locations to destinations such as downtown, the university, and hospitals. The annual cost for each route is the sum of the hourly net costs for base service plus peak service. Service investments are judged by comparing the net cost for different routes after planners have sought more economical operation or additional revenue for individual routes.

Agencies that have recently expanded service could benefit from examining the Edmonton experience when they take up the question of route restructuring. The Capital Metropolitan Transportation Authority in Austin, Texas, faces this decision. The authority had expanded service from 65 to 200 peak buses within eighteen months using a combination of old and new routes. However, performance has disappointed the directors, and they have placed the ambitious service expansion program on hold. The directors have requested an analysis of cost and ridership by route and are considering a complete restructuring of service.

Computer-assisted planning packages are available to assist with route restructuring. These programs match supply (limited by equipment and budget constraints) with demand (based on travel demand studies and on-board surveys) to permit planners to evaluate alternative network designs. The Volvo Interactive Planning System, developed in Sweden and applied in many countries, designs routes that stimulate ridership by reducing travel time and minimizing transfers. When the planning modules are linked with computerized scheduling packages, estimates of labor costs can be obtained for alternative networks.

Transit Scheduling. The implicit goals of scheduling are to provide the highest quality of service while using the least amount of resources. The former is normally achieved by varying scheduled headways according to demand, whereas the latter is achieved through maintaining a schedule with the minimum number of pay hours permitted by the labor contract.

Most transit agencies do not have an explicit objective for scheduling headways between runs. Instead they use a load standard or crowding constraint to indicate when schedules should be revised. The following are examples of thresholds that ensure that service will be accessible, dependable, and safe:

1. The ratio between passengers and seats (loading ratio) for individual lines should not exceed 140 percent during the peak twenty minutes at the maximum load point.
2. Loading ratios should not exceed 100 percent for base periods and evenings.
3. Loading ratios for freeway express service should not exceed seated capacity.

When the loading threshold is violated, schedule changes are initiated. These may take the form of adding service or employing strategies to use existing service more effectively. Turning some buses around before they reach the terminus, "turnbacks," and "interlining," one route with another so that there is duplicated service on some streets, are methods used to provide more service on overcrowded segments. Express service can also be used to move vehicles more rapidly when direction of demand is unbalanced. Schedule revisions must balance the need for service quality and reliability with the requirement to use labor efficiently. Allocation of more service during peak periods would improve service quality and attract more riders, but under existing labor contracts it is difficult to do this without increasing costs disproportionately.

"Runcutting." The effect of service changes on the cost of operation depends on the manner of "runcutting"—the process whereby scheduled service is "cut" into "blocks" and "runs." Drivers bid to operate various runs three or four times annually. These changes, called "shake ups," offer an opportunity to cut runs into more efficient pieces of work. Routes and schedules are normally changed at "shake up" to reflect service demand. Once the schedule has been established, vehicle trips are built. Sufficient vehicle trips must be assigned to each route to meet the time requirements of the schedule. Trip building is a simple but tedious arithmetic process. Once built, trips are grouped into blocks that take into account both layovers between trips and travel time when a block contains trips on more than one route. Blocks are cut into pieces of work and then grouped into runs that one driver can handle. For example, Figure 10 shows a block of work beginning early in the morning and ending in the evening that is cut into two straight runs.

While runcutting involves the assignment of drivers to vehicles, "blocking" involves the assignment of vehicles to routes. Both activities offer many opportunities for increasing efficiency. The problem is to analyze these opportunities in terms of systemwide impacts: should the schedule be changed, or should the allocation of vehicles or drivers be changed? Ideal blocking will include all trips with the minimum number of vehicles, whereas an ideal runcut will combine the blocks for the least labor cost, given the constraints of existing work rules.

A variety of computerized methods are used for runcutting (Hildyard and Wallis, 1981). The most widely used software package is RUCUS (Runcutting and Scheduling), a package developed by UMTA for transit scheduling and runcutting. Released in 1974, RUCUS is used in modified form by many U.S.

and Canadian authorities. It is based on manual scheduling techniques and permits analysts to create and analyze data bases with the aid of several scheduling and runcutting programs. RUCUS has substantially reduced the time required for runcutting and has achieved small improvements in labor efficiency.

More sophisticated programs have been developed using linear programming algorithms (Bower, 1986). These seek to optimize vehicle efficiency in blocking and labor efficiency in runcutting. They also offer alternative solutions by suggesting changes in schedules, trip distributions, and work rules. Such programs are advantageous for transit agencies because they permit testing of proposed schedules and vehicle assignment strategies. They also help management to prepare for labor negotiations because they suggest work-rule changes that may increase labor efficiency.

Much more effort should be devoted to the formal analysis of service supply questions. Better procedures for estimating service demand were developed when service was expanding during the 1970s, but techniques permitting critical analysis of service supply were neglected. Now that transit faces a period of fiscal austerity, planners must use better methods of data collection as well as more analytical approaches for examining route structure, service frequency, and cost. Attention should focus not only on routes identified as substandard but also on successful routes.

Transportation Systems Management (TSM)

Efforts to manage a metropolitan transportation system as a whole provide new opportunities to improve transit performance. A traditional response to excessive, peak-hour, highway demand has been to add lanes or construct alternative facilities; more recent strategies have increased highway capacity by designating lanes for express buses or car pools or have altered demand by encouraging businesses to use flex time or staggered shifts. Such methods, which reduce congestion without expanding highway facilities, are collectively referred to as transportation systems management (TSM).

In September 1975, the U.S. Department of Transportation issued regulations mandating that metropolitan areas develop TSM plans. The regulations declared that "automobiles, public transportation, taxis, pedestrians, and bicycles should be considered as elements of one single urban transportation system. The objective of urban transportation system management is to coordinate these individual elements through operating, regulatory, and service policies so as to achieve maximum efficiency and productivity for the system as a whole" (U.S. Department of Transportation, 1975, p. 42979).

The TSM regulations were a response to the increasing desire among transportation planners and engineers to improve management of existing facilities rather than create additional capacity. This change occurred as professionals realized that:

1. The infrastructure of transportation facilities was essentially "complete."
2. Financial resources for new construction and system expansion were limited.
3. Energy and environmental concerns were changing attitudes toward the automobile.
4. Increased traffic volumes, especially in central cities, new suburban centers, and along radial corridors would have to be accommodated by ridesharing rather than solo driving.

Management of demand is especially valuable when normal market mechanisms are absent. However, attempts to manage demand through pricing mechanisms are met with strong resistance: neither automobile drivers nor transit riders wish to pay the full cost of the facilities and service they use. Regulatory control and persuasion are preferred for balancing supply and demand. As a result, transit is left with somewhat limited strategies for improving service.

Assessment of TSM Strategies. Four groups of TSM strategies have been identified in terms of their influence on demand for vehicle travel and for transportation facilities (Table 12).

Table 12. Prototypical TSM Strategies for a Large, Congested, Transit-Intensive City.

Strategies	Action	Applications Context[a]					
		CBD	OLD HAC	NEW HAC	RES AREA	RAD COR	XTWN COR
1. Reduce Demand	Ride Sharing	X	X	X		X	?
	Pricing	X	?			X	X
	Express Bus, Park-Ride	X	X	?	X	X	X
	Local Transit Improvements	X	X	X	X	X	
	Bicycle Facility Improvements	X	X	X	X	X	
	Pedestrian Facility Improvements	X	X	X	X		
	Paratransit	?	X	X	X	?	?
2. Increase Supply	General Traffic Engineering	X	X	X	X	X	X
	Freeway Management	X	X	X		X	?
	Four-Day Week	X	X	X			
	Truck Restrictions	X	X		?		
	Work Rescheduling	X	X	X			
3. Reduce Demand and Degrade Supply	Auto-Restricted Zone	X	X				
	Parking Management	X	X	X		?	
	Take-a-Lane for High-Occupancy Vehicles	X	X			X	?
4. Increase Supply and Reduce Demand	Add Lane for High-Occupancy Vehicle Facilities					X	

a X Definitely Applicable   HAC High-Activity Center   RES Residential
   ? Possibly Applicable   RAD Radial   XTWN Crosstown
   (Blank) Not Applicable   COR Corridor

Source: Adapted from Wagner and Gilbert, 1978.

1. Strategies that reduce demand for vehicle travel. These include actions that induce travelers to shift from lower-occupancy vehicles (automobiles) to higher-occupancy vehicles (transit and ridesharing) or to nonmotorized travel modes. Pricing strategies such as tolls or parking fees that reduce trip frequency are also included in this group.

2. Strategies that enhance highway supply (that is, improve traffic flow). Included are a wide array of traffic control measures, in the form of minor capital improvements, that allow existing highways to accommodate more vehicles. Ramp metering on freeways that gives priority to transit and ridesharing vehicles is the method most beneficial to transit.

3. Strategies that reduce demand and degrade supply. These actions induce travelers to shift to higher-occupancy vehicles by increasing the travel time for automobiles. Examples are replacement of a traffic lane by a lane reserved for high-occupancy vehicles, auto-restricted zones, and reduction of parking.

4. Strategies that increase supply and reduce demand. For example, a lane may be added (increasing supply) that is reserved for high-occupancy vehicles. Such usage reduces vehicle miles by accommodating more people per vehicle. Removal of on-street parking may have a similar effect if the freed-up space is used for high-occupancy vehicle lanes and drivers are forced to rideshare or use transit because of the parking shortage.

Various strategies are suitable for different areas. Table 12 illustrates how they may be applied in combination to minimize congestion and facilitate ridesharing. Transit systems in major metropolitan areas can use these strategies to their advantage. Transit systems operating in smaller, less congested, metropolitan areas can benefit by encouraging ridesharing programs and paratransit alternatives to the automobile.

Pricing of Parking. Increasing the price that automobile users pay for parking would have the greatest impact on transit. Parking is provided free by most employers and many activity centers, with the exception of the CBD. Consequently, there is little incentive for the traveler to use transit. Automobiles are faster for all but the shortest trips; and if costs that vary with distance traveled (variable costs) are all that the traveler uses when comparing auto costs with transit fares, then there is no financial incentive to use transit unless there are parking charges. When realistic parking fees are established, transit enjoys a cost advantage over automobiles, and this causes impressive modal shifts to occur.

Four groups of governmental employees work in central Los Angeles. Federal, county, and city employees are provided with free parking to the extent that space is available. State employees must pay for parking. Shoup and Pickrell (1980) found that the proportion of state employees using transit or ridesharing was 20 percent above that of all governmental employees. Many more state employees would have switched from automobiles to other transit modes if parking charges had been based on the cost of providing additional parking (marginal cost) rather than the average cost. The state of California continues to price parking according to average cost rather than the marginal cost of building new parking structures. Public agencies require employees to pay no, or very low, parking charges and at the same time voice their concern over traffic congestion, insufficient parking, and underutilized transit service.

Imposing parking charges to discourage automobile use is a controversial strategy. Few officials in America are willing to risk the public's ire by interfering with its "right" to drive when and where it chooses. Americans refuse to consider highway capacity and parking spaces as scarce commodities, the use of which could be allocated efficiently by pricing that reflects the marginal cost of constructing additional facilities. In other countries, such as Canada, Japan, Singapore, and the United Kingdom, parking charges based on marginal cost have been accepted. Requiring parking fees of government employees in Ottawa caused the proportion of employees driving daily to work to decrease from 35 to 27 percent. As a result, the transit agency recorded an average daily increase of about 3,000 trips. Similarly, in Nagoya, Japan, where off-street parking is scarce, increased charges for on-street parking caused a substantial mode shift to transit and reduced morning peak-hour auto travel by 10 percent.

Establishing high-occupancy vehicle lanes on freeways and arterial streets encourages transit use. Traveling by high-occupancy vehicles in such lanes saves the patron time, offsetting the advantages of privacy and comfort available in the automobile. Compared to charging fees for parking, high-occupancy vehicle lanes are difficult to put in place and costly to police. However, as part of an overall TSM strategy that includes restrictions on parking, they can be extremely beneficial to transit.

Implementing TSM. A cooperative strategy between transportation agencies is essential for implementing a regional system. But this requires leadership in metropolitan areas where it is the rule for public agencies, cities, and counties to jealously guard their independence. Successful transit agencies will be those that assume a leadership role in developing a regional strategy. Many TSM strategies have been crippled by feeble implementation. A coherent package of projects is needed to achieve significant reduction in travel demand by automobile, but the projects need not be implemented simultaneously. Because the idea of improved management of transportation facilities departs from the traditional American practice of responding to transportation problems by investing in capital projects, implementation of TSM should be incremental. Strategies that reduce travel time by enhancing traffic flow should be used to complement strategies that encourage ridesharing to the most congested activity centers. But care must also be taken not to confuse the traveling public. Changes must be simple, easily modified, and widely advertised in advance. Ample time must be allowed so that local officials, especially those in traffic enforcement, are aware of the planned program and knowledgeable about the changes it will require. As with the promotion strategies recommended in the marketing chapter that follows, it is prudent to implement a program as an experiment so that difficulties can be corrected before it is officially inaugurated. Attempts to change travel habits can easily become overwhelmed by controversy if planning for change is inadequate.

TSM in Retrospect. Although TSM remains part of the required federal planning process, it no longer has the priority it was accorded in the late 1970s. Rational approaches to planning and budgeting have not worked well in metropolitan planning, where authority is dispersed among many city, county, and special agencies. The chief contribution of TSM has been to raise the issue of whether it is prudent to increase capital investment in rail transit and highways when less costly management strategies can achieve equivalent improvements. Insofar as transit management is concerned, the major contribution of TSM has been the encouragement of regional ridesharing. Other legacies have been bus priority lanes and the increased willingness of transit agencies to contract with private providers for suburban commuter bus service.

Planning for Strategic Actions

Entire books are devoted to the subject of transportation planning, so this chapter merely highlights some methods that deserve managerial attention. The focus here is on short-range planning techniques, because these will be most useful to professionals facing decisions on system improvement and even system retrenchment. Management also has the responsibility for presenting the results of analysis to the governing board as well as obtaining cooperation between planning and operating personnel.

The turnover of planners in transit agencies is high because of the frustration caused by political and organizational obstacles. In half the agencies contacted by Wilson and others (1984), planners reported that there was a level of distrust between scheduling and planning personnel that adversely affected the introduction of needed changes. This was most pronounced in agencies where planning and scheduling were organizationally separate and schedulers could make little direct input into route planning.

Planners are frequently offended by the way in which their recommendations are treated by the governing board. They perceive that technical analysis receives scant attention when it does not conform to the desires of influential groups. Planners can reduce their frustration by viewing planning as contributing to, rather than deciding, policy. The professional planner has an obligation to display the costs and consequences of alternative service proposals. But the final decision must be left to the elected or appointed board. Board members are better able to integrate community desires with technical considerations than are professional planners, because they have many more avenues for obtaining community opinion.

The unwillingness of operating managers to cooperate with planners poses another dilemma. Transit organizations are normally hierarchically structured with little attention given to information sharing at the second and third levels of management. Unless route planning is placed under the supervision of the operating division, there is limited cooperation between those who plan service and those who operate it until the plans reach top management. As a result, service plans are seldom implemented in the manner in which the planning department originally intended. To prevent hard feelings from surfacing, management must foster communication between the scheduling group and the planning group and ensure that the former is involved early in the route-planning process.

Challenging planners and operating personnel to focus on satisfactory rather than on problem routes helps to increase cooperation among them. Operating personnel will naturally resist any reductions in the number of vehicles operated. On routes that are performing below established thresholds, however, there is often little alternative to terminating them, so operating personnel resist proposals to analyze these routes. But on satisfactory routes, there are many opportunities to make service both less costly and more responsive to passenger demand without decreasing the number of vehicles used. TSM options also encourage cooperation, because professionals can enlarge the transit market by adopting innovations that reduce congestion along the corridors of heaviest demand. Transit planners and operating personnel must look back to central city neighborhoods, suburban business centers, and arterial corridors to maintain their market share. These congested areas offer many opportunities to improve transit service. And once the development strategy has been decided upon, the entire agency must cooperate in marketing service.

9

Marketing Public Transit

In this chapter, the general characteristics of public-sector marketing are described, and an integrated structure for marketing public transit is outlined. This marketing structure is meant to be consistent with the strategic approach to management. The importance of market research is emphasized, because a thorough knowledge of the travel desires of different groups is necessary. Unfortunately, however, marketing is usually neglected in transit management. Few transit executives give sufficient attention to customers and their travel needs and how these needs relate to agency goals and services.

Basic Requirements

An integrated marketing program (Figure 11) would include these elements:

- A systems approach that begins with goals and objectives, proceeds with action plans, and includes evaluation procedures that build self-control into the marketing plan
- Market segmentation studies to determine who the regular patrons are, how to meet their needs and desires, and how they respond to services offered
- Integration of service development (including pricing) with promotion and customer service
- A management philosophy that is market oriented and receptive to marketing experiments and that integrates the marketing

Figure 11. Integrated Structure for Marketing.

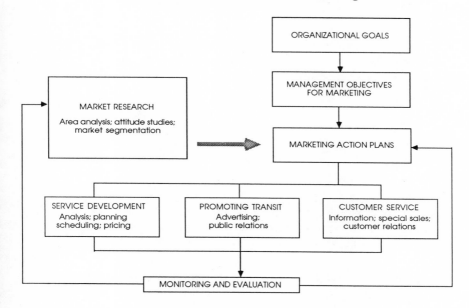

A systems approach to marketing that includes objectives, market research, implementation, and monitoring of results is recommended.

plan into a development and evaluation cycle consistent with the strategic approach to management.

Recognition for the role of the driver in marketing is essential. Drivers control the quality of service and should be trained so that they can provide reliable information to patrons. Too often they are neither asked to comment on service plans nor given explanations for proposed service changes. They are insulated from these decisions by the hierarchical structure of most agencies but must bear the brunt of customer reactions. Allowing employees to participate in planning will increase their satisfaction with work, their acceptance of change, and their willingness to communicate service and marketing plans to customers. Patrons are influenced by the employees with whom they interact. After frequency and reliability of service and fares, driver attitude is the most important attribute determining patron attitudes toward bus travel (Fielding, Blankenship, and Tardiff, 1976).

Marketing in Nonprofit Agencies. Although public transit adopts techniques from private organizations, marketing public transit is more like marketing in nonprofit agencies for several reasons:

1. Transit sells a service rather than a product.
2. Transit is a service for which demand varies during the day and a service that cannot be held in inventory: An empty seat on one run cannot be stored for later use.
3. The profit motive is replaced by a multiplicity of objectives, many of which do not involve meeting the needs of patrons.
4. Transit serves more than one public; there are regular users, occasional users, and nonuser supporters.

Management must be concerned about the image presented to the nonuser public and governmental organizations on which transit relies. As Lovelock and Weinberg (1978) have explained, the multiple objectives and political context of transit make it similar to marketing for county hospitals, libraries, and public universities. Too often management adopts procedures from private-sector firms without realizing how marketing in nonprofit firms and public agencies should differ in order to be successful.

Promotional activities still dominate, with too little attention given to the development of transit services that can be produced efficiently. This is evident in the way in which marketing funds are allocated by transit agencies. Expenditures on marketing vary from agency to agency and appear to be unrelated to operating expenditures, fare revenue, or patronage. For example, Santa Clara County in northern California spends ten cents on advertising for every passenger, San Antonio four cents, and Chicago less than one-half cent. The average for eighteen systems in 1983 was three cents (Booth, 1986). The absence of consistent relationships suggests that comparative planning is not used.

Little attention is given to customer loyalty. Fare and pass programs seldom reward repeated use by allowing additional (free) use during the midday and weekends when transit is uncrowded. Discounts for younger users and for those who are newly employed or completing their education are not used for a marketing purpose. These customers represent potential replacements for the existing core ridership of central city workers. Their allegiance needs to be developed while they are reliant on transit; they should *not* be treated as cheap riders to whom the oldest equipment is allocated.

If transit is to become more self-sufficient, agencies must pay more attention to groups that use transit regularly or are likely to do so. Quality of service is important; for example, riders want fast, reliable service, and they want seats to be available, even during rush hours. But transit service is delivered by many different employees under varying conditions, and management must recognize that it is unlikely to remain consistent. To counter this situation, transit agencies must give special attention to customer services so that trained representatives can sensitively respond to passenger inquiries and comments.

Reliable data on service quality are difficult to obtain. For this reason, the integrated structure for marketing outlined in Figure 11 includes market research monitoring and evaluation at each step. Data should be collected on patronage responses to service and fare changes, so that market research can use past experience to evaluate alternative strategies. Data collection is expensive, but Everett and Watson (1982) have demonstrated how powerful marketing research procedures can be developed with high-quality data.

Organizing for Marketing. An agency that wants to implement a comprehensive approach to marketing must be prepared to use a marketing perspective throughout the organization. A team approach that emphasizes shared responsibility is required. Action plans that originate from the desires of specific market segments must be evaluated with respect to the cost of providing the desired services. Managers of finance and personnel must also be involved when decisions involve changes in fares and/or service level. Coordination between top management is again essential to ensure that market-oriented decisions are conveyed to supervisors and drivers. It is a top-down, strategic process that requires a sharing of responsibility among the upper hierarchy of management and a clear identification of organizational goals, objectives, and policies to guide all employees.

Two important requirements for successful team management are (1) establishment of marketing objectives that represent the goals of the agency and (2) identification of indicators with which to monitor performance against these objectives. Such clear delineation of goals and objectives is seldom evident in public transit agencies in contrast to private ones. The latter know precisely their purpose—to increase their share of the transportation market and make a reasonable return on investment. Employees in public transit agencies seldom understand how their work relates to organizational objectives. As a result, good marketing programs are often frustrated by employees who have not been trained to recognize the relationship between their performance and the achievement of marketing objectives.

The framework for transit performance analysis provided in Chapter Four forms the basis for measuring achievement of marketing objectives. Indicators are listed for measuring transit effectiveness, and these can be adapted to action plans in marketing. For example, an action plan that seeks to increase ridership to a specific industrial or commercial area could measure the number of employees using transit frequently, infrequently, or not at all before and after the marketing program. Monitoring market penetration is another way of assessing achievements. Measurements such as the number of households whose members use transit more than once a week provide a method for evaluating market penetration. Several other indicators have also proven useful in evaluating transit marketing programs:

- Passenger trips per revenue vehicle hour
- Passenger revenue per revenue vehicle hour
- Ratio of revenue to cost for designated service
- Number of persons in frequent-user households using transit
- Passenger trips per population group.

Some people are dependent on transit, others are not. Some locations are well served, others are not. Transit is convenient for some trips, but for others, such as grocery shopping, it is not, and for many people transit is too slow. Groups of people who respond differently to transit ought to be considered separately when an agency develops and markets service. Rather than considering potential users as a uniform group, market segmentation disaggregates consumers on the basis of needs and desires. If a group is large enough to be worth the effort, a transit agency will develop services responsive to its perceived needs. The key principle is to identify target markets, determine their needs, and develop marketing plans that respond to them.

Market Segmentation

Marketing programs should be adapted to groups of people who are differentiated in terms of use of transit, demographic characteristics, trip purpose, and decision-making constraints. Market segmentation begins with personal factors (transit availability and current travel behavior) and links these with trip purpose, constraints, and attributes of service. This, the most widely used approach in marketing, is similar to political polling. Instead of predicting voting behavior, however, it predicts what proportion of the population will travel by transit and identifies those attributes salient to each market segment. Information is obtained by telephone interviews, and responses are further disaggregated by individual characteristics. For example, households are selected for interview by locational characteristics, and the respondents are further identified by sex, age, life-style, and other personal factors.

Another type of survey begins with current travel behavior by asking whether the individual and his or her household use transit service. The user group is further subdivided into frequent and occasional users, whereas the nonuser group is subdivided into nonusers and likely users. Then demographic, attitudinal, and awareness information is obtained for users and likely users. This method has the advantage of focusing attention on the frequent users, who are usually less than 5 to 7 percent of the population. These are transit's customers—the people whose attitudes, travel needs, and responses are important to management. Far too much attention has been paid to the infrequent user and to the nonuser in the vain hope that transit will be able to recapture a significant portion of urban travel. This is unlikely, for even in the period when auto travel was curtailed by gasoline shortages, car pools were a far more popular alternative than transit.

Unless transit agencies adopt marketing strategies to satisfy the needs of these regular customers, transit's proportional share of urban travel will continue to shrink. Even in the period of transit's renaissance between 1970 and 1980, the number of work trips made by public transport declined in most major metropolitan areas. It is therefore essential that marketing research plans give high priority to discovering who the regular customers are. After that, planners can segment these customers into groups, each with its own constraints and preferences. After segmentation, a series of action programs can be designed to suit each segment. In other words, the marketing function should help determine what services will be produced, how they will be scheduled and priced, and how the changes will be promoted to achieve the desired response. The frequent user cannot be regarded as a captive patron. The automobile will continue to compete with transit, and transit must satisfy the needs and desires of its regular customers in those markets in which transit enjoys a comparative advantage.

Transit Markets. There are two principal markets for transit. First, there are commuters who make the work trip from suburb to central city. Personal automobiles are usually available for this trip, but commuters can be attracted to transit by providing them with seats in a clean, comfortable environment on reliable express service using exclusive rights-of-way. But even if this level of service is available, the suburban commuter will choose to drive alone or in a car pool if subsidized parking is available and there are no congested areas to traverse. The second market is the autoless traveler. This person is most likely to be of low income, elderly, or a student and not making a work-related trip. This market segment prefers reliable, low-cost, local service with frequent stops that operates throughout the day.

Choice of transit for each group will be determined by many variables. Trip purpose is important: people making work trips can usually be attracted to transit if their total travel time is less than forty-five minutes. Shopping trips are seldom made by transit because it is difficult to carry purchases onto buses and trains while fumbling for the fare. Recreational trips are also difficult to make on transit. These often involve several destinations and irregular travel schedules. Long trips will seldom be made on transit because it is too slow; a bus traveling congested local streets usually averages no more than ten to twelve miles per hour during peak periods.

Segmentation allows the marketing professional to disaggregate the potential market and select the service development program, the promotional plan, and the customer service strategy best suited to each market segment. San Francisco's BART divides rider groups according to frequency of use to determine service development strategies. A survey conducted in 1974 indicated that BART was losing frequent riders because of service unreliability. Expansion of service and planned increases in train frequency were delayed until the technical problems in train control were solved. During this period, marketing efforts concentrated on retaining existing riders rather than trying to attract new riders.

Because a large percentage of the public is unlikely to use transit, it is more efficient to confine marketing efforts to those segments that are most likely to respond to them and to make the effort commensurate with the likely response. For this reason, it is proposed that market segmentation be conducted before service is developed (Figure 11). Many transit operators use this strategy. For example, in Milwaukee market segmentation has been used to improve customer services. By analyzing relationships between age of patron, trip purpose, and the use of different sources of information, rider segments were differentiated on the basis of need for customer information about service changes.

The Orange County Transit District began monitoring attitudes toward bus service in 1975. Twice each year, a stratified, random sample of 500 residents is selected for telephone interviews. The primary purpose of this survey is to determine the effectiveness of alternative forms of advertising. Sample opinions about proposed service and fare changes are also gathered. The results are then disaggregated into user, potential user, and nonuser households, as well as by demographic and area criteria. These surveys have helped in designing action plans aimed at inducing more members of frequent-user households to use the bus system.

Research on Attitudes. People vary in consistent ways in their attitudes toward public transit and whether they will or will not use it. Knowledge of these attitudes is required when an agency is developing and promoting service for different markets. Many studies of attitudes toward transportation were conducted during the late 1960s and early 1970s. Some were intended to expand demand modeling by providing a behavioral element; others examined attitudes toward transportation improvements. Wachs (1976) reviewed a number of these studies to determine consumer attitudes toward transit service and reached these conclusions:

1. While most operating improvements attempt to reduce in-vehicle travel time, travel-time reliability (schedule reliability) may be a more important factor than total elapsed travel time in determining consumer response to transit improvements.
2. Portions of travel devoted to waiting, walking, and transferring (out-of-vehicle time) are more onerous than time spent actually moving in vehicles.
3. Fare reductions are probably less important than travel time.
4. Raising auto tolls or parking fees may be more effective inducements to transit ridership than small reductions in transit fares.
5. Amenity levels are not important except for temperature control (that is, heating and air conditioning) and assurance of seating.

Three other attitude-related dimensions must also be considered in marketing transit:

1. Permanence of service and regularity of departure times are important because these help patrons to remember the network and reduce reliance on schedules and route maps.
2. Attitude of operating employees is important because they can provide reliable information to occasional users.

3. Attitude of frequent users is important because new riders often obtain information from them.

Evaluation Research. Marketing programs benefit from the monitoring of results from action plans. Monitoring should begin in advance of implementation and continue during implementation so that unintended consequences can be corrected. However, such longitudinal research designs are seldom used in transit marketing research. The case studies and the comparative designs that prevail lack precision and internal validity because the effects of alternative influences are not ruled out. Everett and Watson (1982) outline three types of research design: preexperimental surveys, quasi-experimental surveys (where the marketing professional cannot exercise adequate control over the setting), and valid experiments. Selection of design is determined by the manner in which research questions will be framed and the intended use of the results.

Although experimental precision is beyond the capacity of most agencies, it is important to recognize the need for sophistication in market research and not generalize from results obtained from nonexperimental situations. Useful marketing information can be obtained by adopting a quasi-experimental strategy that

- Implements data collection strategies that remain stable over time
- Designs action plans to solve problems and monitor the results
- Implements new programs incrementally
- Uses a monitoring strategy that modifies the program where necessary and determines whether it ought to be abandoned or expanded.

When there are sufficient funds for valid experimental studies, these should be undertaken with the assistance of consultants. When funds are limited, a less ambitious strategy, such as the incremental strategy, can be used. In every instance, data should be collected in a consistent manner because the results are often useful in other contexts, such as measuring service and price elasticities of demand.

Service Development

Ideally, marketing specialists should have a direct influence on the planning of transit operations. However, it is not uncommon for operations to be planned, implemented, or changed without the advice of a marketing department, leaving it the task of explaining the new service to the public. If operations personnel dominate service development, an integrated marketing plan cannot succeed. Agencies with this philosophy should content themselves with an advertising and public relations program.

To be useful for service development, market segmentation should be sophisticated enough to distinguish among population groups that reside in different sectors of the city. It should also be able to suggest a range of alternative service improvements that would satisfy their needs. Alternatives should then be evaluated on the basis of cost and the ability of the agency to supply the service, because the extent of service desired in any urban region always exceeds the fiscal capacity of transit agencies. For example, many attitude studies indicate that elderly central city residents prefer demand-responsive service. However, few agencies can afford to provide such a high level of public service or possess the small vehicles and computer-controlled dispatching capability needed for demand-responsive service. Demand-responsive paratransit service can serve the needs of the handicapped in central cities more efficiently than can buses fitted with lifts and rapid transit stations equipped with elevators, but it is not an efficient mode for the mobile elderly and other users (Rosenbloom, 1981).

To ensure that service options are carefully evaluated for cost effectiveness and practicality, marketing should be assigned to the manager responsible for service development. When this is not feasible, coordination must be encouraged by the general manager. A cooperative working relationship between operations and marketing is essential. Little is accomplished when marketing promotes service on a designated route, saturates adjoining neighborhoods with schedules and route maps, and then learns that the operations division plans to increase the headway by five minutes or, worse still, alter the route at the next service change.

Marketing that focuses on trip attractors rather than generators is easier to coordinate with operations. High-potential transit attractors should be targeted and a program of service improvements and marketing developed so that each receives attention when funds and equipment are available. Shopping centers, educational institutions, and industrial centers are potential target attractors. Marketing programs should begin with market analysis and then proceed with route analysis and proposed service improvements. New schedules and route signs should be included, and the program should culminate with promotions jointly funded by the transit agency and firms in the target market. Development of the entire sequence requires from sixteen to eighteen months. Even then, a prudent marketing manager will allow two or three weeks for the service to "shake down" before launching the full promotional effort.

Marketing professionals who can translate specialized research methods and results into information understandable to the rest of the organization gain a degree of acceptance because they are then seen and accepted as part of the management team. Focusing on areas where service is already deployed, knowing which service characteristics are salient to the patrons, asking operations how these characteristics might be improved, and then promoting the improvement and monitoring the results are the elements of a successful strategy.

Pricing Transit. Because passenger revenue is vital for matching state and federal funds, responsibility for fare policy is often assigned to the financial department. This is a mistake because it leads to uniform fare policies that are designed to cover deficits rather than fare policies that market service to user segments. Responsibility for pricing should be shared with those knowledgeable about consumer response. Market segments differ in their response to fares, and an effective service development plan should use fares to influence consumer demand in addition to generating revenue.

Fares should reflect the value of the trip to the customer, as well as the cost of providing service. For example, customers place a higher value on a trip to work than on a shopping trip. And because peak-hour, work trips are more costly to provide, higher fares can be justified. Considerable experience has been gained about responses to fare changes on the part of different market segments. But this information, which is summarized in Table 6, is seldom used. Response to fare changes tends to be predicted by using the industry-wide rule of thumb about price elasticity (there will be a 3 percent reduction for each 10 percent increase in fares) rather than by examining the probable impact on different market segments. Elasticity of demand should be calculated separately for each segment with local data collected to verify industry-wide estimates. Monitoring each fare change provides information to improve an agency's strategic intelligence. Only when local data are inadequte should price elasticities from other areas be used to predict probable magnitudes of change.

Unwillingness to utilize information about market elasticities is due primarily to the emotional response to fare changes. Authority to set fares is normally delegated to appointed or elected boards of directors. Opposition to increased fares comes primarily from lower-income residents who are dependent on transit. Issues such as elasticity of demand and market segmentation receive short shrift during emotional public hearings in which equity overwhelms all other considerations. The result is that uniform fares tend to be adopted regardless of their consequences. In Chapter Five, under the section on increasing revenue, it was explained that uniform fares neither maintain ridership nor maximize revenue. These policies discourage marginal riders (recent converts to transit who will soon return to their cars) and levy inequitable burdens upon those who are transit dependent. The persistence of such fare policies illustrates the frustration transit managers must endure when they choose to manage strategically.

The political nature of setting fare policies prevents its use as a flexible service development strategy. When budgets do not balance, it is far easier to curtail frequency or alter hours of operation than to increase fares. Yet the inability of service changes alone to decrease operating deficits means that there will have to be more attention paid to fare policies in the future. Managers must learn to confront these issues even though they are politically unpalatable. Forecasting the need for future fare increases is a helpful strategy, and relating them to cost for different types of service lessens the controversy. Basing recommendations on local observations is preferred, but where local data are insufficient, extrapolating from responses to fare changes observed elsewhere and adjusting them to reflect local conditions can help policy makers think strategically about fare policy.

Pass Sales and Incentives. Another way to market transit is with prepaid passes. Requiring patrons to pay exact fares has created major problems for transit ever since rising crime rates made the need for them apparent. To offset the disadvantages of such fares, most agencies have introduced prepaid tickets and passes. However, neither the potential revenue losses nor the advantages of passes as a marketing device have been examined by most transit agencies.

Transit operators tend to lose revenue from unlimited-use passes. Doxsey (1984) suggests that only patrons who attach considerable weight to the convenience of holding a pass, and little weight to the inconvenience of obtaining it and possibly losing it, buy passes. These patrons anticipate that the value of trips taken will exceed the cost of purchasing passes. The trips taken are estimated to exceed break-even rates by 25 percent in small cities and 45 percent in New York, Chicago, and Los Angeles. The problem is less troublesome for the new rapid transit systems where magnetic fare cards and turnstile entry and exit allow payment based directly on distance traveled and frequency of use. However, bus systems and older rail systems lose money when they issue unrestricted passes, and their fraudulent use often causes embarrassment to public officials. They are also disliked by drivers and ticket collectors because they make fare evasion too easy.

Using passes as a marketing concept tailored to service type and targeted to market segments is advocated by Oram (1983) as an alternative to unlimited plans. He lists the following actions for pricing and marketing pass programs:

1. Restrict the use of the pass to periods of the day (off peak) or to special segments (commuting workers or students).

2. Design passes for market segments and price passes according to the cost of providing the type of service desired.
3. Involve employers in selling and subsidizing passes to offset some of the benefits of free parking.
4. Involve merchants who will provide discounts for bus pass holders in return for promotional inserts and advertising on passes.
5. Set prices for passes relatively high and use introductory and targeted discounts for promotion. If riders do not respond, discontinue the pass.

Coupon discounts targeted at new patrons or promoted as occasional rewards for regular patrons are used in grocery sales, and airlines provide frequent-flier bonuses. Oram recommends that transit imitate such private-sector marketing techniques rather than maintain discounted prices as an incentive for the sale of the unlimited-use pass.

None of his five suggestions is new, and several are already in use. In Bridgeport, Connecticut, for example, three passes were introduced: a commuter pass for the peak-only user; a "fare cutter card" that is valid at all times but requires patrons to pay an additional fare of twenty-five cents instead of the 1983 base fare of sixty cents; and tokens for occasional users. Duluth, Minnesota, offers a fare cutter card that can be used during off-peak hours but requires an additional fare during peak hours. Spokane, Washington, and SCRTD in Los Angeles provide merchant discounts that in some instances more than compensate for the cost of bus travel. The Bridgeport pass program is unique in that the marketing department has carefully analyzed the market for transit and designed a range of pass programs and incentives to attract new users and encourage regular riders to use transit more frequently without a financial loss to the agency. Bridgeport offers an excellent example of a transit agency that dared to experiment with different marketing programs and conscientiously monitored the results. Not all programs were successful; for example, the commuter pass was abandoned after six months. But each innovation has provided the Bridgeport transit agency with new information that has enabled it to manage more strategically.

Promoting Transit

Marketing is confused with promotion in many transit agencies. Although promotion is only one of several marketing functions, it is an important one and should be used to communicate service characteristics to potential riders. Promotional managers need knowledge about market segments, organizational objectives, and service development to promote ridership through advertising and public relations. Linkage to a marketing plan is also essential because there are so many ways in which transit can be promoted.

The transit marketing demonstration in Nashville, Tennessee, was coordinated around a plan to promote the introduction of new and expanded bus services. Radio commercials, route maps, schedules, and news releases were prepared and placed with this objective in mind. Using information gained from market segmentation studies, marketing employees targeted groups along selected travel corridors for saturation coverage after the new service had been introduced and was operating satisfactorily. The entire program was monitored at predetermined intervals through rider responses and personal interviews.

In the ideal situation, transit service is fully developed or improved before promotion begins. But this ideal is seldom attained, and many programs fail because the service does not perform as advertised. Inaugurating new service or raising reliability levels is a lengthy process. Public relations efforts should be mounted to explain these difficulties to patrons, and major promotional campaigns should be waged *after* service has been introduced and is operating smoothly.

Advertising transit is always controversial because it expands the use of public transit, and because additional customers seldom pay their full cost, they create the need for additional governmental assistance. Hiring an advertising firm can alleviate this problem. The firm develops copy and recommends media tactics that keep the agency from appearing to want to influence consumer behavior. However, before choosing an advertising firm, those responsible for marketing must decide to whom the transit agency is trying to sell service and whether or not the type of service that targeted groups desire can be provided. Additionally, there must be answers to these questions: How much money is available for advertising, what should the timing be, how long will the advertising effort continue, and how should the results be monitored? Only when these questions have been answered and assembled as a marketing plan can a professional advertising agency develop copy, recommend media, and estimate costs.

Media advertising is not as effective as direct mail in targeting specific areas. BART in San Francisco found that 90 percent of its riders came from 15 percent of the census tracts in San Francisco. Direct mail was a more efficient means of reaching these frequent users and their neighbors. In cases where routes and schedules are to be changed in bus systems, the target population usually lives within two or three blocks of the route. Inserting new schedules into doorknob bags and paying people to deliver them constitute an effective means of reaching this group. Inclusion of complimentary tickets is a successful tactic where service is new, and it also provides a means of monitoring the response. Procedures to maximize the benefits of these inducements have been explained by Everett and Watson (1982) and should be examined by every transit agency.

Trade-outs and cross promotions are useful procedures for transit agencies. A trade-out is a transaction in which the transit agency provides advertising on a bus or bus bench to other media in exchange for time on radio or television or space in a newspaper to promote transit. This is an effective method in large metropolitan areas where advertising is expensive and difficult to target. Community newspapers and local radio stations willingly engage in trade outs if it can be shown that such exchanges help them to develop a local market. Seattle Metro has gone further and provides traffic information to local radio stations from its radio-equipped buses in exchange for advertising time.

Cross promotions are similar to the merchant discounts discussed under pricing. A fast-food chain will often pay to have its advertising printed on transfers and passes and can usually be persuaded to provide discount incentives. Some transit agencies work with major events such as a circus. They place circus advertising on bus cards and fare passes in exchange for 1,000 or so circus tickets. These are then offered as a promotional device by the transit agency.

Free publicity should not be overlooked as an advertising technique. As a public, nonprofit enterprise that enjoys broad community support, transit can obtain excellent coverage through news releases. Board meetings at which significant developments will be considered should be described in advance as a means of fostering a progressive public image. Care should be taken to have the media describe the agency's point of view when it is proposing to increase fares or reduce service. This is the time when a marketing department that understands the marginal cost of providing different types of service and fare elasticities can set forth the facts before controversy clouds the issue. Market research has shown repeatedly that lack of information discourages occasional use of transit. Controversial events offer an opportunity not only to advance a point of view but also to provide reliable information on services available. Tri Met in Portland has always used this technique skillfully. During a driver strike, for example, it promoted a car pool matching service. The agency was thus able to direct attention away from the controversial labor negotiations and develop support for an alternative mode that has subsequently allowed it to reduce long-distance, peak-only service.

Customer Services

Transit management's failure to attend to consumer needs is especially apparent in customer services. In a period of increasing costs and declining governmental assistance, management has been relatively indifferent to boosting demand by improving the quality of service. Basic user information in the form of timetables, system maps, bus-stop signs, and signs on buses themselves are seldom coordinated as to their message, graphic treatment, and color. They should be simple, legible, and easily understandable, and they should have priority in any marketing budget because there is no sense in advertising services that people do not understand how to use. Telephone information centers in transit agencies are ineptly managed when compared with those operated by airlines. These centers seldom take advantage of the latest developments in communications and computer technology.

Worse still is the attitude toward the patron that management has allowed drivers and station personnel to exhibit. The problem is not that management does not wish to motivate employees to be more "customer oriented." Rather, employee allegiance is divided between management and the union, with the result that supervisory emphasis is placed on maintaining schedules, even though this may mean that drivers ignore passenger questions, do not insist on correct fares, skip stops, and splash pedestrians as they try to make up time. Only by changing the driver's attitude can these problems be overcome. Drivers need to be self-supervising and to feel responsible for the level of service provided. They must be trained to recognize that, like management, they have a stake in the welfare of the agency. Attitudes like these are difficult to foster; it requires skill and considerable effort on the part of managers. Managerial objectives must be conveyed to vehicle operators during training and maintained by incentives throughout an operator's career. There are some very good examples of employee involvement in agencies where management and labor have learned to cooperate. But generating such involvement requires a change to a more open, participatory style that is uncharacteristic of American transit management.

Training and Rewards. The best examples here come from private transit. Before its bus operations were sold, Greyhound Corporation used market research to obtain customers' reactions to different classifications of employees—drivers, desk clerks, and baggage handlers. Complaints were also analyzed for patterns of behavior. These results were used in employee-training programs so that the problems could be corrected. Employees were encouraged to improve overall passenger service by incentive programs based on customer response to the entire work force at a terminal rather than to individual employees. Everybody who worked at a given facility, from telephone information operators to baggage clerks and drivers, was rated by a published achievement matrix. By rating each terminal as a unit, the company encouraged cooperation within and competition between terminals. Winners in the Greyhound Gold program select their rewards from a catalogue with the level of the awards for individuals determined by the terminal manager.

DAVE Systems, which operates thirty-eight transit systems under contract to local agencies, bases its training on programmed learning. Cassettes, videotapes, and personal instruction are combined in a progressive sequence, not only to help with vehicle training but also to instill an appreciation for the importance of service. Since many of DAVE's patrons are elderly, the course includes stress and empathy training and provides techniques for dealing with frail patrons. Once training is completed, all employees are encouraged to obtain Red Cross and CPR certification. DAVE provides employee incentives that are based on employee understanding of the training and on the recommendations of clientele.

Recognition in Public Agencies. Employee morale is a problem in most public transit agencies. Work is repetitive, there are few opportunities for advancement, it is difficult to define unsatisfactory performance, and there are obstacles to rewarding public employees without appearing to be making a gift of public funds. The CENTRO system in Syracuse, New York, has approached this last problem by providing psychological rewards. Management has attempted to improve the employees' self-image by placing emphasis on personal esteem. Employees are encouraged to conceive of their jobs as professions and of themselves as professionals who take personal pride in high-quality performance. The system provides employees with well-tailored uniforms, as well as with briefcases in which to carry schedules and operating reports.

The Metropolitan Transit Commission (MTC) in the Twin Cities uses status as an incentive for superior performance by coach operators and combines this with vacation incentives. The need for employee development became apparent when absenteeism and poor fleet maintenance were causing more than sixty trips to be missed each day. The first step was to obtain the union's agreement for all employees to participate in an attitude survey. The results revealed that employees wanted involvement in decision making, recognition for superior performance, discipline for unsatisfactory behavior, and more helpful supervision. These employees generally liked their supervisors but not the way they supervised. The general manager has noted that the results of the survey were at first quite unsettling to him and other long-term managers (Olsen, 1983). However, the survey clearly helped to change management's approach to supervision of personnel.

The results of the survey were discussed by employee-management committees. These committees, which function like quality circles, have continued in the maintenance and administrative sections where cooperative effort is essential. For the drivers, a plan was developed that recognized the need for self-management and provided a tangible reward—additional vacation leave—for reliable, safe, and courteous operation. Meritorious service is recognized annually as it is in many transit agencies, but MTC provides additional incentives for operators who perform well year after year. They are recognized by Distinguished, Master, and Senior Driver awards.

A Distinguished Driver must have: (1) no more than two sick occurrences during the year; (2) no more than one chargeable request off (as defined in the driver absenteeism policy) during the year; (3) no more than ten days away from work due to sick occurrences and the requests off combined; (4) zero "no shows" during the year; (5) zero chargeable accidents during the year; (6) no more than one nonchargeable accident during the year; and (7) neither chargeable passenger complaints nor written warnings or suspensions during the year. Criteria for achieving Master or Senior Driver status are progressive. To become a Master Driver, an operator must achieve Distinguished Driver status five times, not necessarily consecutively. To become a Senior Driver, an operator must achieve Distinguished Driver status ten times (again, not necessarily consecutively). Recognition, cash awards, and vacation benefits are progressive. It is also intended that the Master and Senior Drivers will assume peer roles in MTC, although they will not necessarily move on to become supervisors. Results from the employee development program in MTC are impressive: missed trips have been reduced, supervisors who could not adapt to the cooperative approach were reassigned, and the union has continued to cooperate by supporting disciplinary action against employees whose failures caused unreliable or unsafe service.

It had been anticipated that only 10 percent of the drivers would achieve Distinguished Driver awards in the first year. In fact, some 26 percent of the drivers achieved the award, and most have maintained this standard for their second year. It appears that workplace democracy can improve organizational effectiveness in transit. As the idea spreads, it will have an important influence on customer service and consumer response.

Marketing Plans

The state of the art in transit marketing is generally unsophisticated. While there are scattered instances in which one or the other of the activities described in this chapter is conducted at a sophisticated level, they seldom, if ever, exist as an integrated marketing plan linked to strategic objectives as outlined in Figure 11. Marketing should be everyone's business, not a separate responsibility of one unit. Plans should be organized so that they are consistent with agency goals and objectives. Programs should begin with research based on market segmentation and then proceed with analysis of service development, service refinement, and pricing at the sector and route level. Coordination with service development is essential. Changes should be promoted through appropriate media that broadcast messages salient to target groups. Promotion must be coordinated with the development of user aids: timetables, maps, bus-stop signs, and signs on the vehicles. Advertising should be a joint undertaking of the transit agency and firms in the area that will benefit from service improvement.

Employee involvement is essential. For most passengers, operating employees represent the agency. When employees feel involved and recognize a mutual interest with management in passenger welfare, they perform better and gain a sense of self-fulfillment in doing so. Training programs should be expanded to emphasize interpersonal relations, knowledge of the system, and marketing. Supervision and incentive programs must encourage superior performance rather than focus on punctuality and adherence to schedules.

Monitoring of marketing effectiveness must be an integral part of the marketing plan. Action plans for service development, promotion, and customer service can be evaluated using the performance measures described in Chapter Four. Effectiveness indicators will be the most useful. However, cost cannot be overlooked. Cost-effectiveness indicators such as net cost per additional passenger or marketing cost divided by fare revenue are helpful when measuring achievements over time or assessing the performance of one agency against that of peer-group agencies.

10

Managing the Political Environment and Responding to Constituencies

Politics in transit is similar to politics in other domains of urban policy. Issues are decided through competition between interest groups. Administration is facilitated when managers understand that groups with more resources, more skills, and/or positional advantages tend to prevail. Such principles are useful to management when working with outside groups, when soliciting community support for policy changes, when establishing relations with boards of directors, or when negotiating with state and federal administrators.

Strategic management does not normally focus on political concerns, but transit agencies have become so dependent on assistance from external sources that their strategic future is now closely bound up with maintenance of favorable relations with financial partners. An important first step in strategic management is assessment of the expectations of constituent groups (Figure 2). This includes monitoring national, state, and local expectations and conducting community relations in ways that will elicit support from customers and politically influential groups.

This chapter focuses on the political nature of administrative decisions. Although successful administrators always emphasize the primary role of their governing board, policies enacted by governing boards are usually so general that administrators must make decisions on when, where, and how policies will be implemented. These decisions are essentially political because they impact different groups differently. When the strategic approach is followed, management will be aware of the attitudes toward transit held by different groups and will be able to anticipate their responses and tailor implementation to minimize opposition or to build a constituency of support. The ability to manage the political environment is essential for public administrators. In transit, this skill is most apparent in community relations, but it is also required when developing support for federal and state legislation.

Transit Constituency

Transit employees, mayors of large cities, and transit managers often find themselves to be political allies, because each has a stake in the passage of legislation favorable to public transit. However, these groups cannot prevail by themselves. Their constituency must be enlarged by identifying the need for transit as a problem shared by other groups. Success in building constituencies is now evident at all levels of government. At the federal and state levels these constituencies have lobbied for increased transit assistance, and at the local level for the adoption of routes and the funding of rapid transit projects.

Central city business associations support transit improvements because rapid transit reduces the travel time costs for suburban residents and enlarges the service area for the CBD. Similar views are shared by metropolitan news media, so that transit has enjoyed generally favorable reporting. Suburban business associations have not been so supportive; they prefer highway improvements. However, with the emergence of suburban business centers such as Tyson's Corner in northern Virginia, City Post Oaks near Houston, and South Coast Plaza and Newport Center in southern California, which have congestion and parking problems as serious as those found in central cities, attitudes have begun to change. These suburban centers joined the transit constituency in 1982 to support a five-cent increase in the federal gasoline tax for highway and transit purposes.

Community Leaders. Prominent individuals in the community often influence the formulation of transit policy and aid in the building of support constituencies. Management of transportation agencies cannot be understood without an appreciation of the role of community leaders. Although their influence is most apparent in the development of new systems, it is also present in ongoing management decisions. Board members of transit agencies often seek the guidance of community leaders and they are able to influence the deployment of service and the selection of suppliers of goods and professional services.

San Francisco's BART would never have been built had it not been for the dedication of executives from major corporations. They contributed the time, money, and skill that initiated the planning and financing studies and then used their positions to persuade local officials and the news media to support these plans. Completed in 1972 at a cost of $1.6 billion, the seventy-one-mile BART system was the forerunner of new rail systems in Atlanta, Baltimore, Washington, D.C., and Miami. Although originally criticized for cost overruns and poor service, BART is now providing reliable service, attracting more than 212,000 weekday passengers on average, and covering 47 percent of its operating costs from revenues. By current standards, BART is a success. Those policy critics who had advocated commuter bus routes instead of rail rapid transit in the mid 1970s are now quiet.

BART originated in the 1950s when automobile ownership was rapidly expanding. Community leaders in the central city feared decentralization and sought ways to improve access between the suburbs and downtown. For this reason BART was planned as "a high-speed, futuristic mode that would transport commuters in luxurious comfort without economic pain" (Webber 1976, p. 37). It also provided the rationale for removal of the commuter rail tracks from the lower level of the San Francisco-Oakland Bay Bridge. Removal of these tracks in 1958—fifteen years before the BART transbay tube was opened—reduced traffic congestion on the bridge. Motorists and truckers traveling from East Bay cities benefited from this step, and cities such as Berkeley, which had opposed removal of the Key System tracks, were promised a superior replacement that would be paid for in part by bridge tolls.

Community leaders enthusiastically participated in the planning studies conducted between 1949 and 1962. For example, the Bay Area Council, an association of prominent executives, established a three-man committee on rapid transit in 1950. All three of these members were executives of leading banks. They endorsed plans that would encourage central city development through construction of a high-speed commuter system oriented to the outlying suburbs.

In November 1962, voters, by a 61 percent margin, approved a $792 million bond issue for construction of the system. This vote just barely achieved the 60 percent margin then required by California to obligate bonded indebtedness against real property. Because the BART District as yet had no staff, business leaders played a prominent role in organizing and promoting the legislation. There was no effective opposition, and business leaders, public officials, and the three major newspapers worked together to sell rapid transit to the voters.

Virtually every major contributor in the effort to build BART had a vested interest in the outcome and later received either direct or indirect benefits from rapid transit: "Bank of America, Crocker Citizens Bank, and Wells Fargo Bank each contributed undisclosed sums of money. All three banks later built their high-rise headquarters near rapid transit stations. Bank of America also received large commissions for handling BART construction bonds worth almost a billion dollars. The members of the joint venture, Parsons, Brinkerhoff, Tudor, and Bechtel, contributed a total of $27,500. This joint venture later received a lucrative $100 million engineering contract for the system. Of the ten largest BART construction contracts, half involved firms which contributed to Citizens for Rapid Transit.

"Rapid transit was endorsed by the Bay Area Council, the chambers of commerce of San Francisco, Oakland, and several other communities, and numerous associations of merchants, business-men, property owners, realtors, and builders" (Fong, 1976 p. 14).

Even the highway lobbyists—a consortium of community leaders that includes automobile distributors, petroleum refiners, automobile clubs, and general contractors—have come to support transit. Initially they had opposed sharing revenues derived from gasoline taxes, but they relented in 1973 when it became apparent that they needed the support of transit to overcome opposition to the Federal Aid Highway Act. Opposition to transit is not nationally organized. Conservatives frequently object to federal and state expenditures for transit in the belief that it should be supported by fares. However, they have never proposed a realistic way to amortize capital expenses so that transit could compete on an equal footing with automobiles. Transit could achieve a higher level of self-support were conservatives to support introduction of road tolls that reflected the cost of constructing roads to handle peak demands. Theories on road pricing are popular with neoconservatives but are seldom adopted by elected officials who share their viewpoints.

Opposition to Taxes for Transit. Serious opposition occurs when a local authority asks voters to approve increased taxes for transit. In part, this is a reaction stimulated by the taxpayer revolts of the late 1970s. However, it is also a reaction by voters against paying in advance for transportation improvements. Voters dislike proposals for future public improvements that entail a direct private cost for which individual taxpayers perceive little short-term benefit. Even transit patrons seldom support transit taxes. They want immediate service improvements and lower fares rather than long-term proposals for new forms of rapid transit. The strongest opposition usually comes from middle-income voters. In contrast, upper-middle-class voters whose preferences for an unpolluted environment and freedom from highway congestion take precedence over immediate concerns for jobs and taxes often support new transit proposals.

Houston, Texas, provides an instructive example of voter reaction to taxes for transit. The Houston metropolitan area grew rapidly in population between 1970 and 1980, and there was an even more rapid increase in automobile traffic. Population increased from 2 milion to 2.9 million, and vehicle miles traveled on freeways increased by 223 percent, while the rate at which transportation facilities were expanded was greatly reduced. The result was that, within the decade, Houston went from a city with excellent mobility to one of the most congested cities in the United States.

Three elections have been held in which transit solutions were proposed. These proposals were rejected in 1974 and 1983, but approved in 1978.

In 1973 a proposal to create a regional transit agency to salvage the failing private bus company was turned down by a three-to-one margin. The private system, which served less than half of Harris County, used an outdated radial network. Voters had not yet perceived highway congestion and energy conservation as problems, nor were they willing to approve a transit district whose funding would be based upon an automobile engine displacement tax. The city of Houston was then forced to take over the system in 1974 to prevent abandonment of routes needed by minority residents.

Concern over the effect of explosive population growth helped change opinions. In 1977 Harris County led the state in industrial and residential growth, in declines in air quality, and in the number of new vehicle registrations (an average of 411 a day) (Kliewer, 1978). Using provisions of legislation passed earlier that same year by the Texas legislature, the Metropolitan Transit Authority (MTA) was created, and the effort to persuade citizens to support transit commenced. A broad spectrum of community leaders and citizen groups participated: suburban commuters who were concerned about congestion, inner-city minorities who could not afford gasoline prices that had doubled in twelve months, and developers of downtown property who had not provided sufficient parking. These groups were asked to consider alternative plans and were then persuaded to support a countywide transportation plan to improve highways as well as transit.

A proposal to add a one-cent sales tax was submitted to the voters in August 1978 and passed by 57 percent. (It passed by a majority in Houston and in most communities in Harris County.) The plan was intentionally general. It focused on immediate improvements, including modernization of the bus fleet and conversion of freeway lanes for bus and van pools. A transitway network, elevated over freeway dividers, was planned, and the possibility of future conversion to rail transit was suggested.

The success of this plan in Houston astonished many, given the national tax revolt currently underway. However, volunteer supporters who were alarmed over increased automobile traffic had helped persuade potential voters, especially those in low-income and minority precincts, to vote for the sales tax. Effective citizen participation had created groups of well-informed supporters who volunteered to persuade friends and neighbors to vote for public transit. MTA moved quickly to implement the bus plan. Routes were reorganized and expanded, and a ten-mile-long contraflow bus and van pool lane was opened along Houston's heavily traveled North Freeway. But problems began to appear in the bus program. The existing fleet was old and mechanically vulnerable, and the fleet of 329 replacement buses proved extremely unreliable due to structural and mechanical problems. Management was ill prepared to cope with the promised service expansion; the fleet of 500 buses had to be maintained in a single, inadequate facility built in 1902 to service streetcars. MTA had promised more service than it could reliably deliver. Proposed improvements soon fell behind schedule, and management and the work force became demoralized when public opinion turned against them. In the summer of 1980 maintenance was so neglected that only one-half of the fleet was available for service. New buses were running with their windows removed because mechanics were unable to keep the air conditioning in service. Supporters of transit in Houston were embarrassed, and their allegiance was lost.

Cooperation between MTA and the Texas Department of Highway and Public Transportation had been more successful. Contraflow lanes on freeways had been opened and construction begun on the Katy Freeway (to the west) and the Gulf Freeway (to the southeast). Thirty miles of high-capacity transitways were planned, about one-half of which were under construction within five years of the election. Although the theoretical capacity of these lanes ranges between 30,000 to 40,000 persons per hour, this is far in excess of the projected 1995 demands of about 10,000 per hour. The projected demand can be accommodated in about 100 buses and 400 van pools. Therefore, it appears that development of the grade-separated lanes, together with the thirty-five park-and-ride lots, will be able to accommodate future travel demand.

Houston also made plans for rail transit. Rather than restricting itself to improving local bus service to complement availability of bus-on-freeway express service, MTA management launched a new ballot proposal to build a rail transit system. The one-cent sales tax proved to be a bountiful source of revenue. Sales tax revenue of $162 million in 1982 exceeded bus system operating costs by almost $64 million. Management saw this surplus as an opportunity to build rapid rail transit and chose to ignore federal opposition to new rail construction. It sought approval from the voters in 1983 for $2.35 billion in revenue bonds, to be repaid by the sales tax. However, the proposal was rejected by a two-to-one margin.

Voters rejected the proposal for many reasons. For example, it was estimated that the approximately eighteen-mile heavy rail system would cost $5.2 billion but that it would be many years before the benefits would be realized. The proposal assumed substantial federal capital assistance at a time when the Reagan administration had stated its opposition to funding new rail transit systems, voters were therefore concerned that they would have to pay the entire cost through additional taxes. Also, business leadership was not as supportive in 1983 as in 1978. These leaders had observed the success of the transitways and had organized van pool programs or encouraged employees to join commuter clubs. This solved commuting problems for workers more satisfactorily than the proposed rail system would have. Only 12 percent of those eligible voted, and turnout was especially poor in the predominantly black precincts northeast and south of the CBD. These areas, together with outlying affluent precincts, voted for the proposal, but not in sufficient numbers to offset the negative votes in the middle-income suburbs.

Two other voting patterns in Houston were typical of current electoral responses to transit issues. More liberal voters in the "univeristy corridor" to the south of the CBD voted in favor of the proposal, and Harris County towns outside of Houston, which were remote from the proposed rail system, voted overwhelmingly against it. The lesson from Houston that all administrators should heed is that it is middle-income voters who defeat transit tax proposals. This is because they are asked to bear a direct cost without commensurate benefits. It is easy for upper-income families and business leaders to suggest spending billions of dollars to construct new rail systems, but for the middle-income voter who seldom travels downtown, future transit improvements do nothing to meet his or her daily travel needs.

Two strategies can help offset the opposition of middle-income voters. First, lower-income voters can be mobilized. Promises of reduced bus fares and improved service were successful in Houston in 1978 as they were in Atlanta in 1971 and Los Angeles in 1980. In all three cities, lower-income voters went to the polls and overwhelmingly voted in favor of the taxes. Second, a strategy of combined highway and transit improvements can be presented. This strategy was successful for Houston in 1978 and for Santa Clara County in 1984. But this strategy is difficult to implement in most metropolitan areas because of the institutional separation between transit and highways. The strategy of involving low-income voters seems to be the most promising approach. However, the combined highway and transit strategy is the only option for suburban counties, which usually have few low-income voters.

Community Relations

Effective community relations help build a constituency for public transit. Every community includes groups with differing attitudes toward transit. There is neither a "power elite" that can impose its will nor a Democratic or Republican approach to transit. Opinions on major issues are formed gradually. They are influenced by the manner in which information is presented and by the views that community leaders such as corporate executives, elected officials, labor leaders, newspaper editors, church officials, and members of the League of Women Voters express about the issues. Too few managers appreciate the importance of community relations, and many sound proposals are rejected because management has failed to use strategies to convey information to the whole spectrum of affected interest groups.

Describing urban politics as an "ecology of games," Long (1958) has compared the way in which individuals join groups to support or oppose issues to the way in which children play games: one day they join one team and the next day another. For example, individuals who form a group to support public transit may find themselves on opposite sides of a public housing issue. Who wins or loses depends on how skillfully groups use their resources— money and/or time—to persuade local officials to endorse "their" point of view. There is no such thing as "the public interest." Rather there are many "interests," and the "public interest" is decided by elected or appointed officials in response to presentations by groups representing differing points of view. However, where there is intense competition between groups, officials seek compromise decisions. When they cannot reach a compromise, they prefer to put off the decision. Requesting another study is a favorite strategy used by elected officials to avoid making a decision when differences between community groups cannot be resolved.

Power is elusive in most local governments. No individual or group can compel others to do its bidding on all issues for very long. Even big-city mayors, elected by the remnants of political machines, no longer dominate issues because they have become dependent on state and federal officials. In nonpartisan governments, one elected official or a small group may gain control for a short period, but soon other elected officials begin to "gang up" to strip that individual or group of power. Even the editor of the dominant newspaper in a community may lose his influence. People may stop reading his editorials or begin to pay more attention to news programs on television. Organized labor became powerful in the 1960s because of the money and time their members could contribute to local officials. However, campaign reporting requirements have exposed labor's influence and elected officials, who also serve on a transit board, have become reluctant to accept contributions from organized labor in fear of adverse publicity. Also, union members now tend to vote in their own interest rather than in accord with endorsements by union leadership.

Building and Maintaining Constituencies. Even though constituencies in favor of public transit do not last long, it is important that management attempt to build community support on controversial issues. User groups interested in service and fare changes are more narrowly focused than community groups and easier to recruit as supporters for transit improvements. However, justifying to them the changes that management wants requires considerable effort. Nonuser groups have a different perspective on the way in which transit improvements will affect their community, and service and fare changes are unlikely to be crucial for them. Management must determine what groups will be directly affected by proposed changes and try to inform them of the consequences well in advance.

Citizen participation must begin early in any planning process. It is important to begin meeting with groups before a major change is announced, otherwise they may feel left out of the process and react negatively because they lack information. Also, the process must be open to change. Several alternatives should be suggested, and citizen groups should be invited to study the merits and adverse consequences of each.

Sufficient time must be provided for groups to learn about alternative plans and arrive at their own decisions, or they will not be able to give the support that every public agency needs. Value analysis has proved to be an effective procedure for making controversial transportation decisions (Fielding, 1972). It enables groups interested in a proposed change to learn about its positive and negative aspects well in advance of a decision. It works best when there are alternative versions of the proposal that vary in location and/or magnitude. Alternatives are helpful because they facilitate development of a compromise that several groups can support. In the aforementioned example from Houston, this procedure was used prior to the successful election in 1978 to build a constituency of support in low-income neighborhoods. Too often, however, citizens are able to participate in decisions about transit only in token ways. The agency has already made up its mind on which alternative it wants and then tries to co-opt citizens' groups into supporting this proposal. This strategy seldom works. It results in confrontations during the public hearings that may delay the entire program.

Public Hearings. Federal regulations require that hearings be held before fare and route changes and prior to adoption of major capital projects. Although burdensome to announce through public notices and to record as legal proceedings, public hearings can serve to clarify the issues. Obtaining declarations of positions from affected groups and public officials is difficult because they tend to avoid controversial decisions. But public hearings force groups to declare themselves so that it becomes apparent whether there is sufficient local support for proposed changes.

It is essential that managers allow sufficient time prior to the public hearing for the citizen participation process to influence elected officials. When there is sufficient time for individuals to learn the positive and negative consequences of alternative proposals, they are more likely to reach a compromise and are better able to present their position to decision makers. Once community opinion has formed, the emphasis shifts to elected and appointed officeholders. If the citizens feel confident that their interests have been accommodated in the proposal, they will be more likely to help transit administrators convince elected officials. Advocacy by citizens conveys a sense of urgency about the issue that encourages elected officials to make decisions that they might otherwise avoid.

Internal Organization. Attitudes within the organization are also important. Ordinarily, little attention is given to aligning the attitudes of middle management with organizational policy. But it is especially important to do this when decisions in controversial areas such as fare policy and route restructuring must be made. Opinions on these issues will differ among professionals. Rather than advocating their own preferences, management employees need to describe the consequences of different alternatives so that citizen groups and elected officials can make informed decisions. It is a staff role to develop the information, whereas it is the elected or appointed official's role to make the decision. It is an error for employees to assume that they have responsibility for decision making.

Employees play a crucial role in diffusing reliable information about controversial decisions. Top management can attend only a certain number of meetings and must rely on middle management to convey consistent information to other groups. The positive contribution of telephone operators, station employees, and drivers should not be overlooked. Alternative proposals should be explained to them so that, when asked, they can provide reliable information to inquirers. These employees provide the only contact with the organization for many citizens. If community relations are made part of their training, then they can respond positively and provide constructive feedback to management. In the Columbus, Ohio, transit agency customer relations are emphasized in driver training. Management attributes part of the agency's increase in ridership to drivers who fed back to management their perceptions of community responses to proposed changes.

Types of Policy. Some policies will be readily accepted by community groups, whereas others will generate adverse reactions. It is important for managers to anticipate both positive and negative reactions. This knowledge can influence both the selection of options and the manner of their presentation. By and large, individuals and groups will react to governmental policy in terms of its impact on them. Over time, they might be persuaded to take a more community-wide point of view, but this can only be achieved when there are socially desirable outcomes. Altshuler (1977) has described technical options for transportation in terms of the degree to which they "disturb" existing policies and behavior. His typology can be adapted to display the potential reaction to various transit policies. Five categories of increasing disturbance follow:

1. Ideal policies that produce services that customers will use and for which they will pay the full operating cost. Privately operated commuter bus or van pool strategies are examples. They are widely supported and noncontroversial.
2. Programs that involve some compulsion but that relieve problems. Peak-hour fares for transit are unpopular, but they do relieve congestion. Restrictions on playing radios or transporting bicycles and surfboards on vehicles come under this category. Transit taxes levied on businesses or the owners of newly constructed office buildings also fall into the same category. The cost is borne by corporate enterprises rather than individuals.
3. Measures that involve substantial public and private cost but can be imposed in a manner that permits the spreading of responsibility. Establishing benefit districts that help pay for

rapid transit is one example. Another is levying taxes on petroleum to encourage conservation of fuel by spreading the responsibility among petroleum producers and importers.

4. Programs where the costs are borne directly and without commensurate benefits. Imposition of parking charges designed to persuade people to use transit or the taking over of a lane for high-occupancy vehicles, causing increased congestion for motorists, are examples.

5. Programs involving substantial cost or interference with established patterns of behavior. Additional sales taxes for transit, the use of part-time employees, or the return of transit to private enterprise fall into this category. Controversial policies of this kind will be accepted only during periods of crisis.

We can illustrate this last point by noting that a fiscal crisis caused implementation of substantial changes in Boston's transit system. On December 6, 1980, the Massachusetts Bay Transportation Authority (MBTA) was shut down by management. It had exceeded the $302 million budgeted for the year, and the state legislature would not grant additional funds without concessions from labor that the unions were unwilling to give. MBTA serves more than 250,000 commuters in Boston and seventy-nine surrounding towns; cessation of service in midwinter had substantial impacts. The Massachusetts legislature reacted in one day by granting a $41 million appropriation. However, it used the opportunity to legislate changes, previously unacceptable to labor unions, that increased "management's right to manage" employees. The MBTA was given more control over work and overtime assignments, which before had been based on union seniority rules. It also gained the right to hire part-time drivers, something other systems have had to negotiate. In addition, union members were stripped of automatic cost-of-living pay increases and inclusion of overtime in calculating pension benefits. Most of these benefits had been achieved through negotiations, and the labor unions appealed to the courts to prevent implementation of the legislative mandates. However, management contends that commonwealth statutes, not federal regulations, determine the manner under which MBTA operates and has implemented the changes. It has been estimated that these changes reduced operating cost by $10 million in the first year.

Crises present opportunities for changes that management recognizes as needed but that in normal circumstances it would be unable to implement. A prudent manager should always have a list of needed changes ready, categorized in terms of the degree of disturbance they might create. Ideal policies are readily implemented; but those that interfere with existing behavior present more difficulties. Opportunities to put the latter into effect seldom arise, but when they do, speed of implementation is essential.

Governing Boards

Governance of transit differs from that of other municipal functions such as highways and public health. Transit is governed more as though it were a public corporation with its own independent governing board or separate advisory board that recommends policy to a general-purpose government. This independence had its origin in the separate revenue stream generated by transit and in the tradition of transit work force unionization when it was illegal for municipal employees to bargain collectively. Separate governance has remained even though the rationale for its existence has changed. For example, the transit system in Nashville is owned by the Metropolitan Government of Davidson County. Employees work for Transit Management of Tennessee and are supervised by a private management company. The county owns the equipment and facilities. It provides an operating subsidy and appoints the board of directors, which approves operating policies recommended by the contract manager.

Five general types of organizational form can be described for transit agencies. These reflect both the ownership of the agency and management structure:

1. General government under public management
2. Special authority under public management
3. General government with contract management

4.   Special authority with contract management
5.   Private ownership under contract to general government or
     special authority.

Perry (1984) used these categories to analyze the efficiency of transit
operated by different organizations. Publicly managed special
authorities were found to be more efficient than those organized as
part of general governments. Contrary to expectations, the relative
efficiency of contract-managed systems was no better than that of
public-managed systems. Private management companies are hired
by one-quarter of the agencies operating fixed-route transit. Their
advantage is the higher level of managerial experience that they can
provide to small and medium-sized agencies. Since management
service companies have no financial risk at stake in managing the
transit agency, it is not surprising that they perform no better than
public management.

     Private companies that contract with public agencies but
supply their own labor and equipment are more efficient operators
if size is disregarded. Perry (1984) found that they were more cost
efficient than all other forms of public management. An explanation for this finding is the small number of vehicles operated by the
thirty-two private firms in this type of organization. This gives
them an apparent advantage over systems managed by public or
contract employees; when size was controlled for, however, private
systems were not significantly different in cost efficiency. Private
systems were also found to be less safe as measured by the number
of miles between accidents. But more research is needed before
definitive conclusions can be reached over the relative efficiency of
public versus private management in the transit industry.

     Composition of the Board. Boards of directors are either
appointed, elected, or some combination of both. Special districts
created by state legislation normally require a combination to
ensure that different municipalities within a regional transit district
are represented along with the general public. The elected members
are appointed by a process specified in the statutes. Some regional
agencies, such as BART in San Francisco and the Regional Transit
District in Denver, elect board members directly. The rationale is

that direct election enhances board concern for transit users. However, the principal contributors to election campaigns are the employees of the agency. Users and the general public pay little attention, and decisions tend to reflect the interests of employee organizations.

Transit boards may have as few as five members or as many as forty. A small board of five to seven members is an advantage for management: different viewpoints can be represented, but the board is not so large that its members cannot meet and resolve policy issues through discussion. Some regional transit agencies are required to select a member from each municipality in the service area. Metro in Seattle has thirty-eight board members (they deal with sanitation as well as with transit). The Metro Council functions by subdividing into committees. Recommendations by committees are seldom rejected by the council because the committee commands superior information.

Function of the Board. Confusion exists over the appropriate role for board members. Enabling legislation is vague, although it normally specifies that the board is responsible for decisions on fares and routes. Confusion also stems from differing interpretations of board functions. The private corporate model confines the board's function to policy setting and leaves day-to-day management to professional employees. The municipal corporate model allows direct involvement of board members in day-do-day operational issues as well as in policy making. Board members from small cities tend to adopt this strategy. They are familiar with a wide range of issues in their communities and have difficulty altering their perspective when they serve on a regional transit board. Board members from large cities or counties are more accustomed to delegating authority.

The private corporate model is more appropriate for transit because of the expertise required for operating decisions. However, a public agency cannot ignore the actions of other individuals and groups as readily as can a private firm. Short-run fiscal planning and adoption of the annual budget enable boards of directors to set overall policy for a transit agency and to monitor progress against the budget. Unfortunately, this kind of policy management seldom occurs, because too much effort is spent gathering information on issues not germane to the primary function of the agency. There is a tendency for boards of directors to target a host of community objectives rather than focus on fiscal and policy issues.

Governing boards have five roles:

1. Discharging fiscal responsibility, which includes the approval of budgets and grant applications, establishment of fares, and approval of labor contracts.

2. Evaluating activities, which includes reviewing budgeted expenditures against objectives, ensuring compliance with laws, adopting service changes proposed by staff, reviewing the executive manager, and maintaining good governmental and community relations.

3. Participating in strategic planning, which includes considering new technology, financial options, organizational development, and compensation for key employees. The ability of boards to fulfill this role will depend both on the capacity and interests of their membership and on the willingness of the executive manager to encourage board participation in strategic planning.

4. Serving as consultants to management on special issues. Board members frequently possess knowledge on legal, fiscal, and political matters that can assist management. Directors of private corporations are sought for their expertise, and this basis for selection could be used to advantage by public agencies.

5. Acting as catalysts for change when management becomes overwhelmed by current issues. Carrying out this responsibility may at times mean removing the chief executive or other key managers. This occurs when management has failed to satisfy the board in terms of key roles.

There is a difference between governance and management. Governance involves overseeing the strategic direction of the agency; ensuring that there are sufficient funds to implement approved plans, monitoring the results, and being a catalyst for the reevaluation of agency goals and personnel. Management plays more of a hands-on, implementation role; it must convert goals into objectives, develop action plans, delegate responsibility, and allocate funds to different departments to accomplish objectives. Budget development and fiscal control, service planning, purchasing supplies and deploying labor, marketing, and community relations are elements of management by which board direction is implemented. From the systems point of view summarized in Figure 2, the governing board should encourage the assessment of possibilities and the evaluation of performance, whereas management should be more concerned with such matters as fiscal planning and performance evaluation. Transit managers place their position in jeopardy when they fail to appreciate these different roles. The most frequent managerial error is the failure to encourage the board to reassess the agency's situation and to think strategically about the future. Board members who become too involved with daily operating issues commit an error of a different kind; they become so involved in the complexity of operations that they do not have sufficient time to think strategically or monitor accomplishments.

Development of transit corporations modeled after the British type of public corporation has been proposed as a solution (Hamilton and Hamilton, 1981). A strong chairman is appointed as well as a board of directors. The chairman is paid sufficiently well to enable him or her to devote full time to corporate affairs. The chairman of New York's Metropolitan Transit Authority (MTA), serves in this capacity, as does the chairman of Chicago's Regional Transportation Agency (RTA). However, the results achieved with this type of state socialism have been no more effective in the United States than they have been in the United Kingdom. Although this model is acceptable in the larger and older metropolitan areas, it has not been welcomed in communities where the nonpartisan, "good government" tradition requires separation between policy making and management.

Employing private management companies is another strategy to separate policy making from management. Some 78 of the 249 agencies operating more than 10 fixed-route vehicles in 1980 contracted with management companies. The largest of these, ATE Management and Service Company, manages over 60 systems.

ATE supplies the top executives while midmanagement, drivers, and mechanics are agency employees. The management company backs up local executives with regional supervisors and national experts. Firms such as Community Transit Service in Santa Ana, California, perform similar service for paratransit agencies. Management companies operate service according to the policies and budget adopted by the board, for which they are paid a management fee.

Staff-Board Relations. Confusion over appropriate roles for the governing board hampers staff-board relations. Staff members consider the board to have a titular role, deciding issues brought to them, whereas board members view themselves as originators of ideas and real decision makers. They object when they are not notified in advance of important issues and not informed of all the consequences of alternatives.

Antagonism can be reduced if staff members view their role as that of presenting options to decision makers. They should outline alternative courses of action and describe the consequences, insofar as these are understood. A recommended alternative can be presented, but discussion of the consequences should make apparent the disadvantages of the recommended alternative as well as its advantages. The decision should then be left to the governing board, which is elected or appointed to represent community interests. Board members are cognizant of differing points of view and better able than staff to decide between competing interests. Tri-County Transit in Orlando, Florida, operates according to this philosophy. Thus, it has adopted a strategic as well as a marketing plan. Its board meets monthly to review budgets and plans and the agency's performance against these plans. Operating decisions are delegated to the contract management team and agency employees. The result has been a consistently high level of performance year after year.

Selection of special contractors is another important board responsibility. These might be engineering or planning firms that perform planning studies or they might be companies that provide services such as transit for elderly and handicapped patrons, facility cleaning, or heavy equipment maintenance. Competition between suppliers is intense, and factors other than bid price must be considered. Staff should analyze the proposals and recommend qualified vendors. It is the board's role to select the provider and to direct staff to develop a contract for service, which the board should review before approval.

A governing board may have its own staff. Normally the agency's attorney and occasionally its treasurer report to the board. Otherwise, all staff report to the general or executive manager. Independent legal counsel is essential, because when the board adopts policy, it needs an independent, legal review of proposals presented by staff before taking action. An independent secretary or treasurer is not essential. For example, the secretary-treasurer for the Greater Cleveland Regional Transit Authority reports to the board and is not a part of management. There is a staff of two in the treasurer's office who assist the board by conducting internal audit and budget control functions. Because the treasurer relies on staff to provide the information needed for auditing, his independence is only nominal. Placing all fiscal responsibility under the general manager appears to be prudent in most instances. An independent auditor can then be hired to review compliance.

Legislative Relations

Whereas most of this chapter has been concerned with issues and actions in local government, management must also be concerned with activities at the state and federal levels. Approximately one-half of the operating assistance for transit comes from federal and state agencies. Managers must be concerned about the continuance of these funds and the federal and state regulations governing their use. They must devote considerable time to meeting with state and federal representatives, and pay special attention to legislators who sit on committees that have responsibility for transit. In Congress, the House Public Works Committee and the Senate Committee on Banking and Urban Affairs have jurisdiction over transit. These committees initiate legislation, but funding allocations are decided by committees that handle appropriations.

Trade associations play an important role in formulating legislation. The primary function of the American Public Transit

Association (APTA) is to represent the industry in Washington, D.C. Through its committees and regional conferences, APTA determines the desires of the industry and works closely with members of Congress and their staffs to make or prevent changes in existing law. In recent years the primary effort has been to minimize reductions in transit assistance. APTA's approach has two thrusts. First, it works closely with staff and congressional representatives on key committees, since this provides an opportunity to structure the legislative response to administrative initiatives. Second, it builds a constituency for the support of transit through local agency members. Messages of support from a congressman's district are far more influential than representations from industry lobbyists. Spreading federal investments in transit to many small cities and rural areas has markedly increased the effective constituency for transit. Although these small systems carry few passengers and receive little money, their support is essential. By this twofold strategy, APTA ensures that it has skilled staff to lobby in Washington in addition to a broad constituency of support.

UMTA is the principal federal agency administering transit programs. Regulations promulgated by the Department of Health and Human Services and the Department of Labor occasionally affect transit, but the majority of federal transit regulation emanates from UMTA. There are ten UMTA regional offices that are responsible for implementing the transit program and deciding whether the performance of grantees is in compliance with federal regulations. Before the regional offices were established in 1976, transit managers lobbied for grants in Washington. Since 1976, far more attention has been given to the regional offices. In addition, federal funds have become more formula based and less discretionary.

State Agencies. State transit programs have always provided fewer discretionary funds than has the federal program. Funds are allocated by formulas based on ridership, taxable sales, and population. Agencies compete to influence the formula in their own interest: operators in major metropolitian areas want formulas based on ridership, whereas suburban and small-city operators prefer allocations based on population. State transit associations have been established in the more populous states but none are as powerful as APTA. Agencies have to safeguard their interests in state politics, so the larger agencies employ their own lobbyists in the state capital in addition to being members of state transit associations.

Members of the governing board can be helpful advocates. As community leaders, they usually keep in close contact with state representatives. These friendly relations are important when legislation is being considered; board members can line up the support of an influential state legislator, and legislators must rely on recommendations by people they trust. Effective managers inform state legislators of important decisions affecting their constituents in advance of the decisions and invite them to attend special events—a courtesy that allows legislators to share the credit for transportation improvements.

Unlike the federal highway program, the federal transit program does not designate a major role for the state departments of transportation. All states perform some functions, but only twenty-five had transit expenditures of more than $1 million in 1981. The major contribution of states has been construction of high-occupancy vehicle lanes and park-and-ride lots, along with the encouragement of van and car pooling. The federal transit program began as a city-oriented program, in the Department of Housing and Urban Development, and was subsequently transferred to the Department of Transportation. Programs were directed toward cities so as to bypass states that were dominated by rural legislators before reapportionment in the 1960s. The MPO was given more jurisdiction than the state in transit funding, and this tradition has remained. Only the federal program to provide transit service for the elderly and handicapped in rural areas has formally involved the states.

Pennsylvania is the most active state in regulating transit. The formula for state subsidies involves an incentive payment for improved service, and this has been the rationale for promulgating state regulations affecting transit service. Very specific directions are given as to the appropriate distances between bus stops and the degree of crowding that ought to be permitted on transit vehicles. But these limitations are not effective because of the difficulty in ensuring compliance. New York requires that transit systems be operated effectively and economically, and its Department of Transportation has developed procedures to measure transit performance through annually reported data. California also relies on performance statistics to evaluate efficiency and effectiveness. Performance audits are required triennially to ensure that state assistance is used appropriately.

Transit operators have not welcomed surveillance by state agencies, because state regulations can conflict with federal regulations. However, compliance is the price that an agency must pay if it seeks state assistance. To allocate state funds for local purposes without regulation would generate criticism if the funds were spent inappropriately. Wisconsin provides the best example of state assistance to local transit agencies. Its Department of Transportation organized training conferences on issues such as insurance, maintenance of small transit vehicles, and service contracting. It also provides specialized services to the many small transit agencies throughout the state. Green Bay Transit, with twenty-nine active vehicles, is an example of a small agency that makes good use of state assistance. Its consistently high level of performance on both the efficiency and effectiveness indicators demonstrates what a small agency can accomplish.

Regional Agencies. Monitoring of compliance with federal and state regulation is left primarily to regional agencies. The Federal Aid Highway Act of 1962 required that planning for federally assisted transportation improvements be conducted in a consistent, coordinated, and comprehensive manner. Responsibility for this planning process was assigned by the states to metropolitan planning organizations (MPOs) in most instances. This gave the MPOs both control over access to federal planning funds and also the responsibility for certifying that transit plans were consistent with regional policies. Transit managers must spend considerable time attending regional meetings so as to ensure that their interests are represented. Policy boards for the MPO must also be considered when developing plans and fiscal programs. Representation may overlap with that of the transit governing board and may include competitors. Managing this interaction requires political skill and

compromise, or else transit plans may become mired in interjuris-
dictional disputes.

Lines of governance have become more obscure with the
creation of regional fiscal control agencies in some metropolitan
areas. These are state-mandated agencies that program the
availability of transportation funds. Thus, in some metropolitan
areas, transit agencies must now submit plans not only to the MPO
but also to a regional agency or commission. In California,
transportation commissions or boards have been created for each
major metropolitan area. In Chicago the RTA serves as the fiscal
control agency and in New York it is the MTA. A similar agency
has been created for Minneapolis-St. Paul: the Metro Council
prepares the comprehensive transportation plan; the Regional
Transit Board controls the flow of state and federal funds and is also
charged with responsibility for planning and constructing a rail
system; and the Metropolitan Transit Commission hires a management contract company to operate the buses. Policies must run the
gauntlet of all these local agencies before being considered by state
and federal agencies.

Impress of Politics

Politics has a pervasive influence on transit management.
Although the structure of a transit agency is similar to that of a
private corporation in that it has an independent board of directors,
the similarity is superficial. As transit agencies have become less
dependent on farebox revenue and more dependent on assistance
from local, state, and federal agencies, their managerial behavior
has increasingly adapted to the requirements of these agencies.
Taking care of the customer is important in transit, but it is also
essential to be attentive to the desires of community leaders, elected
officials, and public administrators. Ensuring that they know in
advance what the transit agency is planning, listening to their ideas
and criticisms, and acknowledging them in every achievement are
essential. Seldom does the manager of a private corporation have to
take care of such a broad array of "customers."

The politics of transit are similar to the politics of urban
governance in America. Numerous groups express their interest on

controversial issues so that the "public interest" must be decided by compromise. There is seldom a consistent policy. National and regional concerns may create a coalition of interests that is sustained for a number of years. An example was the national preoccupation with environmental quality and then energy conservation in the 1970s. At the regional level, concerns over traffic congestion, as happened in Houston, or central city redevelopment, as in San Francisco, can help unify interests in support of transit. However, these coalitions never last long. As soon as the issue appears to have been solved at the legislative level, the coalition disbands. Management is then left to grapple with the more difficult implementation issues without much community support.

Effective citizen participation can help build a constituency. Such participation should begin early in the development of a project, with citizens from a wide range of groups given an opportunity to establish goals and develop alternatives as well as to participate in public hearings. Citizens who are knowledgeable about transit development can also assist in gaining support from other levels of government. Legislators are responsive to requests from influential constituents. They are accustomed to appeals from public administrators, but they are much more likely to give attention to a local issue when they perceive that official requests are endorsed by constituents. Developing this kind of political support is an exhaustive process, but necessary for successful administration.

The rewards for accomplishing these tasks are not generous. Salaries for top management in transit are comparable to similar positions in local governments. Salaries in private firms of similar magnitude are seldom considered in establishing transit management salary levels. When they are, insufficient attention is given to the indirect benefits, such as stock option plans, that are frequently granted managers in private companies. Transit managers do benefit from good pensions if they remain long enough to accumulate equity in the pension plan.

Transit management is an exhausting, stressful way to earn a living. The techniques outlined in this book can make it more satisfying, but transit managers must be content with "psychological rewards" to offset their inadequate monetary compensation.

Incentive payments could help offset the inequities between the management task and compensation. Bonuses for achieving objectives are seldom given in public enterprises, yet they are an important form of compensation in private firms. Public agencies view bonuses, other than token awards, as a gift of public funds. But as Simpson (1985) has shown, this need not be the situation. Public agencies can pay bonuses, and managerial performance would improve if they did. Chapter Four outlined a procedure for formulating performance objectives and measuring them quantitatively. An incentive program for top management could be based on holding increases in the cost per revenue vehicle hour below the regional inflation rate or increasing the proportion of operating cost recovered from passenger revenue. Other indicators that measure improvements in labor efficiency or service reliability could be used to reward assistant managers. Incentive bonuses could offer tangible incentives for management. These might encourage skilled managers to apply for and remain in these positions.

Bonus payments can also be incorporated into contracts for firms hired to manage transit operations. San Diego County, California, contracts for bus service for rural areas and small towns. Proposals are requested every three years for providing a designated number of miles and hours of service using county-owned vehicles. The contractor has to provide drivers, mechanics, and supervisors. Potential contractors are reviewed for experience and reliability, and acceptable contractors are nominated to the board of supervisors. Contract proposals are then analyzed. The firm selected is offered a contract with monthly payments based on the miles and hours offered. A financial incentive is then added for on-time performance, cleanliness of vehicles, and operation of air-conditioning equipment. Random inspections by county staff determine whether or not the standards are being met. For the contractor, achieving the bonus makes the difference between a marginal return on investment and a generous return. In a thirty-six-month period between 1982 and 1985, the private contractor missed the bonus only one month. As a result San Diego County residents are delighted with the service, and the contract has became one of the most sought after in California.

As privatization of some public transit service achieves broader acceptance, boards of directors can use incentive payments to satisfy service demands while ensuring high-quality service. Privatization alone does not produce more efficient transit as some advocates represent. The form of management is only one determinant of efficiency. Private operation can be beneficial under some circumstances, and management should seek these opportunities. Hesitancy over loss of control is understandable, but incentive-based contracting is a method whereby the quality of service can be ensured. In those instances where the contractor is not motivated to provide satisfactory service by the monetary reward, the contract should be canceled.

11

Managing Strategically:
Balancing and Integrating
Responsibilities

Now that each major function of transit management has been reviewed, we are in a position to describe how the pieces fit together. Strategic management is a systems approach to public administration that involves the deployment of resources to achieve goals on the basis of plans, scenarios, and programs (Figure 2). Performance evaluation is used to monitor progress toward goals and as a stimulus for revision of programs. This latter requirement is essential, because without a market test transit programs may remain in place even when they no longer serve a useful purpose. Unless performance is monitored against goals, therefore, management is not strategic.

The cyclical nature of strategic management encourages managers to seek incremental changes within difficult environments. External agencies and local conditions, was well as an organization's capabilities, place constraints on the ways in which managers can respond to service expectations. A competent manager must become familiar with these constraints and learn to distinguish those that can be changed from those that must be endured. The systems approach is an ideal that provides a map of the way different functions fit together, but the plans developed for each agency, and the speed at which they are implemented depend on the opportunities inherent in every situation. Rosenthal (1982,

p. 281) describes successful managers in government as those who are "opportunistic, analytic, and energetic enough to gain control over program directions despite frequent buffeting by the shifting winds of public policy." The systems approach outlined in Figure 2 helps managers to chart a course through difficult environments and to deploy effective service on a daily basis, while still leaving sufficient time to anticipate and plan for change in each annual cycle.

The strategic approach is not new in transit; it is inherent in the SRTP/TIP regulations promulgated by federal agencies in 1975. Plans, programs, and budgets must be developed and updated annually or biennially in order to qualify projects for federal funds. However, monitoring results against goals has not been required. Data have been available in the Section 15 reports required by UMTA, but until the Triennial Review requirements were adopted in 1984, there was no systematic monitoring of the transit services supported by federal funding.

UMTA's monitoring of transit performance does not mean that transit agencies will be managed strategically. Each agency should monitor its own performance in light of its own goals and objectives, because only the agency can alter the deployment of its resources to accomplish goals. Federal and state agencies should require every agency to have a performance monitoring system in place as a condition for receiving governmental assistance. The system should include measures of both efficiency and effectiveness, with responsibility for monitoring assigned to the operating agency.

A wide range of indicators can be used to monitor transit performance. Although most are used to measure individual functions, the following set has been defined for monitoring the major dimensions of transit performance:

- Revenue vehicle hours per dollar of operating expense
- Total passengers per revenue vehicle hour
- Operating revenue to operating cost ratio
- Total vehicle hours per employee
- Total vehicle miles per peak vehicle

- Total vehicle miles per maintenance employee
- Total vehicle miles per collision accident.

Each indicator is defined so that higher scores are better than lower scores. This facilitates comprehension of time-series analysis and comparisons of one agency with another in the same peer group. For example, cost efficiency is expressed as the fraction of an hour for which one dollar of operating expense will keep the agency running; increasing values indicate improved efficiency. If the inverse were shown as cost per hour, efficiency would be improving when indicator values were declining.

Situational Assessment

When appraising transit performance, managers must take into account the situation of their agency as well as its history and geography before attempting to manage strategically. Otherwise they will not recognize either the possibilities or the constraints of their situation. Transit has been revitalized by two decades of government investment: the industry now has modern equipment and facilities, and its employees are generously compensated. But with the transformation, transit has been assigned new goals. It is expected to reduce congestion and air pollution, solve the mobility problems of the transit dependent, provide highly subsidized fares for the elderly and persons with disabilities, and protect employees from any adverse consequences of spending federal funds—such as, reduction of employment opportunities through automation or elimination of the right to bargain collectively. A maze of regulations complicate improvement plans, and managers need to appreciate why these were promulgated, and to whom they are important, in order to incorporate them into strategic plans.

Classifying transit agencies according to size, peak-to-base service demand, and speed makes it possible to group similar agencies together (Figure 3). Knowledge about the achievements of these peer systems helps transit managers set reasonable goals for their agencies. Otherwise, expectations can be distorted by the performance of transit in the largest cities. For example, the urbanized areas of New York, Chicago, and Los Angeles account for

57 percent of the transit market. Eighty-five percent of the service demand occurs in the twenty largest urbanized areas, each dominated by a regional transit agency. And yet the majority of transit agencies are small: 276 of the 336 agencies that report Section 15 data to UMTA have fewer than 100 peak vehicles. These agencies, which operate in both metropolitan areas and smaller cities, have service goals that are quite different from those of the larger regional agencies. Furthermore, comparison of performance in small municipal transit agencies with performance in large regional agencies provides a distorted picture of both.

Using a small set of indicators to monitor performance over time and checking the achievements of one's own agency against those of peer systems form the essence of strategic management. Unless they monitor performance against goals, managers are not managing strategically; they are merely supervising operations. Every transit agency must determine its mission and goals and translate these into objectives whose attainment can be measured. Objectives must be prioritized in terms of local expectations and agency capabilities. Measures of performance can then be selected so that achievement of objectives can be regularly monitored over time within the agency and occasionally monitored against the performance of peer agencies. Managers who adopt this strategic approach are making a personal commitment to manage within the context of their local and organizational constraints.

Public transit requires a strategic approach because of the weakness of the market test for services and because it is constantly subjected to public scrutiny. Service plans for public transit agencies depend on external funding; earning sufficient revenue to cover costs and make a reasonable profit is not the goal of public agencies. These agencies provide all the service they can afford to provide. Rarely do they monitor revenues by route or service type as would a private firm, because their effectiveness is defined by achieving social and environmental objectives rather then by earning revenue.

Performance measurement helps an agency respond to public scrutiny. The ability to describe achievements in terms of performance indicators helps management answer questions from regulating agencies and the press. Without performance indicators, an agency can easily become mired in reporting regulations and disoriented by a press that expects both furthering of social and environmental objectives and economy of operation. The seven indicators proposed earlier represent the principal dimensions of transit performance. They indicate what is actually being accomplished, and they suggest other measures that might clarify what is occurring. For example, the number of miles between collision accidents indicates how safe transit travel is. If the indicator is decreasing, this suggests that there may be a problem in driver training or that a change in operating conditions is needed. Additional statistics can then be obtained on the number of employee hours allocated to driver training to determine whether changes in training requirements might explain the decline in operating safety. Performance indicators provide objective measures about what is happening within an agency so that queries can be reliably answered.

Transit managers must be capable of juggling the competing demands on their time. Trying to comply with federal, state, and regional regulations is only one of their many frustrating, time-consuming chores. News media also demand time for interviews when they suspect that a transit agency is experiencing problems, but they are seldom interested in success stories because public agencies are supposed to be successful. Boards of directors also want information on whether or not an agency is achieving its goals. Using performance measures helps both to satisfy these demands and to create an organizational setting conducive to strategic management.

Budgets in Transit Organizations

Preparing budgets and monitoring achievements are pivotal to the strategic approach to transit management. These activities provide opportunities to compare the relative contribution of departments to agency goals and to solicit comments from directors and the public on priorities. Those who control the budget dominate policy implementation because they select objectives, determine priorities, and monitor progress.

Integration of the annual budget with the three-to-five year transportation improvement program, developed in accordance with the federal SRTP/TIP requirements, is recommended. This facilitates involvement of the policy board in choosing between alternative service strategies, each of which will have different requirements for annual capital and operating expenditures. Policy boards are well suited to the task of evaluating alternatives in terms of community expectations. Public discussion of the SRTP/TIP also diffuses knowledge about strategic plans and what will be required annually to implement them. These discussions make formulation of the annual budget less controversial because board members have already agreed to the major elements. If financial or operating conditions change, the plan can be altered in the annual budget, but there is a continuity to the process that increases trust between board members and professional staff.

The SRTP/TIP requirement, as summarized in Table 1, provides a method for integrating revenue forecasts with the costs of pursuing different service objectives. Alternative strategies or scenarios may be examined, and the most beneficial one selected for implementation. The decision as to what service will be operated, where, and by whom can then be implemented gradually over several years as part of the annual budget process. Conceptualizing the budget as the annual element of a continuing effort to improve transit captures the very essence of managing strategically.

Monitoring performance against the budget ensures that cost overruns do not occur and that expenditures are achieving service objectives. Brief reports after each pay period can determine whether payroll expenditures by category and fare revenues are above or below estimates. Quarterly reports give more information. Financial data are combined with output measures to present the hours and miles of service produced against labor, fuel, and other costs. The question of whether an agency is achieving service objectives is answered by measures of ridership and operating revenue. Procedures to estimate cost and revenue for budgetary purposes are widely used. Performance monitoring provides a method for checking the accuracy of estimates and, if necessary, for modifying procedures before the next budget cycle.

The conceptual approach to finance and budgeting encompasses much more than preparation of the annual budget. It integrates forecasts of available revenue with the estimated costs of proposed service. The transit agency governing board can then give guidance on proposed service and capital investment plans well in advance of the annual budget so that community expectations are also reflected in the budgetary process.

With all the elements of the strategic approach to budgeting so readily available, why do transit agencies so seldom use them in a coordinated strategy? The answer lies in the persistence of the belief that performance should be measured in terms of ridership rather than by cost and revenue indicators. More attention is now given to the efficient production of service, but in any list of agency goals this will fall below the goal of providing effective transit service as measured by ridership. However, if transit is to survive in medium-sized cities and suburban areas, its managers must, above all else, emphasize the goal of increased efficiency. Managers must become more skilled in planning and implementing changes that will match service to fiscal capacity.

Improving Labor Efficiency

Labor accounts for 74 percent of the operating costs of all modes of transit. Wages and benefits for vehicle operators alone account for 36 percent of operating costs. Because the employment conditions of most operators and mechanics and many clerical employees are governed by labor contracts, improvement of labor efficiency requires negotiating with employee representatives for the right to apply more efficient work rules. Few people outside of management appreciate the importance of negotiating the labor contract. The general public and the press pay little attention unless a work stoppage is threatened; they do not realize that levels of service and fares are indirectly determined by the labor contract.

Negotiating a labor contract is an arduous process; preparations for negotiation should begin at least twelve months before expiration of the current contract. A management team should be created to review grievances filed during the expiring labor agreement and to produce a list of changes sought by management. The costs implied by each change should be determined in advance so that management knows how to calculate what each penny of salary increase will mean in cost per service hour and how changes in benefits will affect this cost. Managers have an advantage if they can calculate these costs quickly during negotiations. Employee representatives from international unions have better knowledge about contracts in other agencies than managers do. But management representatives know more about the local consequences of proposed changes and how service can be deployed to minimize cost. They must use this knowledge to approve or reject employee demands.

The inflexible nature of transit work and the tradition of strong unionism tend to set employees against managers and supervisors, so that sharing of agency goals is undermined. Management must seek ways to overcome this obstacle to strategic management because employee attitudes are an important factor in encouraging more frequent use of transit. Managers have tried various strategies for gaining employee involvement, but none of these has been particularly successful with drivers, who operate relatively independently. The most promising strategies have been those that reward reliable attendance and courteous service and at the same time discipline drivers whose work falls below a certain standard. A minority of employees create most of the problems, and every agency should have a monitoring procedure that detects the offenders.

Organized labor has played an essential role in obtaining governmental assistance for transit. Labor organizations influenced the passage of federal legislation in 1964 and 1974 and have participated in the development of most state programs as well. In return, they have demanded legislative provisions that protect existing employees and guarantee the right to bargain collectively with public agencies. International unions have skillfully used these legislative provisions to increase transit labor's share of income while reducing its work load. Transit managers may feel that unions have been excessive in their demands, but without union support, the transit industry might not have achieved the level of governmental assistance that it now enjoys.

Improving Transit Service

Planners have developed analytical procedures that enable management to use labor more efficiently to produce more effective transit service. Productivity is management's responsibility, and the use of planning procedures facilitates deployment of service within budget and labor contract constraints

In an era when resources are limited and fares, on average, cover only 41 percent of operating expenses, procedures that analyze the cost of supplying service are critically important to managers who wish to allocate resources strategically. Estimating the cost of service by allocating costs to (1) hours of service, (2) miles of service, and (3) number of peak vehicles required is a relatively simple accounting procedure. It always surprises me to discover how few agencies use this three-variable model. All the data required for making calculations can be derived from the fiscal and operating records of an agency. Results give average costs for routes and divisions and can be used for planning purposes.

Procedures that analyze route costs in terms of the type and nature of labor assigned provide route-specific costs. These models are more time consuming to calibrate because they require determining the labor costs for each trip assigned to a route. They may be worth the effort when routes are to be restructured and managers need to know the route-specific cost of proposed changes so as to determine whether the proposal, or alternatives to it, can achieve the same benefits for less cost.

Analysis of satisfactory as well as unsatisfactory routes is recommended. Frequently there are opportunities to improve performance on satisfactory routes by restructuring service to lessen crowding or to reduce cost. The only real cost-saving alternative for many unsatisfactory routes is to abandon them, an action that most agencies try to avoid because of adverse political consequences.

Marketing integrates operational and planning considerations. Management should base service development programs on the travel needs of market segments and then proceed with the analysis of existing and proposed service at the sector and route levels. Proposed changes must be analyzed for both operating cost and ridership; if implemented, they should be priced and promoted in a manner acceptable to the target population. Marketing should be everyone's business in a transit agency; it should involve operations, planning, finance, and the employees who meet the public. To attain this level of involvement, management must persuade all employees to pursue agency objectives and should report performance so as to display results clearly.

Politics of Public Transit

The heavy hand of politics rests on all transit functions. Transit has been revived through governmental assistance, and every aspect of it, from finance to operations, planning, and marketing, has felt the weight of government. Although the Reagan administration has eased some reporting requirements, new regulations have been added to help private providers compete for contracts to operate public transit. This has alarmed labor unions and turned employees against management at the very time when cooperation is needed to ensure that transit remains successful in the two markets where it enjoys a competitive advantage over the automobile: in the inner-city suburbs and along congested corridors between the suburbs and high-activity centers.

Managers must recognize the constraints that governmental regulations place on operations and determine productive courses of action that satisfy both the regulators and the expectations of employees and the community. By using the systems approach outlined in this book, managers can incorporate shifts in public expectations and in legislative requirements into agency goals so that changes are brought about gradually without disrupting daily operations.

Continuing education helps employees cope with the uncertainty that can result from the crosswinds of politics. Professional meetings describe changes that are occurring in the industry and acquaint transit managers with the ways in which other agencies are coping with new conditions. Good managers also need knowledge about practices in nontransit public enterprises. On-the-job training can meet part of this need, but it is also an advantage to provide off-site training where managers and supervisors can distance themselves from job pressures and share experiences with other public employees. Some agencies feel that such training courses are a luxury they cannot afford. However, employees are less overwhelmed by their jobs when they realize that their problems are not unique and that they do have a productive role to play in strategic management.

There are political liabilities inherent in a strategic approach. Managers are rarely rewarded for accomplishing service goals, yet they are likely to be criticized, even fired, for failing to accomplish the goals that they themselves have proposed. Care is therefore needed when preparing goals. This is why it has been suggested that goals be formulated and scenarios developed with full participation of the governing board. Resulting plans are then implemented gradually over three to five years according to the availability of funds and with careful monitoring of the public's response. Corrections to the plan can be made through the annual budget process, with operating plans changed more frequently. Service can be expanded or reduced when routes do not perform according to forecasted cost and ridership estimates. Managing strategically does involve taking prudent risks to achieve improvements, but performance monitoring affords some protection.

Managing Strategically

Clarifying agency goals, involving the entire agency in accomplishment of objectives, and monitoring performance are the essence of strategic management. Critical assessment of the situation is required to determine possibilities and limitations. This involves knowledge of external constraints and local expectations in addition to an appreciation of the capabilities of one's organization. Development of goals, objectives, and alternative courses of action or scenarios is a time-consuming, sometimes chaotic activity. The governing board must be involved along with representatives from community interest groups, including transit employees. It can take as long as two years to create a shared vision of the future.

Once a plan has been selected and sources of funding have been identified, implementation is a normal activity involving the day-to-day management of financial, operational planning, and marketing functions to achieve strategic objectives. Opposition should be anticipated. Organizations are composed of individuals with different values, preferences, and degrees of power. Financial and service planners adapt to changes quite readily, whereas operating departments tend to be conservative and prefer to continue with customary procedures rather than think strategically. Opportunities for change must be utilized to move the organization forward. For example, when a new division opens or ridership increases because of a special event, changes can be implemented as experiments. If successful, they can be blended into normal operations as catalysts for further changes. If they fail, they can be abandoned. The object should be to keep the organization moving toward the attainment of goals and the monitoring of achievements against objectives based on these goals.

One of the major differences between private and public transit organizations is their orientation to strategic thinking. Strategic thinking comes naturally to the managers of successful private agencies, since they must coordinate activities in order to produce a reasonable profit and enlarge their market. There is a small set of quantified objectives that are widely shared in private firms because jobs depend on achieving them. Public agencies, by comparison, are budget based. Service is provided to the level allowed by the budget and to satisfy a broad range of goals. These goals are often poorly understood by employees, and transit performance is seldom monitored in a way that can influence the quality of service supplied.

I am currently involved in a study of superior transit agencies in which the performance of over 300 agencies was analyzed using the performance indicators discussed in this book. Seven agencies were identified as consistently excellent performers when compared with their peer groups. Four of the systems are managed strategically on the basis of some of the principles outlined in this book. The other three are organizations with a strong culture of privatization. They are managed by private contractors and proud of traditions inherited from prior private owners; they evaluate service in terms of deficit per passenger rather than ridership. None of these three privately managed agencies is engaged in formal strategic planning. And yet the management of each thinks strategically: the objective to minimize the deficit per passenger is widely shared and related to taking good care of customers and keeping costs low; there are fewer managerial employees in these three agencies than in most, and they perform a variety of tasks.

Relations between management and drivers are amicable, and managers are enthusiastic because they are challenged to achieve objectives that are readily understood and easily monitored.

All seven agencies are stimulating places to visit. Managers are capable and hardworking; and they enjoy broad spans of control. Proposed changes are discussed collectively and then implemented gradually, with the results monitored to detect improvement. Favorable publicity is received because managers are proud of what has been accomplished with governmental assistance and are able to describe achievements in terms of objective performance measures. These seven agencies demonstrate what can be accomplished by managing strategically.

References

Altschuler, A. "The Politics of Urban Transportation Innovation." *Technology Review,* 1977, *79* (8), 51–58.

Altschuler, A. In *The Financial and Productivity Problems of Urban Public Transportation: Hearings Before the Subcommittee on Investigations and Oversight of the Committee on Public Works and Transportation.* Testimony before the U.S. House of Representatives. Washington, D.C.: U.S. Government Printing Office, 1981.

Altschuler, A., Womack, J. P., and Pucher, J. R. *The Urban Transportation System: Politics and Policy Innovation.* Cambridge, Mass.: MIT Press, 1979.

American Public Transit Association. *Preparing for Negotiations, Implementing the Contract, and Contract Administration.* Washington, D.C.: American Public Transit Association, 1983.

American Public Transit Association. *Transit Fact Book.* Washington, D.C.: American Public Transit Association, 1985.

Anagnostoupolous, G., and others. *Financial Forecasting Techniques in the Transit Industry: A Summary of Current Practice.* Report no. UMTA-MA-06-0039-82-1. Cambridge, Mass.: U.S. Department of Transportation, Transportation Systems Center, 1982. (Available from the National Technical Information Service, Springfield, Va.)

Attanucci, J., Burns, I., and Wilson, N.M.H. *Bus Transit Monitoring Manual. Vol. 1: Data Collection Design.* Report no. UMTA-IT-09-9008-81-1. Washington, D.C.: U.S. Department of Transportation, Urban Mass Transportation Administration, 1981. (Available from the National Technical Information Service, Springfield, Va.)

Attanucci, J., Jaeger, L., and Becker, J. *Bus Service Evaluation Procedures: A Review.* Report no. UMTA-MA-09-7001-79-1. Washington, D.C.: U.S. Department of Transportation, Urban Mass Transportation Administration, 1979. (Available from the National Technical Information Service, Springfield, Va.)

Attanucci, J., Wilson, N.M.H., and Vozzolo, D. "An Assessment of the Use of Part-Time Operators at the Massachusetts Bay Transportation Authority." *Transportation Research Record 961,* 1984, pp. 21–28.

Baker, H. S., and Scheuftan, O. *Study of Operator Absenteeism and Workers' Compensation Trends in the Urban Mass Transportation Industry.* Report no. UMTA-PA-0050-80. Washington, D.C.: U.S. Department of Transportation, Urban Mass Transportation Administration, 1980. (Available from the National Technical Information Service, Springfield, Va.)

Bay Area Rapid Transit District. *Quarterly Performance Report on System Objectives, 6* (2). Oakland, California, 1986.

Bonnell, J. R. "Transit's Growing Financial Crisis." *Traffic Quarterly,* 1981, *35* (4), 541–556.

Booth, R. "Bus Marketing Costs: The Experience of Eighteen Section 15 Reporters from 1981 to 1983." Paper presented at 65th annual meeting of the Transportation Research Board, Washington, D.C., Jan. 1986.

Bower, D. J. "Runcutting and Scheduling Software for Fixed-Route Transit Service." *TIME Capsule,* 1986, *4* (3), 10–16.

Bozeman, B. *Public Management and Policy Analysis.* New York: St. Martin's Press, 1979.

Briggs, R. "The Impact of Federal Local Public Transportation Assistance upon Travel Behavior." *Professional Geographer,* 1980, *32* (3), 316–325.

Button, K. J., and Navin, F. "A Public Transportation Demand-Forecasting Model for Vancouver." *Traffic Engineering and Control,* 1983, *24* (1), 27–31.

Cervero, R. "Efficiency and Equity Impacts of Current Transit Fare Policies." *Transportation Research Record 790,* 1981, pp. 7–15.

Cervero, R., and Brunk, J. "Intergovernmental Goals for Public Transit." *Journal of Advanced Transportation,* 1983, *17* (1), 29–47.

Cheng, P. C. *Accounting and Finance in Mass Transit.* Totowa, N.J.: Allenheld, Osmun, 1982.

Cherwony, W., Gleichman, G., and Porter, B. *Bus Route Costing Procedures: A Review.* Report no. UMTA-IT-09-9014-81-1. Washington, D.C.: U.S. Department of Transportation, Urban Mass Transportation Administration, 1981. (Available from the National Technical Information Service, Springfield, Va.)

Cherwony, W., and Mundle, S. R. "Peak-Base Cost Allocation Models." *Transportation Research Record 663,* 1978, pp. 52–56.

Chomitz, K. M., Giuliano, G., and Lave, C. A. *Fiscal and Organizational Impacts of Part-Time Labor in Public Transit.* Report no. UMTA-CA-06-0187-1. Washington, D.C.: U.S. Department of Transportation, Urban Mass Transportation Administration, 1985. (Available from the National Technical Information Service, Springfield, Va.)

Cochrane, R.L.D., and Tyson, W. J. "Project Evaluation in the Context of Multidimensional Corporate Objectives for a Public Transport Undertaking." In J. S. Yerrell (ed.), *Proceedings of the World Conference on Transport Research: Transport Research for Social and Economic Progress.* London: Imperial College, 1980.

Crosby, T. "13(c): To Be or Not to Be." *Mass Transit,* 1982, *9* (6), 16–19.

Curtin, J. F. "Effect of Fares on Transit Riding." *Highway Research Record 213,* 1968, pp. 8–20.

Dalton, D. R., and Perry, J. L. "Absenteeism and the Collective Bargaining Agreement: An Empirical Test." *Academy of Management Journal,* 1981, *24* (2), 425–431.

Danielson, M. N. *Federal-Metropolitan Politics and the Commuter Crisis.* New York: Columbia University Press, 1965.

Doxsey, L. B. "Demand for Unlimited Use Transit Passes." *Journal of Transport Economics and Policy,* 1984, *18* (1), 7–22.

Drucker, P. F. "Managing the Public Service Institution." *The Public Interest*, 1973, *33*, 67–74.

Everett, P. B., and Watson, B. G. *A Review of Transit Marketing Evaluation Practice*. Washington, D.C.: Transportation Research Board, 1982. (Available from the National Technical Information Service, Springfield, Va.)

Fielding, G. J. "Structuring Citizen Involvement in Freeway Planning." *Highway Research Record 380*, 1972, pp. 23–36.

Fielding, G. J. "Transportation for the Handicapped: The Politics of Full Accessibility." *Transportation Quarterly*, 1982, *36* (2), 269–282.

Fielding, G. J., Babitsky, T. T., and Brenner, M. E. "Performance Evaluation for Bus Transit." *Transportation Research*, 1985, *19A* (1), 73–82.

Fielding, G. J., Blankenship, D. P., and Tardiff, T. J. "Consumer Attitudes Toward Public Transit." *Transportation Research Record 563*, 1976, pp. 22–28.

Fielding, G. J., Mundle, S. R., and Misner, J. "Performance-Based Funding-Allocation Guidelines for Transit Operators in Los Angeles County." *Transportation Research Record 857*, 1982, pp. 14–18.

Fielding, G. J., and others. *Indicators and Peer Groups for Transit Performance Analysis*. Report no. UMTA-CA-11-0026-2. Washington, D.C.: U.S. Department of Transportation, Urban Mass Transportation Administration, 1984. (Available from the National Technical Information Service, Springfield, Va.)

Fong, K. M. "BART: Taking the Poor for a Ride." *Harvard Political Review*, 1976, *4* (4), 11–18.

Fulton, P. N. "Are We Solving the Commuting Problem?" *American Demographics*, 1983, *5*, 16–19.

Giuliano, G. "Public Transportation and the Travel Needs of Women." *Traffic Quarterly*, 1979, *33* (4), 607–616.

Gray, G. E., and Hoel, L. A. (eds.). *Public Transportation: Planning, Operations and Management*. Englewood Cliffs, N.J.: Prentice-Hall, 1979.

Grey, A. *Urban Fares Policy*. Lexington, Mass.: Heath, 1975.

Hamilton, N. W., and Hamilton, P. R. *Governance of Public*

Enterprise: A Case Study of Urban Mass Transit. Lexington, Mass.: Heath, 1981.

Hildyard, P. H., and Wallis, H. V. "Advances in Computer-Assisted Runcutting in North America." In A. Wren (ed.), *Computer Scheduling of Public Transport.* Amsterdam: North Holland, 1981.

Hodge, D. "Social Impacts of Urban Transportation Decisions: Equity Issues." In S. Hanson (ed.), *The Geography of Urban Transportation.* New York: Guilford Press, 1986.

Holec, J. M., Jr., Schwager, D. S., and Fandialan, A. "Use of Federal Section 15 Data in Transit Performance Evaluation: Michigan Program." *Transportation Research Record 746,* 1980, pp. 36–38.

Holzer, M., and Halachmi, A. (eds.). *Strategic Issues in Public Sector Productivity: The Best of Public Productivity Review, 1975–1985.* San Francisco: Jossey-Bass, 1986.

Jones, D. *Urban Transit Policy: An Economic and Political History.* Englewood Cliffs, N.J.: Prentice-Hall, 1985.

Kendrick, J. W. *Postwar Productivity Trends in the United States, 1948-1969.* New York: National Bureau of Economic Research, 1973.

Kheel, T. "Politics of Collective Bargaining." In *Urban Transportation Economics.* Special Report no. 181. Washington, D.C.: Transportation Research Board, 1978.

Kirby, R. F., and others. *Paratransit: Neglected Options for Urban Mobility.* Washington, D.C.: Urban Institute, 1974.

Klein, W. F. "Strategic Planning at Work." *Metro Magazine,* 1985, *81* (5), 42–60.

Kliewer, T. "Houston Says Yes." *Mass Transit,* 1978, *5* (11), 16–18.

Lago, A. M., Mayworm, P. D., and McEnroe, J. M. "Transit Ridership Responsiveness to Fare Changes." *Traffic Quarterly,* 1981, *35* (1), 117–142.

Lave, C. A. "Is Part-Time Labor a Cure for Transit Deficits?" *Traffic Quarterly,* 1980, *34* (1), 61–74.

Long, L., and Perry, J. L. "Economic and Occupational Causes of Transit Operator Absenteeism: A Review of Research." *Transport Reviews,* 1985, *5* (3), 247–267.

Long, N. E. "The Local Community as an Ecology of Games." *American Journal of Sociology,* 1958, *64* (3), 251–261.

Lovelock, C. H., and Weinberg, C. B. *Readings in Public and Nonprofit Marketing*. Palo Alto, Calif.: Scientific Press, 1978.

Luna, C. *The UTU Handbook of Transportation in America*. New York: Popular Library, 1971.

MacDorman, L. C. *Extra-Board Management: Procedures and Tools*. Synthesis of Transit Practice, no. 5. Washington, D.C.: Transportation Research Board, 1985.

MacDorman, L. C., and MacDorman, J. C. "The Transit Extra-Board: Some Opportunities for Cost Saving." Paper presented at annual meeting of the American Public Transit Association, Boston, Oct. 1982.

Mayworm, P., Lago, A. M., and McEnroe, J. M. *Patronage Impacts of Changes in Transit Fares and Services*. Report no. DOT-UT-90014. Washington, D.C.: U.S. Department of Transportation, Urban Mass Transportation Administration, 1980. (Available from the National Technical Information Service, Springfield, Va.)

Meyer, J. R., and Gomez-Ibanez, J. A. *Improving Urban Mass Transportation Productivity*. Report no. UMTA-MA-11-0026-77-1. Washington, D.C.: U.S. Department of Transportation, Urban Mass Transportation Administration, 1977.

Meyer, J. R., and Gomez-Ibanez, J. A. *Autos, Transit, and Cities*. Cambridge, Mass.: Harvard University Press, 1981.

Meyer, M. D. "Strategic Planning in Response to Environmental Change." *Transportation Quarterly*, 1983, *37* (2), 297–310.

Miller, J. H. "An Evaluation of Allocation Methodologies for Public Transportation Operating Assistance." *Transportation Journal*, 1979, *19* (1), 40–49.

Miller, J. H. "The Use of Performance-Based Methodologies for the Allocation of Transit Operating Funds." *Traffic Quarterly*, 1980, *34* (4), 555–585.

Montreal Urban Community Transit Commission. *Strategic Plan, 1984–1986*. Montreal: Montreal Urban Community Transit Commission, 1984.

Moynihan, D. P. "The Politics and Economics of Regional Growth." *The Public Interest*, 1978, *51*, 3–21.

Multisystems, Inc. *Route-Level Demand Models: A Review*. Report no. DOT-I-82-3. Washington, D.C.: U.S. Department of Transportation, 1982.

Olsen, L. B. "Driver Incentive Program Pays Dividends to Transit in Minneapolis/St. Paul." *Passenger Transport,* 1983, *41* (38), 6-8.

Oram, R. L. "Peak-Period Supplements: The Contemporary Economics of Urban Bus Transport in the U.K. and U.S.A." *Progress in Planning,* 1979, *12* (2), 81-154.

Oram, R. L. "Making Transit Passes Viable in the 1980s." *Transportation Quarterly,* 1983, *37* (2), 289-296.

Orange County Transit District. *Short Range Transit Plan and Transportation Improvement Program, 1977-1981.* Garden Grove, California, 1977.

Perry, J. L. *Organizational Form and Transit Performance: A Research Review and Empirical Analysis.* Report no. UMTA-CA-11-0027-2. Washington, D.C.: U.S. Department of Transportation, Urban Mass Transportation Administration, 1984.

Perry, J. L., and Angle, H. L. *Labor-Management Relations and Public Agency Effectiveness: A Study of Urban Mass Transit.* Elmsford, N.Y.: Pergamon Press, 1980.

Perry, J. L., Angle, H. L., and Pittel, M. E. *The Impact of Labor-Management Relations on Productivity and Efficiency in Urban Mass Transit.* Report no. DOT/RSPA/DPB-50/79/7. Washington, D.C.: U.S. Department of Transportation, 1979. (Available from the National Technical Information Service, Springfield, Va.)

Peterson, G. E., Davis, W. G., and Walker, C. *Total Compensation of Mass Transit Employees in Large Metropolitan Areas.* Washington, D.C.: Urban Institute, 1986.

Pfeffer, J., and Salancik, G. R. *The External Control of Organizations.* New York: Harper & Row, 1978.

Pickrell, D. H. *The Causes of Rising Transit Operating Deficits.* Report no. DOT-I-83-47. Washington, D.C.: U.S. Department of Transportation, 1983.

Pierce, I. N., and others. "A Formula for Suballocating Operating Assistance Funds." *Transit Journal,* 1976, *2* (1), 31-42.

Pushkarev, B. S., and Zupan, J. M. *Public Transit and Land Use Policy.* Bloomington: Indiana University Press, 1977.

Pyhrr, P. "Zero-Based Approach to Governmental Budgeting." *Public Administration Review*, 1977, *37* (1), 1–9.

Reno, A. T., and Bixby, R. H. *Characteristics of Urban Transportation Systems*. Report no. UMTA-MA-06-0173-85-1. Washington, D.C.: U.S. Department of Transportation, Urban Mass Transportation Administration, 1985. (Available from the National Technical Information Service, Springfield, Va.)

Ring, P. S., and Perry, J. L. "Strategic Management in Public and Private Organizations: Implications of Distinctive Contexts and Constraints." *Academy of Management Review*, 1985, *10* (2), 276–288.

Rosenbloom, S. *Bus Transit Accessibility for the Handicapped in Urban Areas*. Synthesis of Highway Practice, no. 83. Washington D.C.: Transportation Research Board, 1981.

Rosenthal, S. R. *Managing Government Operations*. Glenview, Ill.: Scott, Foresman, 1982.

Sage Management Consultants. *Labour in Urban Transit Operations: Profile and Prospects*. Montreal: Canadian Surface Transportation Administration, Urban Transportation Research Branch, 1978.

Saltzman, A. "The Decline of Transit." In G. E. Gray and L. A. Hoel (eds.), *Public Transportation: Planning, Operations and Management*. Englewood Cliffs, N.J.: Prentice-Hall, 1979.

Schneider, L. M. "Urban Mass Transportation: A Survey of the Decision-Making Process." In R. A. Bauer and K. J. Green (eds.), *The Study of Policy Formation*. New York: Free Press, 1968.

Shoup, D. C., and Pickrell, D. H. *Free Parking as a Transportation Problem*. Report no. DOT/RSPA/DPB-50/80/16. Washington, D.C.: U.S. Department of Transportation, 1980. (Available from the National Technical Information Service, Springfield, Va.)

Simpson, A. U. "Implications of Efficiency Incentives on Use of Private Sector Contracting by the Public Transit Industry." In C. A. Lave (ed.), *Urban Transit: The Private Challenge to Public Transportation*. Cambridge, Mass.: Ballinger, 1985.

Sloan, A. *Managing SEPTA Strategically*. Report no. UMTA-PA-09-0005-79-1. Washington, D.C.: U.S. Department of Transportation, Urban Mass Transportation Administration, 1979. (Available from the National Technical Information Service, Springfield, Va.)

Smerk, G. M. *Urban Mass Transportation: A Dozen Years of Federal Policy*. Bloomington: Indiana University Press, 1974.

Smerk, G. M. "The Development of Public Transportation and the City." In G. E. Gray and L. A. Hoel (eds.), *Public Transportation: Planning, Operations and Management*. Englewood Cliffs, N.J.: Prentice Hall, 1979.

Smith, J., Kiffe, D. L., and Lee, D. A. "An Approach to Ideal Manpower Planning." *Transit Journal*, 1980, *6* (4), 61–77.

Smith, R. L. "Improving Section 15 Passenger Data Collection Techniques." *Transportation Research Record 1013*, 1985, 67–77.

Transportation Research Board. *State Transit Management Assistance to Local Communities*. Synthesis of Highway Practice, no. 74. Washington D.C.: Transportation Research Board, 1980.

Tye, W. B. "The Capital Grant as a Subsidy Device: The Case Study of Urban Transportation." In *The Economics of Federal Subsidy Programs. Pt. 6: Transportation Subsidies*. U.S. Congress Joint Economics Committee, Joint Committee Print, 93rd Congress. Washington, D.C.: U.S. Government Printing Office, 1973.

U.S. Department of Commerce, Bureau of the Census. *Statistical Abstract of the United States: 1974*. (95th ed.) Washington, D.C.: U.S. Government Printing Office, 1974.

U.S. Department of Transportation. "Transportation Improvement Program." *Federal Register*, 1975, *40* (181), 42975–42984.

U.S. Department of Transportation. *Urban Mass Transportation Administration, Statistical Summary*. Washington, D.C.: U.S. Government Printing Office, 1977.

U.S. Department of Transportation. *National Urban Mass Transportation Statistics: 1980 Section 15 Annual Report*. Report no. UMTA-MA-06-0107-82-1. Washington, D.C.: U.S. Department of Transportation, Transportation Systems Center, 1982.

U.S. Department of Transportation. *National Urban Mass Transportation Statistics: 1982 Section 15 Annual Report*. Report no. UMTA-MA-06-0107-84-1. Washington, D.C.: U.S. Department of Transportation, Transportation Systems Center, 1983. (Available from the National Technical Information Service, Springfield, Va.)

U.S. Department of Transportation. *The Status of the Nation's Local Public Transportation: Conditions and Performance*. Report to Congress. Washington, D.C.: U.S. Department of Transportation, Urban Mass Transportation Administration, 1984.

U.S. Department of Transportation. *Expenditure by Fiscal Year and Program*. Washington, D.C.: Urban Mass Transportation Administration, Office of Capital and Formula Assistance, 1985.

U.S. Department of Transportation. *National Urban Mass Transportation Statistics: 1984 Section 15 Annual Report*. Report no. UMTA-IT-06-0310-86-1. Washington, D.C.: Urban Mass Transportation Administration, Office of Technical Assistance, 1986. (Available from U.S. Government Printing Office, Washington, D.C.)

U.S. General Accounting Office. *Standards for Audit of Governmental Organizations, Programs, Activities and Functions*. Washington, D.C.: U.S. Government Printing Office, 1972.

U.S. General Accounting Office. *Soaring Transit Subsidies Must Be Controlled*. Report no. CED-81-28. Washington, D.C.: U.S. General Accounting Office, Community and Economic Development Division, 1981. (Available from the National Technical Information Service, Springfield, Va.)

U.S. President. *Economic Report of the President*. Washington, D.C.: U.S. Government Printing Office, 1986.

Vuchic, V. R. *Urban Public Transportation: Systems and Technology*. Englewood Cliffs, N.J.: Prentice-Hall, 1981.

Wachs, M. "Consumer Attitudes Toward Public Transit: An Interpretive Review." *Journal of the American Institute of Planners*, 1976, *42* (1), 96–104.

Wachs, M. "Ethical Dilemmas in Forecasting for Public Policy." *Public Administration Review*, 1982, *42* (6), 562–567.

Wagner, F. A., and Gilbert, K. *Transportation System Management: An Assessment of Impacts*. Report no. UMTA-VA-06-0047. Washington, D.C.: U.S. Department of Transportation, Urban Mass Transportation Administration, 1978. (Available from the National Technical Information Service, Springfield, Va.)

Walton, R. E., and McKersie, R. B. *A Behavioral Theory of Labor Negotiations.* New York: McGraw-Hill, 1965.

Wang, G.H.K., and Skinner, D. "The Impact of Fare and Gasoline Price Changes on Monthly Transit Ridership: Empirical Evidence from Seven U.S. Transit Authorities." *Transportation Research,* 1984, *18B* (1), 29–41.

Warren, K. J., and Connelly, A. G. "Milwaukee County Transit System's Individual Recognition Award Program." *TR News,* Sept.–Oct. 1986, pp. 9–12.

Webber, M. M. *The BART Experience—What Have We Learned?* Monograph no 26. Berkeley: University of California, Institute of Urban and Regional Development and Institute of Transportation Studies, 1976.

Webster, F. V., and Bly, P. H. (eds.). *The Demand for Public Transport: Report of the International Collaborative Study of Factors Affecting Public Transport Patronage.* Crowthorne, England: Transport and Road Research Laboratory, 1980.

Wildavsky, A. *The Politics of the Budgetary Process.* Boston: Little, Brown, 1964.

Wilson, N.M.H., and others. *Short-Range Transit Planning: Current Practice and a Proposed Framework.* Report no. DOT-I-84-44. Washington, D.C.: U.S. Department of Transportation, 1984.

Index